DO YOU KNOW HILCHOS
SHABBOS?

DO YOU KNOW HILCHOS SHABBOS?

Practical Questions for the Whole Family

Compiled by
Rabbi Michoel Fletcher

MENUCHA PUBLISHERS

Menucha Publishers, Inc.
© 2013, 2015 by Rabbi Michoel Fletcher
First edition 2013
Second edition 2015
Edited by Chaya Silverstone
Cover design by Seth Aronstam
Typeset and designed by Beena Sklare
All rights reserved

ISBN 978-1-61465-091-1

No part of this publication may be translated, reproduced, stored in a retrieval system, or transmitted in any form or by any means, electronic, mechanical, photocopying, recording, or otherwise, without prior permission in writing from both the copyright holder and the publisher.

Published and distributed by:
Menucha Publishers, Inc.
250 44th Street
Brooklyn, NY 11232
Tel/Fax: 718-232-0856
www.menuchapublishers.com
sales@menuchapublishers.com

Printed in Israel by Chish

Any questions or comments may be emailed to rabbimfletcher@gmail.com or faxed to 972-2-991-3027.

HARABBANIM HAGAONIM

HARAV TUVYA WEISS, *SHLITA*   HARAV MOSHE SHTERNBUCH, *SHLITA*

Rabbi Moshe Shternbuch
Chief Rabbi
and Vice President of
the Orthodox Rabbinical Courts
Jerusalem

Rechov Mishkalov 13 Har-Nof Jerusalem Tel: 02-651-9610

משה שטרנבוך
ראב"ד
לכל מקהלות האשכנזים
מח"ס מועדים וזמנים ושו"ת תשובות והנהגות ח"ח
רב בית הכנסת הגר"א, ור"מ במרכז התורה הר-נוף
סגן נשיא העדה החרדית
בעיה"ק ירושלים ת"ו

בעזה"י

[handwritten Hebrew letter]

רח' משקלוב 13, הר-נוף, ירושלים ת"ו. טל: 02-651-9610

Rabbi S.F. Zimmerman
Rov of Gateshead

שרגא פייבל הלוי זיממערמאן
אב"ד דק"ק גייטסהעד

בס"ד

אור לז' טבת תשע"ג

"כל מקדש שביעי כראוי לו כל שומר שבת כדת מחללו"

My friend and colleague, the noted author Rabbi Michoel Fletcher has written a work titled "Do you know Hilchos Shabbos" which is written in question and answer form.

I've perused through large portions of the book and have found that the halachos are presented in a clear and concise manner and properly annotated. The format is very engaging (I have tested the pre-publication edition on my younger children) and serves as a valuable aid in teaching and transmitting these all-important halachos and is suitable for use at the Shabbos table.

ויה"ר שזכות השבת יעמוד לימין הרב המחבר שליט"א להמשיך עבודתו הקדושה מתוך בריאות הגוף ומנוחת הנפש ונחת מבני משפחתו

הכו"ח בכבוד ויקר

27-29 Grasmere Street West, Gateshead, NE8 1TS
Tel: 0191 477 1847   Fax: 0191 477 7688

RABBI MOSHE HEINEMANN
6109 Gist Avenue
Baltimore, MD 21215
Tel. (410) 358-9828
Fax. (410) 358-9838

בס"ד

משה היינעמאן
אב"ד ק"ק אגודת ישראל
באלטימאר
טל. (410) 764-7778
פקס (410) 764-8878

הנני בזה להשמיע בשער בת רבים מעלת מעלת הרב"ג ר' מיכאל פלעטשר שליט"א
ומעלת ספרו הנעים הנעשה בטוב טעם ודעת על הלכות שבת. עיינתי במקצתו
המעיד על כולו, שכולו מחמדים, והוא חיבור נחוץ לכל בית ישראל שהלכות
שבת רפוחים בידם וזהו המלב לרוב רובם של אחינו בית ישראל בעו"ה.
החיבור הזה מסודר באופן שהקל ללמוד מתוכו והוא הלכה למעשה. והגם שקוב"ה
חדי בפלפולה דאורייתא הוא חדי ביתר שאת בהלכה בנוגע למעשה כמא"כ הדי"ן
בפ"ק דברכות וז"ל אוהב ד' שערים המצוינים בהלכה יותר מכל בתי כנסיות ובתי
מדרשות שבעולם.

לכן אמינא שדבר טוב עשה בעמו, וכבר איתמחי גברא בספרו קיצור הלכות ברכות
ויזכה שגם ספרו זה יתקבל בקרב אחינו בני ישראל השואפים לקיים כל מילי דשבת
באופן היות טוב, ולעשות השבת יום מנוחה וקדושה יום מנוחת אמת ואמונה, יום
של מנוחה שלימה שהקב"ה רוצה בה, ויפוצו מעיינותיו חוצה.

וע"ז באתי עה"ח בחמישי בשבת לסדר והגידו לפני ד' יום אחד לחדש אייר ט"ו יום
לעומרינט שנת חמשת אלפים ושבע מאות ושבעים ושלש לבריאות עולם.

משה בהה"ר ברוך ג--ליה באמצעת היינעמאן החונ"פ מתא באלטימאר

REPRINTED WITH PERMISSION

DAYAN GAVRIEL KRAUSZ
Rosh Beth Din, Manchester

118 Leicester Road
Manchester M7 4GF
Tel: 0161 740 4548 Fax: 0161 740 9300

Office:
Tel: 0161 740 9711 Fax: 0161 721 4249

גבריאל קרויס

ראב"ד דק"ק מנשסתר והגליל יצ"ו

מח"ס מקור הברכה

ב"ה

I have known Rabbi ישכר Fletcher א‎כט"‎א‎ for over 40 years. Already as a teenager, he always was very particular to do the right thing, especially as far as שמירת הקדין ואמונה was concerned. His deep שאיפת שמים was palpable from the שאלות he asked both in הלכה as well as in השקפה. Since then he has ascended steeply the ladder of עבודת ה' and has become an outstanding תלמיד חכם and מרביץ תורה. This is evidenced by the many enthusiastic letters penned by residents of רמת בית שמש, where Rabbi and Mrs. Fletcher are deeply involved in הרבצת התורה. The letters speak for themselves, as they all highly praise their sterling achievements.

The latest of his remarkable successes is the forthcoming publication of his "קיצור ברטנורא". although in the course of the last 30 years plus, dozens of prominent ספרים on מסכתות have been published, nevertheless the "קיצור ברטנורא" is undoubtedly a "first". מסכתות are some of the most intricate and complicated הלכה. Nevertheless the author managed in a most impressive manner to elucidate in a concise, clear way most of the הלכות which are applicable day-to-day.

I have to emphasize that although I read through large sections of the קיצור and am, of course, very impressed by it, but equally, significant parts I did not manage to work through. Consequently, by giving this הסכמה, it does not automatically imply that I concur with all הלכות mentioned in the קיצור.

I wish Rabbi Fletcher שליט"א הצלחה רבה in the publication of this important work and it is my fervent hope that it will reach a very wide readership.

הכותב וחותם לכבוד התורה ולומדיה
ביום א', ערב חודש אייר לבני ישראל,
שנת זאת לפך בברכת כוח"ט לכל
כלל בית ישראל,

גבריאל קרויס

REPRINTED WITH PERMISSION

Rabbi Elimelech Kornfeld
Rav of Kehillas HaGra
19/8 Nachal Ayalon
Ramat Beit Shemesh
02 9920485

אלימלך קורנפלד
רב דקהילת הגר"א
נחל איילון 19/8
רמת בית שמש
טל. 9920485 02

י"ח מרחשון תשע"א

ידוע שהסוגיות של הלכות ברכות הן מהחמורות שבש"ס ומאידך הלכות ברכות הנהנין הם חלק חשוב של עבודת כל אחד מישראל בכל יום ויום. ולפעמים כפי גודל הפרסום של החשיבות של הבנה ברורה בהלכות ברכות, כך גדול ההעלם.

ולכן שמחתי מאד לראות גליונות מן הספר החדש שידידי הנעלה מאד, מרביץ תורה ברבים הרה"ג ר' מיכאל פלטשר שליט"א עומד להוציא לאור.
הרב פלטשר שליט"א כבר התמחה במסירות שיעורים בחו"ל וגם בארץ בהרבה מקצועות התורה ובפרט בהלכה, אני עד לכך שדבריו נאמרים מתוך הרבה עמל ודקדוק רב בפוסקים ובמחברים, ובס"ד הם מאד ערבים על שומעיהם ומדריכים אותם לדקדוק בהלכה ברורה.

המסירות שלו למען חיזוק התורה ועבודת השם בשכונתנו הוא שם דבר , ויה"ר שכשם שדבריו עושים רושם עמוק כאן כן יזכה שיפוצו מעיינותיו חוצה, וספרו החדש יתקבל באהבה בקרב לומדי התורה ועובדי השם.

לעילוי נשמת ר' יעקב בן ר' לוי הלוי ז"ל

נולד כ"ז תשרי תרפ"ד

נפטר בשם טוב ט' תמוז שנת

ויעקב איש תם יושב אהלים

Mr. Jacob Duijzend, ז"ל

Our Father and Opa, ז"ל, survived the Holocaust בחסדי שמים in hiding, together with his father — a doctor — in the house of a patient, one of the צדיקי אומות העולם. After the war he was taken under the wings of פועלי אגודת ישראל in Amsterdam, where he lived in the famous PAI House and made connections and friendships that lasted a lifetime. Opa, ז"ל, continued his education and became a lawyer and tax expert. He dedicated his life to תורת ה' ומצוותיו and many מוסדות and Jewish causes profited from his help and support. When the כולל חכם צבי was established in Amsterdam, he attached himself to the אברכים and became a תלמיד of the מחבר שליט"א. There is no better way to remember him than this ספר that guides its readers in the ways of הלכה ברורה.

יהי זכרו ברוך

In Memory of

Cissie Czar שמחה בת זלמן ע"ה

Emily Czar חיינה בת זלמן ע"ה

Leah Czar לאה בת זלמן ע"ה

May this sefer, which will help Jews learn about
kedushas Shabbos, be a source of merit for these ladies who
lived modestly and had no expectation
that their memories would be perpetuated.

לע"נ

R' Myer Freedman ר' מאיר ב"ר סיני

He taught limudei kodesh in Manchester and led the services
over many years in Stenecourt Shul.

Mrs. Sophie Freedman מרת בת שבע לאה בת ר' פסח

She was the headmistress of Cassel Fox Jewish Primary School
and taught limudei chol in Stand Grammar School.

לע"נ

John and Phyllis Rose of London
יהושע בן נחום מאיר   פרומית בת אהרן

Bella Silverman of New York
בילה בת שמואל יצחק

In Memory of

**Monty and Julie Aronson / Burton
of Glasgow, Scotland**

משה אהרן בן קלמן יוסף ע"ה
יולי בת חיים ע"ה

לז"נ

ר' אליעזר יונה ב"ר יעקב מאיר ע"ה

והאשה איידל סימא בת ר' משה הכהן ע"ה

ר' צבי ב"ר יהודה אריה ע"ה

In Honor of My Dear Parents

Maurice and Esther Shapiro

Contents

Acknowledgments 17
Introduction 23
Do You Know *Hilchos Shabbos*? 27
    Kavod Shabbos — Honoring Shabbos 31
    Erev Shabbos 36
    The Shabbos Candles 41
    The Three Meals of Shabbos 46
    What We May Read on Shabbos 52
    Walking and Talking on Shabbos 57
    Avoiding Distress 61
    Earning Money on Shabbos 65
    Acquiring Items 69
    Measuring 75
    מוקצה — What We're Not Allowed to Move, Part I 77
    מוקצה, Part II 82
    אמירה לעכו"ם — Requesting a Non-Jew to Do a *Melachah* 90
    חורש — Plowing 99
    זורע — Sowing 104
    קוצר — Uprooting 109
    מעמר — Gathering Together 114
    דש — Threshing, Squeezing 119
    זורה — Winnowing 126
    בורר — Separating 130
    טוחן — Grinding 136

מרקד — Sifting	143
לש — Kneading	148
בישול — Cooking, Part I	154
בישול, Part II	160
גוזז — Shearing	169
מלבן — Laundering	173
מנפץ, צובע — Combing Raw Fiber and Dyeing	182
The Weaving *Melachos*: טווה, מיסך, עושה בתי נירין, אורג, פוצע — Spinning, Warping, Constructing Heddles, Weaving, Unravelling Threads from Fabric	188
קושר — Tying Knots	194
מתיר — Undoing a Knot	200
תופר — Sewing	207
קורע — Tearing	213
צד — Trapping	219
שוחט — Slaughtering	226
מפשיט, מעבד, משרטט — Skinning, Tanning, and Ruling Guidelines	232
ממחק — Smoothing	238
מחתך — Cutting	243
כותב — Writing	249
מוחק — Erasing	255
בונה — Building	262
סותר — Demolishing	267
מעביר — Kindling a Fire	274
מכבה — Extinguishing	279
מכה בפטיש — The Final Hammer Blow	288
הוצאה — Transferring Objects from One Domain to Another	296

The Beauty of Shabbos 306

Index 311

ACKNOWLEDGMENTS

It is a great *zechus* to write a *sefer* on practical halachah.[1] How much more so on the halachos of Shabbos, which is the *bris olam*, the everlasting covenant between Hashem and the Jewish people.

Words cannot fully express my appreciation and thanks to Hashem for giving me the opportunity to complete this *sefer*. "*Katanti mikol hachasadim*" — I am humbled by all His kindnesses to me, "*meodi ad hayom hazeh*" — throughout my life.

In the acknowledgments to my first *sefer*, *Do You Know Hilchos Brachos?*, I mentioned teachers and rabbanim who taught me in Gateshead Yeshivah, the Amsterdam Kollel, and since. In these acknowledgments I would like to mention teachers from my youth to whom I am indebted. One of my early teachers in Manchester, UK, was R' Dovid Henry, *z"l*, who was tragically *niftar* at a very young age. I distinctly remember learning from him the first mishnah I had ever learned, the first mishnah in *Megillah*. Because of the encouragement he gave me to learn in my earliest years, he has a part in this *sefer* and in everything else I have achieved. *Yehi zichro baruch.*

Another early teacher of mine was R' Myer Freedman, *z"l*. He helped teach me to read from the siddur and Chumash. He and his late wife, Sophie, *a"h*, were both well-known in Manchester, as Sophie

---

1. See *Pele Yoetz Asufa* and the *haskamah* of Rav Moshe Heinemann, *shlita*.

was the headmistress of the Cassel Fox Jewish Primary School.[2] *Yehi zichram baruch.* Their son-in-law Dr. Philip Stemmer, *n"y*, of London, encouraged me when I first attended Yeshivat Kerem B'Yavneh and has always generously supported my *harbatzas Torah*. May he and his family be blessed with good health and success for many years.

R' Gabriel Brodie, *sheyichyeh*, was the *mara de'asra* of Stenecourt Shul in Manchester for over sixty years until his very recent retirement. He encouraged me, first when I was a young congregant in his shul, and later, after I went to yeshivah, by inviting me to give *derashos* and *shiurim* whenever I came to Manchester. It was these opportunities that gave me the confidence to pursue a career as a *marbitz Torah*. His late wife, Marga, *a"h*, who was *niftar* recently, was also very active and popular within the wider Jewish community of Manchester. May R' Gabriel be granted good health to enjoy his "retirement"[3] *bis hundert un tzvantzig*.

I am particularly indebted to HaRav Yaakov Montrose, *shlita*, author of the *Halachic World* series. He carefully reviewed every chapter of this *sefer* and often made helpful comments and *he'aros* based on his extensive knowledge of *halachah lemaaseh*. Without his approval I wouldn't have had the confidence to publish a *sefer* that

---

2. The name of the school, Cassel Fox, stems from the generosity of two gentlemen, Mr. Cassel (my late great-grandfather) and Mr. Fox, who bought the building to house Jewish German refugees during the Second World War. They fought to maintain its strictly kosher and Orthodox standards against community activists who wanted it to become less Orthodox. Eventually the building was no longer needed for refugees, partly due to the efforts of my late grandfather, Mr. Joe Cassel, who enabled the refugees to learn a trade, marry, and settle down as *baalei batim* in the Manchester Jewish community. Mr. Cassel and Mr. Fox then donated the building to be used as a school, which it still is today, albeit under different auspices.
3. He still gives weekly *shiurim* in Manchester.

contains hundreds of *piskei halachah*. Sometimes we worked hard on the precise wording, since even a slight incorrect nuance in a *sefer* on halachah can give a wrong impression and lead to mistakes.

HaGaavad HaRav HaGaon R' Tuvya Weiss, *shlita*, *av beis din* of the Eidah HaChareidis, Yerushalayim, honored me by reviewing some of the chapters of the *sefer* and writing his personal *berachah* for its success. He further honored me by giving me a *berachah* for the success of all my efforts to spread "Torah and *Taharah*" in Klal Yisrael. I am indebted to him.

HaRav HaGaon R' Shraga Feivel Zimmerman, *shlita*, the *rav* and *av beis din* of Gateshead, UK, kindly gave of his valuable time to read through most of the proposed text. His approval and written *haskamah* was also a vital element in allowing me to present a *sefer* on halachah *lemaaseh* to the Jewish public.

HaRav HaGaon R' Moshe Heinemann, *shlita*, one of the most prominent *poskim* in the United States, also kindly read through a significant part of the proposed text before giving his written approval.

HaRav HaGaon R' Mattisyahu Salomon, *shlita*, read through some of the text and expressed warm encouragement for the success of the sefer, as quoted on the back cover.

HaRabbanim HaGeonim Rav Moshe Shternbuch, Dayan Gavriel Krausz, and Rav Elimelech Kornfeld, *shlita*, did not have the time to read through the text, but having seen my previous *sefer* and written their *haskamos* on it, expressed their confidence that this *sefer* also will be *amitah shel Torah*. They gave me their explicit permission to reprint their previously given *haskamos* in this work. I am indebted to them too.

The Gemara in *Taanis*[4] tells us that someone who learns Torah on his own will become foolish. Therefore I want to mention all those who

---

4. 7a.

learn with me in my daily *shiurim* on Gemara and Halachah. Without these wonderful people, there is no question I wouldn't have been able to acquire the knowledge that comes from *pilpul chaverim* over many *masechtos* and subjects in Halachah.[5] In alphabetical order, they are: Arthur Littman, Asher Lazarus, Avi Strahl, Avrohom Shmuel Bickel, Betzalel Lippman, Dovid Markowitz, Moshe Goodman, Shemariyahu Rabin, Sholom Meir Herman, Tzemach Richter, Yaakov Leschen, Yaakov Rubin, Yaakov Schoemann, and Yosef Marks.

Another exceptional group of people, managers in a busy international firm, Foxcom Satellite Communications, close their computers in the middle of the day to study Gemara with me. They are Jack Hotz, Yaakov Ben-Harosh, Steve Weil, and Jason Nussbaum. If *Minchah* is so important because one is interrupting one's daily activities to daven,[6] how much more precious in the eyes of Hashem is learning Torah in the middle of a workday.

I would also like to thank the ladies who attended my *shiurim* on *hilchos Shabbos* over several years and for whom I first prepared many of the practical questions that form the basis of this *sefer*. It was some of these women who asked me to put the questions into print so others could enjoy and gain from them.

I would like to mention my late mother-in-law, Mrs. Goldie Beigel, *a"h*, for whom the year of *aveilus* has just concluded. The two of us always enjoyed an excellent relationship and she encouraged her children, grandchildren, and great-grandchildren to continue *bederech Yisrael Sabba*. She indeed merited to see *banim uvnei banim oskim beTorah ubemitzvos*.

Baruch Hashem my own mother, despite her advanced age, has

---

5. The Maharam's commentary on *Shas* finishes suddenly at one point because he explains that he hadn't taught that section in his yeshivah.
6. See *Kitzur Shulchan Aruch* 69:1.

begun a new "career" teaching in the Yesodai HaTorah Primary School in Manchester, UK. My sister works very hard for the Southport Jewish Community, UK, with her family. May they both be blessed with good health and success.

"*Ba'ah Shabbos, ba'ah Menuchah.*" I must thank Rabbi Hirsch Traube and his entire team at Menucha Publishers for so excellently preparing and printing this *sefer*. May this be a success and may we work together in the future to produce other high-standard *sefarim* for the benefit of the Jewish people.

I would like to give a special thanks to Mr. Seth Aronstam for the beautiful cover design.

Finally, *acharonah acharonah chavivah*, my wife has an equal share in all my learning and teaching. Our children and children-in-law are all making important contributions in the Jewish communities where they live together with their families. In the *zechus* of Shabbos, may my wife and I be granted many more years together in good health and to see continued *yiddishe nachas* from our family.

In the *zechus* of *shemiras Shabbos* may all of Klal Yisrael see *yeshuos venechamos* and the coming of *Mashiach tzidkeinu bimheirah beyameinu*. Amen.

Michoel Fletcher
Ramat Bet Shemesh
Motzaei Shabbos Kodesh *Parashas Mishpatim*
Rosh Chodesh Adar 5773

INTRODUCTION

Who has time to spare? We are so busy. Hopefully men have fixed times for learning, but how much can one learn in an hour or two, relative to what we need to know? Women have many responsibilities too and spare time is at a premium.

Baruch Hashem for Shabbos, our weekly escape from the pressures of the outside world.

Baruch Hashem for Shabbos, our weekly opportunity to interact with our families.

Baruch Hashem for Shabbos, our weekly pit stop to recharge our spiritual batteries.

It is the halachos of Shabbos that create the framework for our Shabbos activities. Clearly we need to know the halachos to observe Shabbos properly and in order to gain the most from it. There are excellent *sefarim* already available for those who have the time for serious study of the halachos of Shabbos from beginning to end. But how many of us have that time? If we have such *sefarim* they are almost invariably put away in our bookshelves only to be brought out when we want to look something up.

This *sefer* is designed for people with more limited time who want to learn or review the halachos of Shabbos in a stimulating way. It can be learned in a formal context or in an informal way, for instance at the Shabbos table or at Shabbos groups. A question-and-answer format is popular with all age groups. Even those who are experts in *hilchos Shabbos* will find the *sefer* a good way of discussing the halachos with their families.[1]

There are nearly five hundred questions, many of which are asked frequently within families all over the Jewish world. The answers are not short text-book answers but are personalized, advising the questioner what to do in that particular situation. The characters are named so that we can relate to them as ordinary people. They are not perfect, just like us. The *sefer* does not claim to be exhaustive but hopefully it will encourage people to study the halachos in more detail if they have the opportunity.

What is perhaps unique about this work is that while it is a serious *sefer* with many *piskei halachos*, it's written in an informal, reader-friendly style. The answers sometimes suggest how we can encourage our children and how to interact with family members. There is even a touch of humor; after all, one of the key ways of trying to ensure that our children will want to build their own Jewish homes is by infusing our homes with *simchah*, particularly on Shabbos and at the Shabbos table. The first chapters concentrate on honoring Shabbos and other positive mitzvos of Shabbos, before going on to activities that we do not do on Shabbos. This order gives people a more positive feeling about the day.

In difficult situations, I try to find halachic solutions. Needless to say the answers are carefully researched and have been approved by *gedolei harabbanim* and *talmidei chachamim* in Eretz Yisrael and in *chutz laAretz*. All the sources are noted and the notes themselves sometimes contain important information.

---

1. See the *haskamah* of Rav Zimmerman, who learns the prepublished version of this *sefer* with his family. I heard that before one Shabbos when the *rav* and his family were going away, the children insisted on taking this *sefer* with!

I hope this *sefer* will contribute to a greater knowledge of *hilchos Shabbos*, a higher level of observance of the laws, and a more positive attitude to the wonderful gift that Hashem has granted us.

The Family's Names

Moshe is the father of the household, representing Jewish tradition from Moshe Rabbeinu.

Malka, the mother, represents every Jewish mother, the queen of her household.

Chaim and Chaya are the young children, the future life of the Jewish people.

Avi the toddler is a hint to my late father, R' Eliyahu ben Chaim Shmaryahu, *z"l*; to my late father-in-law,[2] R' Moshe Isser ben Eliezer, *z"l*; to my many teachers, including the late Rav Shlomo Brevda, *zt"l*, who was *niftar* recently;[3] and to *Avinu she'baShamayaim*, who, in His great kindness, has granted me the tremendous *zechus* to complete this, my second *sefer*.

Michael Fletcher
Elul 5775

On the Printing of the Second Edition (Fourth Printing)

Baruch Hashem, just about three thousand copies of *Do You Know Hilchos Shabbos?* have been sold. It is enjoyed by Jews in many countries around the world and many people have written to say how much they enjoy it and are learning from it.

---

2. See the *Taz* in *Yoreh Deah* 240:19 that says that one's father-in-law is also called Av.
3. See *Melachim II* 2:12, where Elisha called his rebbe Eliyahu "Avi, Avi."

Before the fourth printing, I thought I could respond to comments of some of the readers by making a few changes. The main addition is the index, professionally done by Mr. Levi Bookin of Yerushalayim, to enable people to find the topic they are interested in with ease. I also made a very small number of changes in the text itself and in some of the notes. The only changes of halachic significance are in chapter 13, note 16; chapter 19, answer 9; and chapter 20, answer 4.

May the *sefer* continue to inspire readers, young and old, in the future.

DO YOU KNOW HILCHOS SHABBOS?

There are twenty questions in the following short story. How many can you answer correctly? The answers are found in this *sefer*.

It had been a busy Erev Shabbos at the Goldsteins'. Moshe was delayed at the office, Chaim had come home from *cheder* with a grazed knee, Chaya couldn't find the belt that went with her new dress, and the cleaning lady's childen were sick so she couldn't come.

It all wouldn't have mattered so much, except for the fact that they'd invited their neighbors the Cohens (because Mr. Cohen was away on business), two seminary girls, and of course old Mr. Black, who's quite a regular since his wife went into the old age home.

But *baruch Hashem*, "*ba'ah Shabbos ba'ah menuchah*," and at *licht bentchen* everything was spick-and-span.

The first question we had was about Chaya's belt, which she finally found. Can she thread it through the belt loops[1] and tie it into a bow?[2] Then Chaim decided he needed a new Band-Aid. Can he have one?[3]

---

1. Ch. 45, question 2.
2. Ch. 31, questions 2 and 4.
3. Ch. 32, question 8.

We are short of *lechem mishneh*. Can we take a challah out of the freezer?[4]

I can't remember the seating plan. Good thing I fixed it to the fridge. But who's going to read it out?[5]

Mrs. Cohen gave me a bottle of wine, which she said was to pay me back for the one we lent her last week. Can I accept it?[6]

Oy vey. I left the bathroom light *off* and the bedroom lights *on*. Can I call in the non-Jewish neighbor to help?[7]

I don't believe it — Chaya left some coins on the couch, just where I relax after the meal. Is the couch a *bassis*?[8]

We're only five minutes into the meal and Moshe has spilled the wine. I wiped up the red wine with a red napkin and one of the seminary girls gave me a funny look. Did I do something wrong?[9]

Then Mr. Black wanted his avocado mashed the way his wife used to make it. The whole table discussed the problem until Mrs. Cohen came up with a simple solution. What was it?[10]

Moshe said he wanted to add some more mayonnaise to his chopped liver. Is that allowed?[11]

Three minutes peace, and then tragedy. Avi started with his carrot. If there's one thing Avi doesn't like, it's carrot in his soup. Can he take it out and pass it on to me?[12]

This is getting beyond a joke. Moshe found a broken bone in the

---

4. Ch. 4, question 6.
5. Ch. 5, question 8.
6. Ch. 40, question 9.
7. Ch. 13, questions 4 and 5 (there are two answers).
8. Ch. 12, question 12.
9. Ch. 28, question 7.
10. Ch. 21, question 2.
11. Ch. 23, question 7.
12. Ch. 20, question 5.

chicken. The *rav*'s out of town, but Moshe said, "Let's get out a ruler. Seeing that it's for a mitzvah we're allowed to measure how far along the bone it's broken." Another funny look from the seminary girl. Was she right this time?[13]

Baruch Hashem I had some spare meat and then we had some nice singing and a *devar Torah* expounding on the theme of *"Ba'ah Shabbos ba'ah menuchah."*

Chaim went off to read (or so I thought) and we had some sensible conversation, until a red-faced Chaim reemerged, with Mr. Black's hat looking more like a flying saucer than his best Shabbos hat. Can he fix it?[14]

The meal was drawing to its conclusion. There was a bit of a problem when Avi wanted to put his ice cream right on the hot apple pie. Is he allowed?[15]

Mr. Black brought some peanuts. Could we shell them?[16]

Somebody forgot to say *retzei* in *bentching*. Does he need to repeat the *bentching*?[17]

We needed to bring over two mattresses from a neighbor. We made an eiruv last Pesach — it's just that new people have moved in downstairs and they weren't included in the eiruv. Does that matter?[18]

By the time all the guests left I was really exhausted. But *baruch Hashem* for my wonderful husband. He'd secretly washed all the dishes we needed for the next day and stood there with some beautiful jewelry with a note attached: *For the world-champion balebusteh.* But could I accept it?[19]

---

13. Ch. 10, question 1.
14. Ch. 45, question 4.
15. Ch. 24, question 7.
16. Ch. 18, question 2.
17. Ch. 4, question 10.
18. Ch. 46, question 9.
19. Ch. 9, questions 2 and 4.

Scoring:

19–20 correct answers: Excellent.

16–18 correct answers: Very good.

12–15 correct answers: Good.

5–11 correct answers: A good start.

0–4 correct answers: Enjoy learning *hilchos Shabbos*.

Whatever mark you achieved, you'll enjoy learning this *sefer* by yourself, with a friend, or with your family. Test yourself when you've finished and see how much you've learned. *Hatzlachah*!

CHAPTER 1

KAVOD SHABBOS — HONORING SHABBOS

1. *It's Tuesday morning and I've just seen a nice cut of meat at the butcher's. Should I buy it for Shabbos?*

   Yes, buy it. The Gemara[1] says that it was the conduct of Shammai to buy for Shabbos anything special that he saw during the week. Although Hillel used to leave everything until Erev Shabbos,[2] the *Mishnah Berurah*[3] says that this was because of his high level of trust in Hashem. He relied on all his Shabbos needs being available on Erev Shabbos. Other people should conduct themselves like Shammai.

2. *My neighbor is ultraefficient — her Shabbos is ready by Wednesday. I get up very early on Friday and do everything for Shabbos. Who is a better balabusteh?*

   Better not compare yourself to your neighbor. Other things being equal it's better to do things on Erev Shabbos when it's clear

---

1. *Beitzah* 16a.
2. Ibid.
3. 250:2.

you're doing them in honor of Shabbos.[4]

3. *Moshe has come home with a new chumrah — not to use the washing machine on Erev Shabbos. I've never heard of it. Is he right?*

The *Shulchan Aruch*[5] brings from the Gemara[6] that Ezra decreed that we should wash our clothes on Thursday in honor of Shabbos. There is a dispute whether the purpose of the decree was to wash on Thursday and not Friday in order to be free to make other Shabbos preparations on Erev Shabbos, or just to make sure we have clean clothes for Shabbos. Everyone agrees that it is preferable to wash on Thursday in order to do other preparations on Erev Shabbos.[7] Even though today washing clothes is not as time-consuming as it used to be, it is definitely preferable not to do laundry on Erev Shabbos unless it is strictly necessary.

4. *I've got a helper who'll get the house ready for Shabbos while I go to the beach with the children. Isn't this a good arrangement?*

It may sound good, but even the greatest of our sages actively prepared for Shabbos themselves.[8] This did not compromise their honor; on the contrary, preparing for Shabbos themselves, even with hard physical work, gave *them* honor. If you have personal reasons for taking the children out on Erev Shabbos and your Shabbos will be enhanced if you had quality time with them, at

---

4. Ibid.
5. *Orach Chaim* 242:1.
6. *Bava Kama* 82a.
7. See *Magen Avraham* 242:3, *Mishnah Berurah* 242:5, and *Shaar HaTziyun* 16.
8. *Shulchan Aruch, Orach Chaim* 250:1.

5. *Chaim wants to taste every one of the Shabbos dishes. I told him that one is enough. Am I right?*

The *Mishnah Berurah*[9] does say that it is a mitzvah to taste all the Shabbos foods to check if they taste right, but it can be done by one person rather than the whole family. This practice is also a *segulah* for long life as it says, "*Toamehah chaim zachu*,"[10] and according to this reason more than one person could do it but it's probably not practical that the children taste all the foods — unless you have a lot of kitchen staff! Besides, listening to one's parents also brings a promise of a long life, as it says, "*Lemaan yaarichun yamecha*"[11]!

6. *Homemade challos are nice, but it's so much easier to send Moshe to the supermarket. What should I do?*

Three reasons are given for the beautiful custom of the *baalas habayis* to bake her own challos on Erev Shabbos: to perform the mitzvah of taking challah; to make sure it is *pas Yisrael* and not *pas palter*;[12] and to make up for the sin of Chavah, which caused the eventual death of Adam HaRishon, who was known as the challah of the world.[13] I would add a fourth reason — they taste

---

9. 250:2.
10. "Those who experience it [literally, taste it] will merit life" (Shabbos *Musaf*).
11. "Honor your father and mother so that the days of your life will be increased…" (*Shemos* 20:12).
12. Bread baked by a non-Jew, which is not ideal even if it is kosher (*Shulchan Aruch, Yoreh Deah* 112:2).
13. *Shulchan Aruch, Orach Chaim* 242:1, Rama; *Mishnah Berurah* 6.

much better! If, in your personal circumstances, it is impossible to bake challos at home, you'll have to buy. From the way you ask your question, it sounds as though, with encouragement, you could find the time. Go for it!

7. *Chaim says you only have to wash your hands and face, not your feet, in honor of Shabbos. This week I told him if he doesn't wash his feet, he's not wearing his new Shabbos shoes. But what do I say next week?*

If Chaim has dirty feet, he has to wash them. Besides, it's a mitzvah to wash one's whole body in honor of Shabbos, if possible.[14] Doesn't Chaim want to be like the holy Tanna Rabbi Yehuda Bar Ila'i, who[15] on Erev Shabbos washed himself in hot water, dressed himself in his finest clothes, and waited to bring in Shabbos looking like a *Malach Hashem Tzevakos*?

8. *I can never remember this: In what order do you cut your nails?*

Starting with the left hand, counting from the thumb: fourth finger, second, fifth, third, thumb. Right hand: second, fourth, thumb, third, fifth. In other words, moving from left to right making sure not to clip two adjacent nails consecutively.[16] Some hold that one should do the right hand before the left.[17]

9. *My neighbor cuts her nails on Thursday. I learned not to. Do I say anything?*

---

14. *Shulchan Aruch, Orach Chaim* 260:1, *Rama.*
15. *Shabbos* 25b.
16. *Rama* 260:1.
17. *Piskei Teshuvos* 260:7 (enlarged edition).

You are right.[18] Telling someone else they're making a mistake, however, needs a great deal of diplomacy and sensitivity. I suggest that you gently mention to her that you heard that you shouldn't cut your nails on Thursday and that maybe you should both check up with the *rav*. I suspect that she was also taught not to cut her nails on Thursday but she misheard or has forgotten or miscopied somebody's notes in seminary.

10. *Our fourteen-year-old likes to have her shower at the last minute. What do I tell her?*

Reread the first two sentences of the previous answer. The *Mishnah Berurah*[19] points out two possible consequences of washing close to Shabbos — combing hair, which involves the *melachah* of *gozez* (pulling out hair); and squeezing the towel or washcloth, which is part of the *melachah* of *melaben* (washing clothes). Braiding or styling hair is another issue, brushing off a stain on her dress, cleaning teeth, turning off her bedroom light, etc., are others. Of course we're not talking about deliberately breaking Shabbos, *chas veshalom*, but just beforehand, just about, "Oh, is it already after *shekiah*?"

Maybe the tactic here would be to quote the well-known *segulah* of bringing in Shabbos before the required time to give merits for recovery from illness or to help other people in need. Learn a halachah or two of *hilchos Shabbos* at the Shabbos table without looking at anyone accusingly. Your daughter will mature, eventually.

---

18. *Mishnah Berurah* 260:6.
19. Ibid. 1.

CHAPTER 2

EREV SHABBOS

1. *It hasn't rained for six months. Can my garden sprinkler continue to work over Shabbos?*

   Watering a garden on Shabbos involves the *melachos* of *zorea* (sowing) and possibly *choresh* (plowing).[1] It is permitted to prepare a *melachah* on Erev Shabbos that will continue by itself on Shabbos, and the example of water sprinklers is mentioned explicitly.[2] There are a number of exceptions, particularly in the area of preparing hot food for Shabbos. See chapter 25, "*Bishul*," part II, for more details. Other exceptions are alluded to in the following few questions.

2. *It's Friday afternoon and I've just spotted a mouse. Can I ask Moshe to put out the mousetraps before Shabbos?*

   This is also permitted and mentioned explicitly in the *Shulchan Aruch*.[3] However, an animal that was trapped on Shabbos is *muk-*

---

1. Shulchan Aruch, Orach Chaim 336:3, Rama; Mishnah Berurah 26; Shaar HaTziyun 18.
2. Shulchan Aruch, Orach Chaim 252:5.
3. Ibid. 252:1.

tzeh and it will have to be left where it is until after Shabbos.[4] If the dead animal causes a disturbing smell, it can be moved to the nearest area where people do not congregate.[5]

3. *I've just taken out my Shabbos dress and there's a big stain on it from last week's cholent. Can I quickly wash it and put it in the dryer before Shabbos?*

The Rama[6] brings the opinion that although we are normally allowed to prepare a *melachah* on Erev Shabbos for Shabbos as we explained in answer 1 above, it is forbidden if people can hear the noise and possibly suspect that a Jew is doing a *melachah* on Shabbos. A washing machine definitely falls into this category but a dryer is somewhat quieter and could be permitted if people in the next room or outside cannot hear it. There are differing views about the status of clothes that are wet at the beginning of Shabbos but that will definitely be dry during Shabbos.[7] A Shabbos garment that is urgently required is not considered *muktzeh*.[8]

4. *Without an alarm clock, Moshe will never wake up in time for Shacharis. Can he set it before Shabbos to go off in the morning?*

As mentioned above, a machine that produces noise is not allowed to run on Shabbos, even if it was set before Shabbos. However, the Rama himself[9] says that this is only *lechatchilah*.

---

4. Ibid. 308:39.
5. Ibid. 34.
6. Ibid. 252:5.
7. *Orchos Shabbos*, vol. 1, 13:72, note 124.
8. *Shulchan Aruch* 301:45, *Mishnah Berurah* 162.
9. 252:5.

Where there will be a loss one can be lenient. To avoid missing *Shacharis* in shul, and the mitzvah of *krias Shema*, etc. is certainly a reason for leniency.[10]

5. *Tomorrow the Yankees are playing an important match and there's a live commentary on "Voice of America." Is there any leniency to put the radio on a Shabbos clock so that I can listen?*

Let's leave aside the issues of *bitul Torah* (wasting time that could have been used for learning Torah) and this being an inappropriate way of spending Shabbos. In terms of *hilchos Shabbos* this is also forbidden for the reasons we mentioned above. Missing the Yankees is certainly not regarded as a loss in halachic terms.[11] Only in an emergency situation when one needs information that could help avoid danger is it permitted. In such a case one would leave the radio on a low volume rather than use a Shabbos clock.

6. *We make a living by selling cola from a vending machine in Times Square. Do I have to immobilize it before Shabbos?*

This is a question of *lifnei iver* (causing someone to sin). Since most of the people who will be in Times Square over Shabbos will not be Jewish, the machine can be left operating.[12]

---

10. Some compare an alarm clock to a clock that chimes on the hour, which the Rama himself says is permitted. This is because everyone knows that it is set before Shabbos. However, this comparison is dubious because many people set their alarm clock just before they go to sleep depending on when they need to get up in the morning. But the *heter* mentioned in our answer is straightforward.
11. See *Minchas Yitzchak* 1:107.
12. *Shemiras Shabbos KeHilchasah* 29:28.

7. *I sell products online. Can my website take orders on Shabbos?*

   This case is even better than the last one. You are doing nothing to encourage people to contact your website on Shabbos and you personally are not responding to a would-be purchaser. It is permitted.[13]

8. *There's a cruise leaving next Thursday and I could really do with a vacation. Is there a problem?*

   There is a potential problem. The *Shulchan Aruch*[14] says that to begin a sea journey within three days of Shabbos is not allowed except for a *devar mitzvah* because it's likely that seasickness will interfere with *oneg Shabbos*. The Rama[15] says that we are quite lenient as to what constitutes a *devar mitzvah* and although a pleasure trip would not be permitted, it could be allowed if this cruise is the only chance for an exhausted person to rest.

9. *My tooth needs to be extracted and the dentist gave me an appointment for next Friday. Should I take it?*

   We can learn from the previous source that we shouldn't do anything within three days of Shabbos that will interfere with our *oneg Shabbos*. If you're not in pain now and the tooth extraction will cause pain over Shabbos, try to get an appointment after Shabbos. If this is the only appointment available and there is a good medical reason for the tooth to be extracted, you can take the Erev Shabbos

---

13. According to most opinions. If your website serves mainly Jewish customers it is better to close it down for Shabbos. See Rabbi Yosef Y. Kushner, *Commerce and Shabbos* (New York: Feldheim Publishers), pp. 184–188.
14. *Orach Chaim* 248:1.
15. Ibid. 4.

appointment, as it would constitute a *devar mitzvah* as mentioned above.[16]

10. *I'm a professional seamstress, and with one hour to go before Shabbos, someone called to ask me to do a quick fix on his Shabbos suit. What should I say?*

The Gemara[17] says that one who works on Erev Shabbos after the time of *Minchah* will see no *berachah* from his work. This is brought in the *Shulchan Aruch*.[18] There is a dispute[19] whether this refers to *Minchah Gedolah* (half an hour after midday) or *Minchah Ketanah* (two and a half hours before Shabbos). One hour before Shabbos is, therefore, certainly included. The *Mishnah Berurah*[20] says that, according to several authorities, it is forbidden according to the halachah and is not just a case of not seeing a *berachah* from such work. If, as in this case, the work is for something needed for Shabbos, we may do it, but not for payment, unless the worker needs the money to pay for her own *oneg Shabbos*.[21]

---

16. *Shemiras Shabbos KeHilchasah* 32:33, note 97.
17. *Pesachim* 50b.
18. *Orach Chaim* 251.
19. Ibid.
20. Ibid. 5.
21. Ibid.

CHAPTER 3

THE SHABBOS CANDLES

1. *Some people light two candles; others light more. Which custom should I follow?*

   If your family tradition is to light two candles, it is certainly a worthy custom that symbolizes the two aspects of the mitzvah of Shabbos — *zachor veshamor*.[1] There is also an increasingly popular custom to add on an extra candle for each child one is blessed with. This symbolizes the extra light that all Jewish parents hope and pray each child will bring to the world through his or her Torah and mitzvos. This practice, in turn, will hopefully inspire the children as they sit at the Shabbos table. If you do adopt this custom, you must continue it. However, if you're lighting away from home, the custom is to light just two candles.[2]

2. *Moshe wants me to light with olive oil. Is it any better than candles?*

   My first response is that if your husband wants you to light with olive oil, light with olive oil. One of the reasons for kindling lights for Shabbos is to promote *shalom bayis*,[3] so agreeing to your hus-

---

1. *Shulchan Aruch, Orach Chaim* 263:1.
2. *Shemiras Shabbos KeHilchasah* 43:3.
3. *Shabbos* 23b.

band's request would be particularly appropriate and certainly add to your *shalom bayis*.

As to whether there is an intrinsic halachic difference between lighting with oil or candles nowadays, I would say that there is not. Both are reliable and produce a clear light. Some may think that tall candles have more of a "presence" on the Shabbos table than oil lights, which adds to their *oneg Shabbos*.

However, we are told[4] that one who is conscientious in kindling Shabbos lights will merit the blessing of sons who are *talmidei chachamim*. Oil is traditionally associated with Torah study.[5] Other sources also speak of the significance of lighting with oil.[6] Thus, there are good reasons why an increasing number of Jewish families are reverting to the traditional oil lights, especially since nowadays olive oil, ready-made wicks, wick holders, and convenient and attractive glass holders are readily available and simple to use.

3. *Is there any reason why we can't do a swap — Moshe will light the candles and I'll make Kiddush?*

Can a man kindle the Shabbos lights and a woman make Kiddush for the family if the situation demands it? Yes. Should you do a swap? No, for at least two reasons.

First, the *Shulchan Aruch*[7] states explicitly that the mitzvah of kindling the Shabbos lights should be done by the woman of the house. It is her privilege and responsibility. The man's role in this

---

4. Ibid.
5. *Sanhedrin 94b*.
6. *Midrash Tanchuma*.
7. *Orach Chaim* 263:3.

mitzvah is the preparing of the wicks.[8] Kiddush is also traditionally the responsibility of the man who is the *baal habayis*. Second, the question itself reflects a desire to alter the traditional Jewish family structure. Our sources say that a woman should treat her husband as a king and then he will treat her as his queen. This way, everyone comes out a winner.

4. *We're invited out for the Shabbos evening meal. Where do I light?*

If you say you're invited out, this implies that you're eating there and coming home after the seudah. Obviously your hosts' home is within walking distance, probably quite close. If so, it's better to light at home, wait until it's dark or nearly dark in order to have benefit from the lights, and then go to your hosts who no doubt will have their own lights on or near the table.[9] If you have to leave your house while it's still light outside, you can still light at home, assuming it is after *plag haminchah*,[10] but make sure the candles are long enough that they'll still be burning when you come back.

If you're invited for the whole Shabbos, the custom is for a married woman guest to light near the hostess's lights.[11]

5. *Can I light and then take a taxi?*

The Ashkenazic custom is that under normal circumstances when a woman kindles her Shabbos lights, she accepts Shabbos,

---

8. *Mishnah Berurah* 263:12.
9. *Shemiras Shabbos KeHilchasah* 45:8 and note 36.
10. This lighting of the candles will be an acceptance of Shabbos even in a case of special need (see next answer); *Shulchan Aruch, Orach Chaim* 263:4.
11. See note 9.

after which she may not do anything that is forbidden on Shabbos. In a case of special need, a woman may light with the intention that she is not yet accepting Shabbos and therefore she could still go in a taxi, etc.[12] What is regarded a "special need" is a subjective question on which a *rav* should be consulted.

6. *That's a shame. One light has gone out. Can I relight it?*

As in the previous answer, the Ashkenazic custom is that once a woman has lit her Shabbos candles, no *melachos* are allowed. However if there is someone else present who has not accepted Shabbos, you can ask him to rekindle this light.[13]

7. *Now that I've lit, I feel hungry. Do I have to wait until Moshe comes home and makes Kiddush?*

No, you don't need to wait. You can make Kiddush yourself, eat an olive-sized (approximately 30 cc) piece of cake and other food if you want to, as long as you will still have an appetite for your Shabbos seudah. Once we've accepted Shabbos, we're not allowed to eat or drink before Kiddush.[14] In a case of need, some *poskim* allow one to drink water or even tea until sunset.[15] A woman who needs to eat or drink for medical reasons should not accept Shabbos when she lights her candles, as above, and then she can eat or drink until sunset.[16]

---

12. *Shulchan Aruch, Orach Chaim* 263:10; *Mishnah Berurah* 44.
13. *Shulchan Aruch, Orach Chaim* 263:17. Obviously this is only if it is still before the official time that your community accepts Shabbos.
14. Ibid 271:4, *Mishnah Berurah* 11.
15. *Shemiras Shabbos KeHilchasah* 43:45.
16. Ibid. 43:47.

8. *Our shul davens early in the summer. Do I have to light early as well?*

Your husband is bringing in Shabbos early for reasons of convenience, rather than a formal desire to accept *tosefes Shabbos*. Although he accepts Shabbos upon himself in the course of davening, this does not obligate you and your family to accept Shabbos at that time, at least according to one major opinion.[17] Having said that, there is a possibility that you may not do *melachos* for him, like cooking the Shabbos seudah.[18] To avoid confusion and also because of a major dissenting opinion,[19] I advise you to light the candles when your husband is accepting Shabbos and enjoy some extra *kedushas Shabbos*. In case of difficulty, consult your local *rav*.

9. *I haven't davened Minchah yet. Shall I daven first or light first?*

You should definitely daven *Minchah*, which belongs to Erev Shabbos, first, before ushering in Shabbos with your lighting of the candles.[20]

10. *Oy vey! The light's still on in the children's bedroom. Can I ask Chaya to turn it off?*

If Chaya has not accepted Shabbos, you can ask her.[21] But I would think it appropriate and likely that a daughter accepts Shabbos when her mother lights. Try a neighbor, or if there are non-Jews around, you can certainly ask them. For the rules of asking non-Jews to do *melachos* on Shabbos itself, see chapter 13 on the subject.

---

17. *Iggros Moshe, Orach Chaim* 3:38.
18. Ibid.
19. *Shevet HaLevi* 7:35.
20. *Shulchan Aruch, Orach Chaim* 263; *Mishnah Berurah* 43.
21. See note 13 above.

CHAPTER 4

THE THREE MEALS OF SHABBOS

1. *I'm on a diet. What is the minimum amount of challah I need to eat?*

    You should try to eat a little over the volume of an egg (about 60 cc) of challah at each of the three meals. At a minimum eat a *kezayis* (the volume of an olive), which is just under 30 cc.[1]

2. *When there is a kiddush in shul, Chaim is never hungry for lunch. What do I tell him?*

    Tell him how much Hashem wants him to enjoy his Shabbos meals, and that's why the halachah tells us not to eat a big meal on Erev Shabbos — so we'll have an appetite for the Friday night seudah.[2] In the same way, we mustn't spoil our appetite for our Shabbos morning seudah by eating more than a small amount at a kiddush, no matter how tasty the food is![3] The minimum one has to eat at a kiddush to fulfill the halachah of

---

1. Shulchan Aruch, Orach Chaim 291:1; Mishnah Berurah 2.
2. Shulchan Aruch, Orach Chaim 249:2.
3. Shemiras Shabbos KeHilchasah 54:37.

Kiddush bemakom seudah is discussed in the *Shulchan Aruch*.⁴

3. *Some people have fish for every meal. Should we do that?*

   It's a mitzvah to honor Shabbos by eating important foods. The *Mishnah Berurah*⁵ says it is "good to eat fish at each of the three Shabbos meals." Some suggest that by eating fish we demonstrate our full acceptance of the words of our *chachamim*, who taught us that fish do not need *shechitah*. Therefore, assuming you like fish,⁶ you should take on this custom (*bli neder*). If we eat fish at the seudah, followed by meat or even chicken soup, we must remember to eat and drink something between the fish and the meat and use different or newly washed cutlery.⁷

4. *Is it a mitzvah to eat chocolate on Shabbos?*

   It's not a mitzvah to eat chocolate as such. One way we honor Shabbos is by eating delicacies, which includes all tasty foods. Ideally we should have the specific intention to eat *lekavod Shabbos* and even say the words "*lekavod Shabbos kodesh*" before saying a *berachah* (where appropriate). It's good to say "*lekavod Shabbos kodesh*" even when we buy the food for Shabbos.⁸

5. *I really didn't feel well last night and couldn't eat anything. Have I lost the mitzvah of the three meals?*

   If you didn't have a seudah on Friday night, you can have three

---

4. *Orach Chaim* 273:5.
5. 242:2.
6. Ibid.
7. *Shulchan Aruch, Yoreh Deah* 116:3.
8. *Mishnah Berurah* 250:2.

seudos on Shabbos day. If you didn't eat anything on Friday night, you also did not fulfill the mitzvah of Kiddush, even if you heard it. Therefore you should say the full Friday night Kiddush (without "*Vayechulu…*") before eating your first seudah.⁹

6. *I've only got one complete challah. Can I use one from the freezer to make up lechem mishneh?*

There is a dispute about using a challah that is frozen and therefore inedible for *lechem mishneh*.¹⁰ *Lechatchilah* make sure to take the extra challah out of the freezer in advance so it will have thawed by the time of the seudah.

Please note three relevant points:

a. If different foods in the freezer are mixed together, we may only take out a small bun that will thaw in a few minutes, not a larger challah that will take an hour or longer, because of the *melachah* of *borer* (separating¹¹), which is dealt with in chapter 20.

b. If there is any frost on the challah, we may not thaw it near a source of heat because of the *melachah* of *bishul*, which will be dealt with in chapter 24, "*Bishul*," part I.

c. A freezer is likely to contain *muktzeh* items, like flour, raw meat, raw fish, etc., so items we may need on Shabbos, such as spare challah or ice cream, should not be underneath these

---

9. *Shulchan Aruch, Orach Chaim* 291:1; *Mishnah Berurah* 5.
10. *Shemiras Shabbos KeHilchasah* 55:12 and note 39.
11. *Orchos Shabbos*, vol. 1, 3:55 and note 54. This is the view of Rav Yosef Shalom Elyashiv and Rav Nissim Karelitz, that even though one has to take food out from a freezer earlier in order for it to be ready for the seudah, it is not called "*samuch leseudah*." However Rav Pesach Eliyahu Falk in *Zochor Veshomor*, "*Hilchos Borer*," is lenient on this point.

items. It's a good idea to have an opened box of matzos available for *lechem mishneh* and unexpected guests.

7. *The challos joined together as they rose in the oven. Can I count them as two for lechem mishneh?*

    Yes, but it is better to separate them.[12]

8. *Mrs. Mizrachi always has hadassim in her house on Shabbos. Why?*

    There is an important mitzvah to say one hundred *berachos* every day. On Shabbos we do not say the weekday *Shemoneh Esrei*, which contains fifty-seven *berachos*. We make up some of the shortfall with the four Shabbos *Shemoneh Esreis* and three seudos, but we are still missing a few. The *Shulchan Aruch*[13] says we should eat different fruits and enjoy different fragrances to complete the hundred *berachos*. Many Sephardim have the beautiful custom of bringing *hadassim* into their homes for Shabbos so they can make the *berachah* "*borei atzei besamim*" on the scent of the *hadassim* whenever they come into the house. This is why Mrs. Mizrachi has *hadassim* in her home. It is important to remember that we may not say an unnecessary *berachah* in order to make up our one hundred *berachos*.[14]

9. *Can women be more lenient about shalosh seudos/seudah shelishit than men?*

    No, women are equally obligated in this very important mitzvah

---

12. Ibid 55:6.
13. *Orach Chaim* 290:1.
14. See my *sefer Do You Know Hilchos Brachos?*

as the *Shulchan Aruch*[15] says explicitly. The *Mishnah Berurah*[16] comments that all the mitzvos of Shabbos apply equally to men and women. He further says that women also benefited from the miracle of the manna, which is the source of the mitzvah to eat three meals on Shabbos.

10. *Why do many people call the third meal shalosh seudos? Doesn't that mean "three meals"?*

Yes, *shalosh seudos* does mean "three meals."[17] So why is one meal called "three meals"? It's a mitzvah to eat the Shabbos meals in honor of Shabbos, rather than for the simple pleasure of delicious tastes. We cannot be sure we're eating the Friday night seudah in honor of Shabbos, because we're hungry. We may eat the Shabbos morning seudah also because we're hungry. However, we're often not hungry for the third meal, especially in the winter. We eat it because the halachah says we must honor Shabbos by eating three meals. So we're eating this meal in honor of Shabbos and this in turn shows our intention that eating the first two meals was also in honor of Shabbos.

This meal is therefore worth three meals in that through it we receive the reward for three meals eaten in honor of Shabbos. Hence the traditional name *shalosh seudos* — "three meals." There's just one difference between it and the first two meals of Shabbos: If we forget to say *retzei* in *birkas hamazon* of the first two meals, or even if we're not sure whether we forgot to say it,

---

15.   *Orach Chaim* 291:6.
16.   291:26.
17.   *Sefer Taamei HaMinhagim.*

we have to repeat the whole *birkas hamazon*.[18] But if we forget to say *retzei* in the *birkas hamazon* of *shalosh seudos* we don't need to repeat it.[19]

---

18. *Shulchan Aruch, Orach Chaim* 188:6 and *Mishnah Berurah* 16. If one remembers before saying "Baruch…haolom ha'el…" one can say a special *berachah* as a substitute for *retzei*. However, see *Mishnah Berurah* 23 and *Biur Halachah*, s.v. "*ad*," for a discussion on the precise details.
19. *Shulchan Aruch, Orach Chaim* 188:8; *Mishnah Berurah* 31.

CHAPTER 5

WHAT WE MAY READ ON SHABBOS

1. *I don't go to work on Shabbos and I've always described myself as "shomer Shabbos." Now someone tells me I'm not even allowed to read the financial section of the newspaper. I'm happy to take this on. But why?*

   I'm glad to hear you're a *ben aliyah*, willing to raise your standard of Shabbos observance. *Yasher kochacha*! Up till now you obviously thought that on Shabbos we merely don't "go to work." Now you've learned that on Shabbos, work mustn't come to us in any shape or form. Reading financial reports in the newspaper, reading financial documents — in fact, reading about anything to do with an activity forbidden on Shabbos is not allowed. To safeguard this, even the reading of other nonessential texts was forbidden, with certain exceptions.[1]

   The rationale for this prohibition is evident. Hashem's wonderful gift to the Jews, Shabbos, forbids us from doing any of the thirty-nine main types of work. This gives us one day a week to remind ourselves of our real purpose in life. I call it a "spiritual pit stop" to refill our spiritual tanks, to give our *neshamos* the

---

1. *Shulchan Aruch, Orach Chaim* 307:13–17.

inspiration to survive another six days in the material world in which we live. It also gives us a chance to check that we're going on the right road toward our ultimate destination. Wouldn't this purpose of Shabbos be all but negated if we spent our time reading and thinking about this same material world from which we're trying to escape?

2. *My wife's always planning ahead so she likes to read the latest recipes on Shabbos. Is that a problem?*

Observing Shabbos may be a challenge but it should not be regarded as a problem. Encourage your wife to read some of the inspiring Torah-related articles and books that are so available nowadays. Recipes can be read at other times. If she is preparing for a Shabbos meal or another *seudas mitzvah* there is room to be lenient.[2]

3. *My neighbor said that if you read forbidden material silently, it's allowed. Is she right?*

No.[3]

4. *We keep all our bar mitzvah and wedding invitations in one drawer. Can I read through them on Shabbos to make sure we don't forget one?*

We can read anything to do with a mitzvah, including invitations to *simchos*.[4] It is an important mitzvah to participate in someone

---

2. *Shemiras Shabbos KeHilchasah* 29:46; *Orchos Shabbos*, vol. 2, 22:148, note 223.
3. *Shulchan Aruch, Orach Chaim* 307:13.
4. *Orchos Shabbos*, vol. 2, 22:148, note 200.

else's *simchah* and share the joy of the *baal simchah*. We know how much we value it when other people take the trouble to come to our *simchos*.

5. *We keep rabbinically approved science books in a certain room where we're not allowed to learn Torah. Do we have to remove them before Shabbos?*

Don't remove them. To read books of general knowledge is permitted according to the strict halachah.[5] Here they can perform a useful function if they distract a person from thinking about Torah.

6. *It says on the paroches in shul that we donated it in memory of Zeidy. Am I allowed to read that on Shabbos?*

In principle it is permitted to read words embroidered on a *paroches l'ilui nishmas* somebody, as this elevates the *neshamah* of the deceased.[6] It would not be allowed if you feel sad when you think of your *zeidy*, as we have to avoid things that distress us on Shabbos. Maybe in years to come, you'll be inspired when you remember your *zeidy*, rather than sad, and then it will be permitted.

7. *What am I allowed to read on Shabbos?*

We're certainly allowed and encouraged to read books and articles on Torah topics, life stories of *Gedolim*, inspirational books that describe people's *emunah* and *bitachon* in difficult situations,

---

5. Shulchan Aruch, Orach Chaim 307; Mishnah Berurah 65.
6. Orchos Shabbos, vol. 2, ch. 22:136, note 206; Shemiras Shabbos KeHilchasah, ch. 28, note 108.

stories of *hashgachah pratis*, stories from which we can learn *middos tovos*, etc. Today we have such a plethora of publications on these topics that we can choose whatever we find most interesting and inspirational; this way, any spare time on Shabbos that we have to read will be most usefully spent.

8. *When we're going to have guests on Shabbos, I write a list of all the dishes I've prepared and when to serve them. I also prepare a table plan. Moshe said I'm not allowed to read the list on Shabbos. What am I supposed to do?*

The halachah[7] sees in this situation the risk that a hostess might change her mind about something and erase what she has written. For this reason, either somebody else who has no authority to make any changes can read out the list, or even the hostess herself, if someone is standing nearby to "guard" her from transgressing Shabbos.

There is still the general prohibition of reading nonessential material that is only permitted in the case of a mitzvah. In this situation a mitzvah would be a *seudas mitzvah* such as Shabbos *sheva berachos* or a bar mitzvah. If the guests have nowhere else to eat or she's invited them to draw them closer to Jewish observance, it is also considered a *seudas mitzvah*. She may read the list under the conditions of the previous paragraph.

9. *The mailman has brought an express letter on Shabbos. May I read it on Shabbos?*

We may not accept a letter or parcel from a mailman who is standing outside our house on Shabbos. This would constitute

---

7. *Shulchan Aruch, Orach Chaim* 307:12; *Mishnah Berurah* 47.

an act of taking something from a public to a private domain, which is the *melachah* of *hotzaah*. We have to ask him, respectfully, to put it down inside the house. We may not sign for a letter or parcel delivered by a non-Jew on Shabbos.

If a very important item is sealed, we may be allowed to hint to the non-Jewish postman to open it. (See *"Amirah Le'akum,"* chapter 13.) An express letter might contain vital information and if one comes on Shabbos we're permitted to read it silently just to check the contents.[8]

10. *Okay, I won't read the paper on Shabbos, but I do like to see the births, engagements, and death notices sections of the community newsletter. Any leniency?*

You can read the births and engagements announcements, if you might meet the *baalei simchah*, in order to wish them mazal tov. Leave the death notices until after Shabbos.

---

8. Ibid., 14.

CHAPTER 6

WALKING AND TALKING ON SHABBOS

1. *I heard the rabbi said something about the way we should walk and talk on Shabbos. What does this have to do with the laws of Shabbos?*

   Have a look at the end of the *haftarah* of Yom Kippur morning. Yeshayahu HaNavi[1] tells us to honor Shabbos by refraining from our weekday pursuits. We should even walk and talk in a sanctified manner befitting someone in the close presence of Hashem, which we are on Shabbos.[2] When we do this, the Navi promises us, we will enjoy the most sublime pleasure of closeness to Hashem, we will be honored by all the nations of the world, and we will merit to receive our full inheritance in Eretz Yisrael as promised by Hashem to Yaakov Avinu.[3]

2. *Moshe's late for the minyan. Is he allowed to run?*

   Yes, we are allowed to run for a mitzvah.[4]

---

1. *Yeshayah* 58:13.
2. See *Nefesh Shimshon, Shabbos Kodesh*.
3. *Bereishis* 28:14.
4. *Shulchan Aruch, Orach Chaim* 301:1.

3. *It looks like rain. Do we have to get wet?*

   No, we are also allowed to run to avoid getting wet.[5]

4. *They say walking is very good for your health. Is Shabbos afternoon a good time?*

   A leisurely walk is permitted even if we are doing it for exercise. However, walking fast enough to cause one to perspire is not allowed.[6] If one's doctor has ordered daily walks for important medical reasons, e.g., recuperation from a heart attack, even a quick walk would be permitted.[7]

   Although a leisurely walk is generally allowed, bear in mind that it's very important not to waste time on Shabbos. Depending on individual circumstances it may be appropriate to enjoy a walk on Shabbos afternoon,[8] but we should also spend as much time as possible going to *shiurim* and learning.

5. *Chaim loves running round the park. Do I have to stop him?*

   No, you don't need to stop him. Children, who enjoying running and jumping, may do so on Shabbos.[9]

6. *We had a seminary girl for Shabbos. When I told her I'd give her a call during the week she gave me a funny look. Why?*

---

5. *Shemiras Shabbos KeHilchasah* 29:4.
6. *Shulchan Aruch, Orach Chaim* 301; *Mishnah Berurah* 7.
7. *Shulchan Aruch, Orach Chaim* 301; *Mishnah Berurah* 7. Obviously we can rely on the lenient opinions in a case of necessity.
8. I remember my late rebbe, Rav Moshe Schwab, *zt"l*, and his late rebbetzin, *a"h*, often going for a Shabbos walk in Saltwell Park, Gateshead.
9. *Shulchan Aruch, Orach Chaim* 301:2.

As mentioned above, we have to sanctify Shabbos by speaking differently from the way we do during the week. This includes not saying that after Shabbos we'll do something that's not allowed on Shabbos. Since we're not allowed to use the telephone on Shabbos, we're not allowed to say, "I'll call you after Shabbos." You may say, "I'll speak to you after Shabbos."

7. *I don't understand. My uncle is a rabbi and when he came for Shabbos he said he's flying to New York on Monday. Why was that allowed?*

It is only forbidden to talk about doing an activity if the activity is undoubtedly forbidden on Shabbos. "Flying" (unless you're the pilot) means sitting in one's seat on an airplane. This in itself is not a forbidden act on Shabbos and therefore it is permitted on Shabbos to say that one will be flying during the week.[10]

8. *Can I tell my neighbor that our vacation home cost two hundred dollars a week?*

If your neighbor is thinking of renting that vacation home or a similar one, you may not say how much you paid. If the price has no longer any practical significance, it is allowed.[11]

9. *What about saying, "I'm hoping to go to Yerushalayim next Wednesday"?*

We are allowed to say we're hoping to "go" to Yerushalayim after Shabbos because there is no mention of any activity that is

---

10. Shemiras Shabbos KeHilchasah 29:66; Rav Pesach Eliyahu Falk, *Zochor Veshomor*, "Discussing Weekday Affairs and Discussing the Forbidden," p. 12.
11. Shulchan Aruch, Orach Chaim 307; Mishnah Berurah 26.

forbidden on Shabbos. Although Yerushalayim is outside the *techum* (the maximum distance we may walk on Shabbos under normal circumstances) if there were small huts along the way in which watchmen stayed to guard fields, etc., it would be permitted to walk there on Shabbos. Even if there are no such huts, it is permitted because there could be. However, to say, "I'm hoping to drive" or "catch a bus," etc., would not be allowed.[12]

10. *We may have finally found a shidduch for Rochel. The young man's parents are in town for Shabbos. Can we invite them over to discuss "details"?*

For a mitzvah that could otherwise be lost, we may discuss matters otherwise forbidden on Shabbos.[13] So invite your would-be *mechutanim*, and I hope there will soon be a mazal tov.

---

12. *Shulchan Aruch, Orach Chaim* 307:8; *Mishnah Berurah* 30.
13. *Shulchan Aruch, Orach Chaim* 306:6.

CHAPTER 7

AVOIDING DISTRESS

1. *What is this mitzvah of being happy on Shabbos? And if I'm not...?*

   Of course a Jew should always be happy — "*ivdu es Hashem besimchah*" — but on Shabbos it is particularly appropriate. Shabbos is the time when we strengthen our trust in Hashem. We have more time to remember that He created the world and brought us out of Mitzrayim. The extra *pesukei dezimrah* we say on Shabbos and the *zemiros* we sing at the Shabbos table mention Hashem's many kindnesses to us. All this naturally makes us feel relaxed and happy.

   Besides, on Shabbos we are in Hashem's presence. When a king comes to visit, he wants to see his subjects happy, which adds to his honor. Similarly it is an honor for Hashem that we are happy especially on the day that we are in His close presence.

2. *I heard that Yenta got that teaching job that my daughter was after. When shall I give her the news?*

   We are not allowed to cause anybody to be unhappy on Shabbos. Seeing that your daughter will be unhappy to hear that Yenta got the job rather than her, Shabbos is not the time to break the news to her.[1]

---

1. *Shulchan Aruch, Orach Chaim 307; Mishnah Berurah 3.*

3. *The newspapers often print obituaries of great rabbanim. They're always educational but it's upsetting to realize what we've lost. May I read them on Shabbos?*

   If reading obituaries makes you sad, which is normal, especially if there is a description of the moment of death, don't read them on Shabbos.

4. *Our rebbe always cries during davening. Why is that allowed?*

   Tears of spiritual elation are permitted. Rabbi Akiva cried intensely when he read *Shir HaShirim*.[2]

5. *Moshe has the flu and he asked me to say Tehillim for him. Is there a problem?*

   Saying *Tehillim* or davening for somebody who is not in danger is not allowed on Shabbos because focusing our attention on illness naturally makes us sad. Where there is imminent danger, it is permitted, like any other form of *pikuach nefesh*.[3]

6. *The chazan in our shul has a wonderful voice but by the time we get home it's after one o'clock. Shall we go to the early minyan?*

   We are not allowed to go without food or drink on Shabbos until after *chatzos hayom*,[4] even if we do not intend to fast.[5] Some *poskim* allow it if we are involved in learning or davening.[6] A cup of

---

2. Shulchan Aruch, Orach Chaim 288, Mishnah Berurah 4.
3. Shulchan Aruch, Orach Chaim 288:10, Mishnah Berurah 28.
4. Midday according to halachah, halfway between sunrise and sunset.
5. Shulchan Aruch, Orach Chaim 288:1, Mishnah Berurah 2.
6. Shulchan Aruch, Orach Chaim 288:1, Mishnah Berurah 2.

coffee or tea before davening solves the question of fasting.⁷ So you don't really need to go to the early minyan. But remember — Shabbos is not a time for enjoying a concert, even by a chazan. If he inspires you to greater *kavanah* in your *tefillos*, there's something to talk about.

7. *Shabbos afternoons are my time for hospital visiting. Is this okay?*

   Because visiting the sick can be quite distressing, Shabbos is not the ideal day to visit if there is any other option.⁸ If you know sick people who will be particularly lonely on Shabbos and would especially appreciate a visitor, it is permitted.⁹ The correct greeting to give to a sick person on Shabbos is "*Shabbos hi milizok urefuah kerovah lavo* — In the merit that we realize the sanctity of Shabbos that we don't want to disturb even by crying out in prayer, Shabbos itself will bring a speedy recovery."¹⁰

8. *I haven't gone to the shivah house all week. Can I pop in on Friday night?*

   Going to a shivah house is similarly inappropriate on Shabbos. The custom is not to allow it even if we had no opportunity to visit during the week.¹¹

---

7. *Shulchan Aruch, Orach Chaim* 89:3, *Mishnah Berurah* 22. See *Ishei Yisrael, Hilchos Tefillah* 13:25 and note 69, who brings that the custom today is to allow milk and sugar, if necessary, seeing that most people drink tea and coffee like that.
8. *Shulchan Aruch, Orach Chaim* 287:1; *Mishnah Berurah* 1.
9. *Shulchan Aruch, Orach Chaim* 287:1, *Biur Halachah*.
10. Rav Mattisyahu Salomon in his introduction to *Halachos of Refuah on Shabbos* by Rav Yisroel Pinchos Bodner and Rav Daniel B. Roth.
11. Rav Dovid Ribiat, *The 39 Melochos* (New York: Feldheim Publishers, 1999), p. 126.

9. *Can I play chess on Shabbos, yes or no?*

It sounds as though you don't understand that something may be permitted, but not advisable. Think of eating a bar and a half of chocolate — permitted but not advisable. Shabbos is given to us for extra Torah learning and sanctity, not for playing long games of chess.

However, someone who is not able, for whatever reason, to spend the time learning and needs "something permissible to do," may play chess. A bad loser who might end up feeling sad on Shabbos, is not allowed to play.[12]

10. *We think it's a good idea to play some games with the children on Shabbos. It's what they call "quality time." How can we make sure all the kids enjoy it and gain from it?*

I agree it's a good idea to spend quality time with our children on Shabbos. Too often children are left to their own devices on Shabbos while their parents go for a *shluf*, which is a recipe for all sorts of undesirable consequences. I always played a game with the children when they were young on the long winter Friday nights. Whatever we played, we had a system that none of the children lost. There was a first winner, a second winner, a third winner, etc. All the "winners" were duly rewarded with a celebratory song and a prize. Everyone went to sleep happy.

---

12. *Iggros Moshe, Yoreh Deah*, vol. 3, 15:2.

CHAPTER 8

EARNING MONEY ON SHABBOS

1. *I've been asked to lein next Shabbos morning in shul. Can I ask to be paid?*

    Although we are not normally allowed to earn money on Shabbos or Yom Tov, the custom is to be lenient in the case of a mitzvah.[1] There is an extra reason to be lenient with a *baal korei* since it is usually understood that he has to prepare the *leining* before Shabbos.[2] Professional *baalei korei* and chazanim often have an agreement to officiate during the week, i.e., Monday and Thursday or Rosh Chodesh. This is the preferred arrangement, since their wages are being paid *behavlaah*[3] for the week's or month's work. This is another leniency mentioned in the *Shulchan Aruch*.[4]

    A person who is in a position to do a mitzvah purely *leshem Shamayim*, especially on Shabbos, and will do it equally

---

1. *Shulchan Aruch, Orach Chaim* 306; *Mishnah Berurah* 24.
2. *Shemiras Shabbos KeHilchasah* 28:61.
3. Literally, the wages for Shabbos are "swallowed up" in the wages for the week or month.
4. *Orach Chaim* 306:4.

conscientiously without payment, should not ask to be paid.[5]

2. *Chani is babysitting while I go to the kiddush. Can I pay her for her work?*

No, you should not pay her. You may give her a present after Shabbos to show your appreciation.[6] Explain clearly that it is not a payment, to avoid causing Chani to transgress the halachah inadvertently.

3. *My neighbor will babysit for me on the first day of Rosh HaShanah if I do the same for her on the second day. Is that allowed?*

This is permitted because it is not a contractual arrangement. If for some reason you can't babysit for your neighbor on the second day, she is not going to expect payment for her services on the first day. *Shemiras Shabbos KeHilchasah*[7] gives a more technical reason why this is allowed.

4. *We're paying fifty dollars to stay in the Cohens' empty apartment over Shabbos. What's wrong with that?*

If you would be staying there just on Shabbos, payment would not be allowed.[8] Staying in the Cohens' home "for Shabbos" obviously includes some time just before and after Shabbos itself, so it is allowed. It is advisable to specify to the Cohens that the agreement includes one or two hours before and after Shabbos.

---

5.   *Pirkei Avos* 1:3; *Shulchan Aruch, Orach Chaim* 306; *Mishnah Berurah* 22.
6.   *Shulchan Aruch, Orach Chaim* 306; *Mishnah Berurah* 15.
7.   Ch. 28, note 121.
8.   *Shulchan Aruch, Orach Chaim* 246; *Mishnah Berurah* 3.

5. *The caterer has sent in a bill for the kiddush last Shabbos. I told him I'll pay for the food but I'm not paying for his service since it was on Shabbos. He said he'll take me to the beis din. Who's going to win?*

   If you want to avoid acquiring a bad name, I suggest paying up before going to *beis din*. Clearly the caterer worked both before and after Shabbos for you and is therefore entitled to be paid under this leniency of *havlaah*.

6. *The mohel will come from out of town for Yom Tov but he wants two hundred dollars in advance for his trouble. Should I look for somebody else?*

   He isn't charging two hundred dollars to do the bris; he wants two hundred dollars to leave his family over Yom Tov! Seeing that you, and not the mohel, have an obligation to arrange the bris, you should be glad he's prepared to come. Book him!

7. *The bank pays interest every day if I'm in the black. What about my Shabbos earnings?*

   This is a question that all the *poskim* grapple with. On a normal Shabbos it is not a problem because the bank works out the interest from midnight to midnight, which always includes some of Erev Shabbos and some of Motzaei Shabbos. The trouble is in the case of a two-day Yom Tov, and when Shabbos and Yom Tov are on consecutive days. The best solution is to work out how much is being paid to you per day and give that amount to tzedakah.[9]

8. *My nephew will house-sit for us on Shabbos while we're out, for free,*

---

9. *Piskei Teshuvos* 306, note 75 (new edition).

providing I'll lend him our car on Sunday afternoon. He says we should grab the opportunity. I'm not so sure.

When your nephew says he'll house-sit for free, he doesn't really mean "free," but without a cash payment. His house-sitting is on the condition of borrowing your car Sunday afternoon — another form of payment. Even assuming he has a license and insurance and is a very careful driver, this is not allowed because you would be paying him for work done on Shabbos. If he would be house-sitting on Erev Shabbos or Motzaei Shabbos as well, this would be permitted, as in question 4.

9. *Our non-Jewish neighbor is prepared to help us over Shabbos when required, but we must pay him for every job. Is that allowed?*

    Yes. A Jew is not allowed to earn money on Shabbos, but we can pay a non-Jew (after Shabbos, of course) for work he did on Shabbos for us.[10] (In chapter 13 we discuss when we are allowed to ask a non-Jew to work for us on Shabbos.)

10. *Sarit was a tremendous help over Yom Tov when we had the family over. Can I give her a gift to show my appreciation?*

    Yes, you can give her a gift, as in the answer to question 2 above.

---

10. *Shemiras Shabbos KeHilchasah* 28, note 112.

CHAPTER 9

ACQUIRING ITEMS

1. *It's the first day of Succos; our beloved Chaim has just dropped my esrog and the pitom has fallen off. How on earth am I going to get a new esrog on Yom Tov?*

    I'm glad you still love Chaim. Life is full of challenges. I'm not sure if you're worried about getting a new esrog or if you are concerned with the rabbinic prohibition against making a *kinyan* (acquisition) on Shabbos.

    If you can't find an esrog dealer, you'll have to ask a friend to "give" you his esrog in order to fulfill the mitzvah, and then you will have to legally "return" it to him. For this important need of Yom Tov you are allowed to make a *kinyan*.[1] You probably know that halachically we need to acquire the *arbaah minim* on the first day of Succos (first two days in *chutz laAretz*) to fulfill the mitzvah.

    If you can find a dealer who has a kosher esrog still available, you are also allowed to acquire it. In this case, seeing that you intend to pay for it, you have to be careful not to discuss the price on Yom Tov.[2] Just assure him that you will settle up after Yom Tov.

---

1. *Mishnah Berurah* 306:33.
2. Ibid. 323:20.

2. *We're invited out for Shabbos dinner and, as the saying goes, "You can't go empty-handed." Can we take a bottle of wine for the hosts?*

You are correctly concerned about the rabbinic prohibition of giving a present on Shabbos, which comes under the general category of making an acquisition on Shabbos.[3]

The correct solution is either to deliver the wine to your host before Shabbos or ask someone (not a member of your household) before Shabbos to lift it up, with the intention of acquiring it on behalf of your host.

Failing these two solutions, if there is a reliable eiruv, you may take to your hosts on Shabbos an item of food or drink that will add to their *oneg Shabbos*. A bottle with a cap that leaves a ring when opened, is halachically problematic; it's better to choose a different gift.

Note: A wedding or bar mitzvah present that, although not *muktzeh*, is not intended for Shabbos use, should be delivered before Shabbos or acquired on the recipient's behalf on Erev Shabbos.[4]

3. *I'm just visiting this town for Shabbos, but no one has invited me for a seudah. Can I get a meal from the kosher restaurant on Shabbos even though I didn't arrange it beforehand?*

I can't believe it — you're a stranger in town and no one has invited you to eat with them? Find the *rav*. I'm sure he'll arrange something.

Bedieved, your solution is acceptable. Just don't mention the price. Simply just assure the owner that you'll settle up after Shabbos.

---

3. Ibid. 306:33.
4. See *Orchos Shabbos*, vol. 2, 22:44–50 and notes 61–64.

At some places the owner asks for some kind of deposit, so people leave an identity card or passport. Essential documents like these are *muktzeh* on Shabbos, so you shouldn't have them on you in the first place, let alone hand them over to someone else. *Letei'avon.*

4. *My new, not-yet-frum mother-in-law wants to give me a present at the Shabbos sheva berachos. Help!*

   I hear your concern. To upset your new mother-in-law is the last thing you want. However, a solution is at hand. Accept it with a smile, but you should have in mind that you don't want to acquire the gift until after Shabbos; it will remain your mother-in-law's property over Shabbos. Eventually, when your mother-in-law, we hope, becomes a *shomeres mitzvos*, you can suggest going to a *shiur* together on *hilchos Shabbos*. Learning this *sefer* would also be a good start!

5. *Today is our daughter's Shabbos sheva berachos and I need more fruit for the fruit salad. I'm on good terms with our local Pakistani-owned corner store. Can I pop in, get what I need, and pay him tomorrow?*

   Although we have seen that under certain conditions we are allowed to acquire items for a Shabbos need, going to your Pakistani-owned corner store for more fruit is not an option. First, there is a possibility that the fruit was picked that day; therefore they are *muktzeh*, even in a case of doubt.[5]

   Second, if you go into a store, onlookers may assume you're going to pay like everybody else. This is *maaris ayin* (an action

---

5.   *Shulchan Aruch, Orach Chaim* 322:3; *Mishnah Berurah* 5.

that looks forbidden).[6] It is also *uvdin dechol* (a weekday activity).[7]

No, just make do with what you have. In the merit of your *shemiras Shabbos* everyone will praise you for the fantastic *sheva berachos* — fruit salad included!

6. *Chaim has been learning excellently. Can I give him a prize on Shabbos?*

Although we learned above that we're not allowed to give a present on Shabbos, for a mitzvah that can only be done on Shabbos it is permitted.[8]

If the prize will only have such a good effect if it is given on Shabbos, for instance, it is a Shabbos afternoon group that only meets on Shabbos, it would be allowed. But if it would have the same effect if it were given during the week, don't give it on Shabbos.

7. *I forgot to tovel the new challah knife. I heard that sometimes you can give an un-toveled item to a non-Jew to own temporarily. Can I do that on Shabbos?*

This is exactly what the *Shulchan Aruch*[9] advises us to do in such a situation. The *Mishnah Berurah*[10] explains that even though we are not allowed to give a present on Shabbos, since here it

---

6. The *Shulchan Aruch HaRav* 252:13 permits even going to a store of a non-Jew on Shabbos. He may mean that the store is officially closed but the storekeeper is opening it just to give this item to the Jew. This would answer the query of *Shemiras Shabbos KeHilchasah* 29, note 47.
7. *Mishnah Berurah* 252:33.
8. *Mishnah Berurah* 306:33.
9. *Orach Chaim* 323:7.
10. 323:34.

is required for Shabbos, it is permitted.[11] The *Mishnah Berurah* adds that this way of using a vessel without *toveling* it, is only permitted on a very temporary basis.[12]

8. *It's early morning Shabbos Erev Pesach, and I found some chametz. Can I sell it to the non-Jewish neighbor?*

   Just giving it to the non-Jew would not be a problem, since you are doing it to avoid the prohibition of owning chametz on Pesach.[13] However, we are are not allowed to do a full transaction, like selling an item, even for a mitzvah.[14]

9. *I know I shouldn't, but it's bein gavra legavra (in between the sections of the Torah reading) and my neighbor and I have just agreed on a business deal. Can we shake on it?*

   While I'm sure Rabbi Levi Yitzchak, the Berditchever Rebbe, would be very impressed — *He's making business deals during the leining, but he still doesn't want to mechallel Shabbos* — I don't think I'm on his level. If the king's messenger were reading out

---

11. In order for this to be effective, the non-Jew should acquire the item halachically by lifting it up (*kinyan hagbaah*).
12. The *Mishnah Berurah* 323:35 says that after Shabbos, one should *tovel* it without a *berachah*. However, Rav Yaakov Montrose pointed out that this is if one just keeps using the vessel without making a *kinyan* to reacquire it, as per the *Shulchan Aruch, Yoreh Deah* 120:9. However, if you would reacquire from the non-Jew with a *kinyan* after Shabbos, you should definitely *tovel* it with a *berachah* as per the *Shulchan Aruch*, ibid. 120:11.
13. We have to be careful not to lift up the chametz to give to the non-Jew to take it out because then we would be participating in the *hotzaah* from a *reshus hayachid* to the *reshus harabbim* by doing the *akirah*.
14. *Mishnah Berurah* 444:20.

a proclamation from the king, would you dare chat with your friend about something else? Here the *baal korei* is reading the *devar Hashem*, the words of the King of Kings from the holy Torah, and you're discussing business! And on Shabbos, about which it says, "Regard it as if all your work has been completed"[15]? And in shul, the *Beis HaMikdash Me'at*?

Having said all that, the Berditchever is definitely right — it's better not to *mechallel Shabbos* on top of everything else. So I'll answer you: No, don't shake on the deal. Closing a deal in a way that is regarded as commitment by both sides is a business activity that is not allowed.[16] But please, do me a favor, try and follow the *leining* from now on.

10. *If we're not allowed to buy things on Shabbos and Yom Tov, why do they sell the aliyos on Rosh HaShanah morning?*

Buying aliyos is indeed a *shailah* with various views being brought by the *poskim*.[17] The conclusion is that where this is the custom, one shouldn't say these people are doing wrong. The selling of seats in the shul, however, is not allowed.[18]

---

15. *Mechilta* brought by *Rashi* on *Shemos* 20:9.
16. *Mishnah Berurah* 323:1 (even a verbal agreement).
17. *Mishnah Berurah* 306: 33.
18. Ibid.

CHAPTER 10

MEASURING

1. *Moshe and I are building up our shalom bayis by studying the sefer 10 Minutes a Day to a Better Marriage.[1] Can we use the egg timer on Shabbos, so we each have exactly five minutes?*

First, a short introduction. Measuring is another case where our rabbis were worried that one thing leads to another, as we often write measurements down. Another time that measuring goes together with a *melachah* is if we were cutting a piece of material to size for a customer, which is forbidden according to the Torah, we would be likely to measure it. Therefore, measuring is rabbinically forbidden. Any form of it is forbidden, whether with a tape measure, a thermometer, even strides, etc. Only in the case of a mitzvah is measuring allowed.

An egg timer is used for measuring and is therefore not allowed. Although improving *shalom bayis* is certainly an excellent project, surely a clock would suffice. We are allowed to bring in a clock from another room. Needless to say, a battery-powered or electric timer is forbidden on Shabbos.

Having said all this, may I suggest that in the honor of Shabbos, you could be a bit generous with each other and not insist on split-second equality.

---

1. By Dr. Meir Wikler (New York: ArtScroll/Mesorah Publications, 2008).

2. Can I take a thermometer into the dining room to see if it's too cold?

   No, but you can read one that's already there.

3. The doctor said our baby needs to be weighed before and after his feed. Can I do that on Shabbos?

   This is obviously a mitzvah and is permitted.[2]

4. Can we play dreidel on Shabbos Chanukah?

   I'm afraid not. Any game where the winner actually wins something is considered similar to a business transaction and is not allowed.[3] If you normally share out the "winnings" equally among all the players, it would be allowed.

5. There is a choice of two people to daven Musaf for the amud. Can they draw lots?

   Drawing lots is not allowed.[4] Since this is for a mitzvah rather than for material gain, we are allowed to do a minor form of lottery, such as opening a *sefer* and the first one to find his initial at the top of the page, wins. Incidentally, if two people want to daven for the *amud* because they both have *yahrtzeit* on the same day, it can be a greater merit for the deceased to give the *amud* to the other person rather than having a dispute about it.

---

2. Shulchan Aruch, Orach Chaim 306:7; Shemiras Shabbos KeHilchasah 37:5.
3. Shulchan Aruch, Orach Chaim 338:5, *Rama*; Rav Dovid Ribiat, The 39 Melochos, p. 978.
4. Shulchan Aruch, Orach Chaim 322; Mishnah Berurah 24.

CHAPTER 11

מוקצה — WHAT WE'RE NOT ALLOWED TO MOVE, Part I

1. *Why do we have to have the laws of muktzeh at all? Aren't thirty-nine melachos enough?*

   There are several good reasons why our rabbis instituted the halachos of *muktzeh*. The Rambam[1] explains that just as Shabbos is different from the days of the week in terms of speaking and reading, etc., so it should be different in terms of which items we move, even in our own house.

   He also explains that these halachos help us avoid doing work that is prohibited on Shabbos. For instance, if we were allowed to hold a pen, we might just forget and write something. Just as we're thankful to the one who places a rope a little distance from a cliff edge so we won't fall off, so should we be thankful to our rabbis for making a fence around the Torah so we won't transgress its laws. The Torah itself gives the rabbis the authority to make laws to protect the Torah and we're obliged to keep them.[2]

---

1. *Hilchos Shabbos* 24:12.
2. *Devarim* 17:11.

2. *Chaim is scratching his head with a pen again. Is that allowed?*

As mentioned above, one type of *muktzeh* is a prohibition to move items that are usually used to do *melachos*. Therefore a pen, which is usually used for writing, may not be used even for a permitted act like scratching one's head. The only leniency in this type of *muktzeh* is that if the only way of doing this action is with this instrument, it is allowed.[3] For instance, I want to crack a nut but I don't have a nutcracker. In such a case I may use a hammer even though a hammer is usually used for building. I'm sure Chaim can find a permitted way of scratching his head; better still, he should wash his hair on Erev Shabbos so he won't need to scratch!

3. *Can I carry my key in my wallet for safekeeping?*

Money is also *muktzeh*, as it is usually used to make purchases. A wallet that almost always contains money is also *muktzeh*.[4] Even if there are no coins in this wallet, it still falls into this category. Theoretically, if there is no other way of keeping the key safe, it would be permitted to keep the key in it.[5] But it's more likely that another method could be found.

4. *We don't have a nutcracker but our neighbor does. Do I have to knock on his door or can I use a hammer to crack the nuts?*

We said above that if there is no nutcracker available, we may use a hammer. Now the question is how much effort we have to make to find a nutcracker to avoid using the hammer. The *sefer*

---

3. *Shulchan Aruch, Orach Chaim* 308:3; *Mishnah Berurah* 12.
4. *Shulchan Aruch, Orach Chaim* 310:7, *Rama*; *Mishnah Berurah* 27.
5. *Shulchan Aruch, Orach Chaim* 310:7, *Rama*; *Mishnah Berurah* 27.

Halachos of Muktza[6] quotes Rav Moshe Feinstein, who said we are not obligated to borrow from a neighbor in this case. If we ourselves have no nutcracker, we may use the hammer.

5. *Chaya left the nail scissors at the end of the Shabbos table. Can I take them off?*

We may also move this type of *muktzeh* if it is in a place required for another purpose.[7] Do you need this area at the end of the Shabbos table?

If you do, you may move the scissors and put them somewhere else. If not, not. The fact that the table does not look *Shabbosdik* with the scissors is not a halachic justification for moving it. If there is a special need — for instance, small children will cause damage to themselves or others if the *muktzeh* item is within reach — you can push it to the ground in an unusual way, for instance, with your elbow, and then kick it out of reach.[8] No doubt you will gently remind Chaya to make sure she puts away her *muktzeh* items *before* next Shabbos.

6. *My Shabbos dress is in the dryer. Can I take it out?*

The door of the dryer is in the way of you reaching your dress. Therefore you may open the door to get your dress out. Closing the door afterward depends on whether people need to walk in that space on Shabbos.

A garment that was wet when Shabbos came in could be

---

6. By Rabbi Yisroel Pinchos Bodner (New York: Feldheim Publishers, 1985), "Kuntress HaTeshuvos" 5.
7. *Shulchan Aruch, Orach Chaim* 308:3.
8. As per the opinion of *Mishnah Berurah* 311:30. If it is not a case of need the *poskim* are *machmir* like the opinion of the Chazon Ish.

muktzeh the entire Shabbos. It is questionable whether that applies to clothes that certainly are going to get dry during Shabbos, like those in a dryer or in the hot sunshine.[9] However, a garment that's required for Shabbos is definitely not *muktzeh*[10] even if it is still wet.

7. *It's a bit cold with the fan facing this way. Can I move it?*

Good question. A fan falls in the category of items that may be moved in order to use either the item or the space they presently occupy.[11]

Needing the cooler air produced by the fan is clearly making use of it and is allowed. What if you don't want the cooler air, but you still want to turn the fan away? Rav Moshe Feinstein does allow it.[12]

8. *My neighbor's using his umbrella as a walking stick. Can I wish him "good Shabbos"?*

I'm assuming you have an eiruv in your area, otherwise we'd have to discuss whether he's allowed to use anything to help him walk in the street.[13] In terms of *muktzeh*, if he needs a walking stick and doesn't have anything suitable besides his umbrella, he

---

9. *Orchos Shabbos*, vol. 2, 19:384 and note 563.
10. *Shulchan Aruch, Orach Chaim* 301:45; *Mishnah Berurah* 162.
11. *Iggros Moshe, Orach Chaim* 3, *teshuvah* 39.
12. Rabbi Yisroel Pinchos Bodner, *Halachos of Muktza*, p. 52. Perhaps this is because you need the place that is currently being made unusable by the fan (Rav Yaakov Montrose).
13. A person is only allowed to use a walking stick in the street if he or she needs one even at home (*Shulchan Aruch, Orach Chaim* 301:17; *Mishnah Berurah* 64).

may use it, as in the case of the hammer. If he is not allowed to use his umbrella, it may or may not be wise not to greet him in the usual way. If he doesn't know the halachah, surely you can make him aware of it without insulting him. "*Divrei chachamim benachas nishma'im.*"[14]

9. *I'd like to put our artificial plant on a different shelf. May I?*

   An artificial plant has no connection to any *melachah* and may be moved for any reason.[15]

10. *The girls left their skipping rope in the yard. Can I bring it in?*

    In terms of *muktzeh* there's no problem. However, sometimes a front yard is not surrounded by a high enough wall to be considered a *reshus hayachid*[16] and you wouldn't be able to carry the rope inside. Even in a backyard, if the item has been left for some time and is more or less embedded in the ground, removing it would allow the grass to grow again. This would be forbidden because of the *melachah* of sowing.[17]

---

14. "People accept the words of the wise if they are said gently" (*Koheles* 9:17).
15. *Shulchan Aruch, Orach Chaim* 308:4.
16. See ch. 45, "*Hotzaah*," answer 1.
17. Rav Dovid Ribiat, *The 39 Melochos*, p. 252.

CHAPTER 12

מוקצה, Part II

1. *My new, expensive camera was left out before Shabbos. Can I put it away?*

   Another type of *muktzeh* is items that I wouldn't normally move on Shabbos because they are valuable and I'm worried about possible damage.[1] This type of *muktzeh* is called "*muktzeh machmas chisaron kis.*" Expensive electrical items are in this category, which may not be moved even if they are in the way.[2] If an expensive item may get damaged if left out, you could move it with your foot or some other very unusual way.[3]

2. *Avi found a packet of envelopes. Can I take it from him?*

   An inexpensive item, which the owner wouldn't use for another purpose because it might get damaged, still falls within the type of *muktzeh* mentioned above.[4] A packet of envelopes is useful if you need an envelope, which we all do from time to time. So I would ask Avi to be a good boy and put the envelopes on a side

---

1. Shulchan Aruch, Orach Chaim 308:1.
2. Ibid.
3. Ibid. 311:8, Mishnah Berurah 30.
4. Mishnah Berurah 308:3.

table. I'm sure he'll be happy to oblige.

3. *It's Shabbos Erev Pesach and Chaim is using the box of shemurah matzah as a goalpost. Help!*

   Yes, the *shemurah* matzah is definitely *muktzeh*. I think this is a case for Chaim to be sent to bed and only come down for the Seder! By that time, the matzah won't be *muktzeh* anymore!

4. *My neighbor wants to look at the wedding photos. May she?*

   An item that has a permitted use, even if it is valuable, is not *muktzeh*. We may look at pictures, even irreplaceable ones like wedding photos. However, if it is a valuable item that you never move, like a precious ornament, it is *muktzeh*.[5]

5. *This flower looks gorgeous. Can I take hold of it to smell it?*

   Flowers in a vase at home are not *muktzeh* and you can hold them to your nose. Don't take them out of the water unless you're sure they're fully opened because you wouldn't be allowed to put them back.[6] Flowers growing in the ground are not *muktzeh* and may be held.[7]

   If the flowers are growing on a tree, e.g., a blossom, don't move them, as all parts of a tree are forbidden to be used on Shabbos.[8]

6. *If someone doesn't move this negel vasser, it'll end up all over the carpet. Can I pour it out?*

---

5.   Kitzur Shulchan Aruch, Orach Chaim 88:6.
6.   Shulchan Aruch, Orach Chaim 336, Mishnah Berurah 54.
7.   Shulchan Aruch, Orach Chaim 336, Mishnah Berurah 48.
8.   Shulchan Aruch, Orach Chaim 336:1.

Yes, pour it out. *Negel vasser* is not usually used for anything else, but strictly speaking there is no prohibition to use it.[9] Therefore it is not *muktzeh*.

7. *The orange peels are all over the table. It looks disgusting! Can I tidy them away?*

   The rabbis allowed us to remove leftover food and other things that would otherwise be considered *muktzeh*, if they are offensive to people in the vicinity. This is called *"graf shel re'i."* So tidy up your orange peels.

8. *Moshe insists on spitting out the peach pits. Is that really necessary?*

   There is a source for Moshe's spitting out his peach pits, although it is not necessarily required. Anything that is not a vessel of any kind, has no designated use, and is not food even for animals is *muktzeh*. A peach pit would appear to be in this category. So how can we take pits out of our mouths?

   Many *poskim*[10] find halachic justifications for removing the pit by hand, especially if people consider it very impolite to spit.[11] Maybe Moshe should be *machmir* when he's on his own but not when he's with other people.

9. *The earpiece came off my glasses. Can I wear the glasses until they're fixed?*

---

9. Shulchan Aruch, Orach Chaim 338:8; Biur Halachah, s.v. "assur."
10. *Orchos Shabbos*, vol. 2, ch. 19, note 201; *Shemiras Shabbos KeHilchasah* 20:26.
11. See *Chagigah* 5a: "Hashem will judge people for hidden things," for instance, spitting in front of someone who is disgusted by this behavior.

I'm afraid not. Sometimes a breakage occurs that could be repaired by a layman. Such a repair would definitely be forbidden, so our rabbis instituted a special type of *muktzeh* to decrease the risk. They said that both the item that needs repairing and the piece that came off are *muktzeh*.[12] So in this case, if the earpiece has come off and we have the correct screw to attach it back on, we are not allowed to wear the broken glasses. A possible solution in an urgent case would be, without touching it directly, to wash or kick the screw down a drain, so that repair is now impossible. The glasses cease to be *muktzeh* as explained and can now be worn.[13]

10. *The toilet seat came off. Can I just place it on the toilet?*

    Again, I'm afraid not. Something that was attached to a building is definitely *muktzeh* if it comes off on Shabbos.[14]

11. *I always leave a siddur on the tray under our candlesticks but now a neighbor told me I'm making a mistake. Who's right?*

    Let's start at the beginning. Fire is *muktzeh* and therefore the flames of your candles are *muktzeh*. As a result, your candlesticks and the candlestick tray are also *muktzeh*. Assuming your candlesticks are on your table, if you haven't got your challos on the table, the whole table will be *muktzeh*.[15] All this is because of the halachah of a *bassis* — that something that physically supports *muktzeh* becomes *batel*[16]

---

12. *Shulchan Aruch, Orach Chaim* 308:16.
13. Heard from Rav Pesach Eliyahu Falk.
14. *Mishnah Berurah* 308:35. If a child won't use the facilities without the seat and it will cause a situation of *kavod habriyos*, one could place the seat down, if possible in an unusual way.
15. *Shulchan Aruch, Orach Chaim* 310:7.
16. Generally translated as "annulled."

to the *muktzeh* and becomes *muktzeh* itself. If you don't want to move the candlestick tray during Shabbos it won't matter, but often one wants to change the tablecloth, especially to prepare the table for a *milchig shalosh seudos*, and to do this you need to lift up or move the candlestick tray.

Your solution is based on the halachah[17] that if the tray is supporting not just the candlesticks, but something more valuable or at least more valuable for Shabbos use,[18] like a siddur, etc., the tray does not become *muktzeh*.

However, some *poskim*[19] are of the opinion that if the tray is only used to hold the candlesticks, and especially if it is designed with these candlesticks in mind, even if you put a siddur or any other valuable item on the tray, the tray remains *muktzeh*. So maybe both you and your neighbor are quite right. It depends on the type of tray you are using.

12. *Oh, no! I was just about to relax on the couch and I noticed that Chaya left some coins on it. What do I do now?*

There are two questions here, of course. First there is the question of the coins that are *muktzeh*. Second, the couch that, according to our previous answer, should be a *bassis* to the *muktzeh* and is therefore *muktzeh* as well.

Well, you'll be relieved to know that in just a few moments you'll be able to relax on the couch. In terms of the couch, this

---

17. *Shulchan Aruch, Orach Chaim* 310:8.
18. *Mishnah Berurah* 277:18.
19. Rav Moshe Feinstein in his *sefer Tiltulei Shabbos*. *Orchos Shabbos*, vol. 2, 19:288, note 420, brings that Rav Shlomo Zalman Auerbach held that seeing that it is customary to put a siddur, etc., on the tray, even a specially designed tray does not become a *bassis*.

halachah of becoming a *bassis* only applies if the *muktzeh* item was deliberately put on the other item for that item to hold it up over Shabbos. If it was put there but then forgotten, the halachah of *bassis* does not apply.[20]

There is a view that if the *muktzeh* item was put on something on Erev Shabbos even by mistake, the halachah of *bassis* does apply.[21] But it seems logical to say that when the *muktzeh* is put on a couch or chair that is regularly used on Shabbos, it was clearly not the intention to leave the *muktzeh* there over Shabbos; in such a case a *bassis* will not be created. Besides this, a person cannot make someone else's item a *bassis*,[22] a child cannot create a *bassis*,[23] and a few coins cannot make a couch — which is much more valuable than the coins — into a *bassis*.[24]

In terms of the coins, all you have to do is lift up the couch, or a single cushion if that's what they're on, and shake the coins onto the floor.[25] Now you can relax!

13. It's Shabbos Chol Hamoed Succos and Moshe left his lulav and esrog in the way. Can I move them?

The lulav is *muktzeh* because it has no use on Shabbos, but the esrog, because we are allowed to smell it on Shabbos, is not *muktzeh*.[26]

---

20. *Shulchan Aruch, Orach Chaim* 309:4.
21. *Mishnah Berurah* 309:18.
22. *Rama* 309:4.
23. *Shemiras Shabbos KeHilchasah* 20, note 173.
24. *Mishnah Berurah* 310:31.
25. *Shulchan Aruch, Orach Chaim* 309:4.
26. Ibid. 658:2; *Mishnah Berurah* 5. On the other days of Succos we don't smell our esrog because of a doubt about whether to say a *berachah* (*Shulchan Aruch, Orach Chaim* 653). On Shabbos, if we smell the esrog, we definitely say the *berachah*, "Hanosein rei'ach tov bepeiros."

14. *I just noticed a lovely fresh apple under our apple tree. Can I eat it, to help me reach my hundred berachos for today?*

I'm glad you're trying to say your hundred daily *berachos*. See the introduction to my *sefer Do You Know Hilchos Brachos?* for a number of reasons why saying *berachos* with proper feeling and understanding is so important. Also see my essay "The *Brachah* of a *Brachah*," in the supplementary section of the new edition of *Do You Know Hilchos Brachos?*, for the great significance of saying one hundred *berachos* every day. However, you might well have to give this lovely fresh apple a miss. Any fruit that fell off a tree on Shabbos, even if you're not sure whether it fell off on Shabbos or before Shabbos, is forbidden to be eaten and is *muktzeh*.[27]

15. *Gevalt. I left the dry cleaning in the car. Is there any way I can get it out?*

In theory we could discuss the possibility of you getting your dry cleaning out of the car, but in practice it won't be possible. Let's discuss the theory. A car is an item usually used to do *melachos*; it's sometimes used for sitting in or for storage. It belongs to the type of *muktzeh* called "*muktzeh shemelachto le'issur*." We discussed other examples of this type of *muktzeh* above; we said it may be moved if we need to use it for a permitted purpose or because we need the space where it is at the moment. The car door is in the way of you putting your arm inside the car to get out your dry cleaning. Therefore in theory it might have been possible for you to open the door, similar to opening the door of your dryer as we discussed above.

---

27. Shulchan Aruch, Orach Chaim 322:3; Mishnah Berurah 5. Mishnah Berurah 6 reminds us that even if we know the fruit fell off the tree before Shabbos, we may only bring in one at a time. See the details in ch. 17, "Me'amer."

However, there are a number of difficulties. The main problem is that opening our car doors usually turn on a light inside the car. Turning the key probably sets off electric currents, for instance, to other doors that also become unlocked. Where there is no eiruv and the car is in the street, you won't be allowed to bring anything in. Once you get your clothes out of the car, if the space of the open door is not strictly required, you might not be allowed to close it. Also, although people do sometimes go inside a car to talk, the purpose is nearly always to drive. Therefore there is the issue of *maaris ayin*, doing something that looks forbidden even if it is technically permitted. And the Torah says,[28] "*Veheyisem nekiim meHashem ve'adam*—You should be innocent in the eyes of Hashem and Yisrael." So practically speaking, you'll have to find something else to wear. If not having these clothes will cause you great embarrassment,[29] you can ask a non-Jew to get them for you.[30]

---

28. *Bamidbar* 32:22.
29. Once a (not so) young man was so embarrassed that he didn't have his *bekisheh* that he felt he could not daven in his usual *stiebel*. He davened in a small shul in another area…where he met the grandfather of a (not so) young lady. The two were married within a short time!
30. Because of *kavod habriyos*. The *issurim* are *mi'deRabbanan*. The lights coming on are *shelo miskaven*. See ch. 13, "*Amirah Le'akum*."

CHAPTER 13

אמירה לעכו"ם —
REQUESTING A NON-JEW TO DO A MELACHAH

1. *Why can't I call in a non-Jew to help me on Shabbos? Isn't it traditional to do so?*

Your question reflects a very popular misunderstanding of the halachos of when and where we can ask a non-Jew to do for us something that we may not do on Shabbos. In fact, unless special circumstances apply, there is a specific prohibition involved.[1] Even more, even in a case where a non-Jew does something for us without being asked, there can still be a prohibition to have benefit from the non-Jew's action.[2]

Many people imagine that this is perfectly permitted or even a Jewish tradition. This misunderstanding has come about for historical reasons. There are certain leniencies in cases of need, such as in the extreme cold of bitter Eastern European winters. People and especially children could easily become ill without a fire to heat their homes, so it was

---

1. *Shulchan Aruch, Orach Chaim* 307:1; *Mishnah Berurah* 8.
2. *Shulchan Aruch, Orach Chaim* 276:1; *Mishnah Berurah* 1.

permitted to ask a non-Jew to light a fire on Shabbos morning.³ Those who grew up without Jewish education simply assumed that non-Jews could be asked to do any *melachos* for us. They didn't realize that the leniencies are very restricted. Even this case of heating the house to avoid illness is hardly relevant today, with modern heating, unless the system is faulty.

There are several reasons for these prohibitions. The Rambam⁴ writes that if we were allowed to ask non-Jews to do *melachos*, Shabbos would become less important in our eyes and we would come to do *melachos* ourselves. This reason is quoted by the *Mishnah Berurah*.⁵ Unfortunately, the Rambam's explanation has come true; many of those children who grew up in households where non-Jews did all kinds of *melachos* without restriction became the Shabbos desecrators of the next generation.

2. *I'm suffering from a very bad migraine. Can I ask my non-Jewish neighbor to drive to the pharmacy to get some medication?*

As we mentioned, a non-Jew may be asked to do certain *melachos* that we may not do ourselves, in a case of illness.

If a person is slightly ill, that is, he is not forced to lie down, but is in some pain or discomfort, a non-Jew may do

---

3. *Shulchan Aruch, Orach Chaim* 276:5; *Mishnah Berurah* 38–45. If we explicitly say to a non-Jew not to do a *melachah* for us but he nevertheless does it, there is no prohibition to benefit from the *melachah* (*Mishnah Berurah* 276:36).
4. *Hilchos Shabbos* 6:1.
5. 276:2.

something that is forbidden *mi'deRabbanan*.⁶ If the person is ill to the extent that he is *nofal lemishkav*, so weak or in so much pain that he has to lie down, or he has a serious, non-life-threatening illness,⁷ the non-Jew may even do what is forbidden *min haTorah*.⁸ A severe migraine fits into this latter category and therefore the non-Jew can even be asked to drive to a pharmacy to get medication.

3. *It's freezing. Can the non-Jewish neighbor put the heating on?*

    As mentioned above, a threat of illness induced by extreme cold is enough to allow us to ask a non-Jew to do even a *melachah min haTorah*. However, being cold does not mean being somewhat uncomfortable, but cold to the extent that there is a real threat of illness.⁹ Where there are children, old people, or sick people one can be more lenient.¹⁰

4. *Oh, no! I didn't turn on the dining room light before Shabbos. Can I ask my non-Jewish neighbor to come over to turn it on?*

    Before we answer your question, may I ask where your Shabbos candles are? One of the purposes of the mitzvah of Shabbos lights is to ensure that you won't be in the dark over

---

6. *Shulchan Aruch, Orach Chaim* 307:5.
7. If the illness is life-threatening we can and should ask a Jew to do the required *melachah* unless we are sure that the non-Jew will do what is required without delay. See *Rama* 328:12, but see also *Mishnah Berurah* 37.
8. *Shulchan Aruch, Orach Chaim* 328:17; *Mishnah Berurah* 47.
9. *Shulchan Aruch, Orach Chaim* 276:5; *Mishnah Berurah* 42.
10. Ibid.

Shabbos.¹¹ So although they don't give as much light as our electric lights, it shouldn't be dark in the room.¹² Now back to the crux of the question: For two reasons, we may not ask a non-Jew to turn on a light for us. We already mentioned the basic prohibition of asking a non-Jew to do a *melachah* and also the prohibition to benefit from such a *melachah* if it was done for us even if we didn't ask. However, the halachah does make some exceptions that might be applicable in your case.

First, we may not ask the non-Jew to do a *melachah*, but we may mention our problem to him. If he understands by himself what we would like him to do and he does it, we have not transgressed the halachah.¹³

For instance, we can say to the non-Jew that it's dark in our house and he might well understand that we want him to turn on the light. If he asks us whether he should turn on the

---

11. *Shabbos* 25b.
12. Once I was in London over Shabbos and there was a power outage. The non-Jews were all in the dark but the Jews all carried on with their Shabbos seudah by the light of their Shabbos candles. As it says in *Parashas Bo* during the plague of darkness, "And for all the Children of Israel there was light in their dwelling places." (The week I am preparing this chapter is *Parashas Bo* 5773!)
13. *Mishnah Berurah* 307:76. See *Orchos Shabbos*, vol. 2, 23:19, note 53, in the name of Rav Shlomo Zalman Auerbach, that one shouldn't even ask the non-Jew to come to one's house and then tell him the problem because this is regarded as a "command," which is not allowed. Rather tell him the problem immediately and hope he will come to the house. However, I have heard in the name of Rav Osher Weiss that, in his opinion, it is only in connection with a fire that calling a non-Jew to one's house is the equivalent of asking, because it is obvious what you want him to do. In a case where it is not obvious, one can ask him to come.

light, we may not say yes or even give any gesture[14] to show that we agree. Non-Jews who are experienced at helping Jews on Shabbos quickly understand what we would like them to do. This might solve the first issue of not asking a non-Jew to do a *melachah*.

However, the prohibition of benefiting from the *melachah* will often preclude this solution. Clearly if it was pitch-dark and the non-Jew has turned the light on, I would benefit significantly, which is not allowed. But if there is some light anyway from the Shabbos candles or from street lamps, which enables me to see and possibly even read, the increased convenience of the extra light is not prohibited.[15] If it is merely a dark winter's day and the extra light would just make things a bit more pleasant, it would also be permitted.

But we have to remember that if the secondary light — such as the Shabbos candles or some daylight coming in from the outside — no longer exists, for instance just before the end of Shabbos, we may not read or do other things that are only possible because of the non-Jew's actions, even though he turned the lights on many hours ago.[16] Also this is only under the condition, as we said above, that we didn't ask the non-Jew to do the *melachah*. We simply mentioned the

---

14. *Chayei Adam, Hilchos Shabbos* 62:2.
15. *Mishnah Berurah* 307:76.
16. *Shulchan Aruch, Orach Chaim* 276:4.

problem and the non-Jew did the *melachah* of his own volition.¹⁷

5. *The light's on in Chaya's room. Can the non-Jewish neighbor turn it off?*

Again, since we may not turn the light off, we may not ask the non-Jew to do it. We can only say that we cannot sleep with the light on or something similar. However, the prohibition of benefiting from the *melachah* does not apply here. Having light instead of darkness is a clear benefit, but darkness instead of light is not regarded as a proper benefit.¹⁸

6. *The lights are off in the shul and no one can see to daven Maariv. Can the caretaker put them on?*

Asking a non-Jew to do a *melachah* for the purpose of a mitzvah is discussed in the *poskim*. If the *melachah* is on a rabbinic level it is certainly permitted.¹⁹

If the *melachah* is on a Torah level there is an argument

---

17. All this is according to the custom and as written in *Iggros Moshe, Yoreh Deah*, vol. 3, *teshuvah* 47:2. However, some *poskim* do not allow hinting to a non-Jew at all. Their objection is based on the *Magen Avraham* 252:10 and the *Mishnah Berurah* 276:11, which seem to contradict the *Mishnah Berurah* 307:6 quoted in note 259. See *Orchos Shabbos*, vol. 2, ch. 23, note 24.
18. *Shulchan Aruch, Orach Chaim* 334:25; *Mishnah Berurah* 61.
19. *Shulchan Aruch, Orach Chaim* 307:5; *Mishnah Berurah* 23.

brought in the Rama.[20] The conclusion in the *Mishnah Berurah*[21] is that it is not allowed even in a case of great need. However, where we are dealing with a mitzvah that affects a group of people, certainly a large group, and there is no other location in the vicinity where they could daven, it is permitted.[22] In your case, therefore, when at least a minyan is waiting to daven *Maariv*, and there is no alternative location, you can ask the caretaker to turn the light on.

7. *Shalosh seudos is inside the fridge. Can the non-Jewish neighbor open it, even though I forgot to take the light bulb out of the the fridge and the light will definitely go on?*

This is a most interesting question. We may not do even a permitted act, if it definitely causes a *melachah* to be done. This is the Talmudic concept of *psik reisha*. Therefore it should be forbidden to ask a non-Jew to do such an act. However, some opinions say that the halachah of *psik reisha* is not so strict when *amirah le'akum* is involved.[23]

Here also the intention of the non-Jew would be to open the fridge door and not to turn the light on, even though the light

---

20. 276:2.
21. 276:24–25. The concluding words "*mitzvah derabbim*" imply that the leniency applies to any *mitzvah derabbim* and not just the quoted case of a broken eiruv. This is also the *pesak* of the *Iggros Moshe, Orach Chaim* 3:42.
22. *Mishnah Berurah* 276:25.
23. Ibid. 253:99.

goes on automatically. It is true that there are other opinions[24] and if there is no particular need, it would be better to be strict. In this case where your entire *shalosh seudos* is in the fridge there is a strong basis to be lenient.[25]

8. *A stray cat has come into our yard and it looks starving. Can I ask the non-Jewish neighbor to give it some milk?*

   You are correct that we may not feed animals on Shabbos if we have no responsibility for them. However, to ask a non-Jew to do so in order to help an animal in distress is permitted.[26]

9. *It's a very gloomy day and a visiting non-Jewish neighbor put the lamp on. Can I daven Minchah by its light?*

   We mentioned in answer 4 that if there is only slight benefit from the non-Jew's *melachah*, for instance, he has increased the light but it was possible to read even before he turned the light on, there is no prohibition.

---

24. *Mishnah Berurah* 253:51 says that others are strict. *Mishnah Berurah* 276:30 seems to be *machmir*. *Orchos Shabbos*, vol. 2, 23:68, note 136, brings that Rav Shlomo Zalman Auerbach and Rav Yosef Shalom Elyashiv held that since the way of turning on the light of a fridge is by opening the door, it is not considered a *psik reisha* but a direct act.
25. See *Iggros Moshe, Orach Chaim* 2, and the opinion of Rav Shmuel Auerbach in *Orchos Shabbos*, vol. 2, 23:68. If it is during the daytime or there is another light on in the kitchen where the fridge presumably is, it is probably *lo ichpas lei* (of no interest) that the light goes on, which is another reason to be *meikil*. See *Shaar HaTziyun* 253:43. I have also heard in the name of Rav Chaim Kanievsky that the custom is to be lenient.
26. *Mishnah Berurah* 305:69.

10. *As I was walking down the street, a non-Jewish neighbor called out that he had just boiled up a kettle of water to make tea, and asked me to join him. May I?*

Although we have explained that we are not allowed to benefit from the *melachah* of a non-Jew unless it is similar to the circumstances of the last answer, it is normally permitted if the non-Jew did the *melachah* for himself or for another non-Jew.[27] For instance, I am allowed to benefit from a light a non-Jew put on for himself. However, where there is a danger that the non-Jew might have done more or will do more on another Shabbos for the Jew, we may not have benefit. In this case it might be true that the non-Jew boiled the water for himself, but he might just have spotted you coming up the road and boiled more water in case you would join him. And even if he didn't, he might do so on another Shabbos. Therefore it would not be allowed. This prohibition is only if the non-Jew knows the Jew and therefore there is this danger. If he doesn't know the Jew it would be permitted.[28]

---

27. *Shulchan Aruch, Orach Chaim* 276:1.
28. Ibid. 325:11. I am not discussing whether drinking tea with non-Jewish neighbors is the most suitable way of spending Shabbos.

CHAPTER 14

חורש — PLOWING

1. *My Jewish neighbor likes to do his gardening on Shabbos afternoon. He says farmers plow; he's just looking after his garden.*

   Unfortunately your neighbor is making a serious mistake. Even an amateur gardener is likely to transgress *melachos* such as plowing and sowing many times over if he does his gardening on Shabbos.

   Pick the right time to suggest gently that he garden on another day. On Shabbos afternoon you could go to a *shiur* together.

2. *I like to sit in the yard on Shabbos afternoon but there is a bump in the ground on the exact spot where I put my chair. Can I just flatten it out?*

   No, this is forbidden because it is included in this *melachah* of *choresh*. Making a hole or groove in the ground or flattening the ground in any place in which one could potentially sow a seed is not allowed.[1]

---

1. See the introduction to *Mishnah Berurah* in *Shulchan Aruch, Orach Chaim* 337.

3. *The garden would look beautiful if it weren't for that big pile of stones in the middle. Can I take the stones away in my wheelbarrow?*

   First, the stones will be *muktzeh* unless they were put there deliberately to form a seat or they were prepared for some kind of game or other use.

   Second, removing a pile of stones from the ground is a form of preparing the ground for possible sowing of seeds and is also prohibited because of *choresh*.[2]

4. *Grandpa's walking stick has a point on the end that makes holes in the ground as he walks along. He says he won't be able to get to shul on Shabbos if he can't use his stick.*

   Of course this question is only relevant if there is no problem with carrying in the street. He can use a stick in the street only if he needs it even to get around at home or if there is a kosher eiruv. There is room to be lenient about the holes in the ground, seeing that Grandpa has no interest in making a hole and he is in fact damaging the ground.[3]

5. *What about pushing a stroller over soft ground in the winter — isn't that going to be a problem?*

   Again, assuming there is an eiruv where you live, it is permitted. The conclusion of a discussion in the Gemara on the subject[4] is that a wheel that makes a groove by compressing the earth is not "plowing," as a seed would not take root there. Although this is

---

2. See *Mishneh Torah, Hilchos Shabbos* 8:1; *Chayei Adam, Hilchos Shabbos* 10:3; Rav Pesach Eliyahu Falk, *Zochor Veshomor,*"Choresh," C(i).
3. *Shulchan Aruch, Orach Chaim* 301:17; *Biur Halachah*, s.v. "she'eino."
4. *Beitzah* 23b.

not brought in the *Shulchan Aruch*, it is brought by all contempory *poskim*.[5] It is nevertheless advised that one should be careful to turn corners gently to avoid digging up bits of earth, which would be forbidden.

6. *The hotel we go to has a "Crazy Golf" course in the grounds. Can we play on Shabbos?*

Ball games that involve rolling or bouncing a ball on the ground are forbidden because of the danger that one might flatten out the ground.[6] This is forbidden outside even on a firm surface because another time one may do the same thing on a soft surface. Playing on a table, e.g., table tennis, is permitted. Ball games are also allowed inside a modern house, even on the floor, as nowadays all indoor floors are solid.[7] It is important to remember that one should not simply forbid children to play certain games on Shabbos without suggesting other games that are permitted.

7. *The hotel has a private beach. Can I walk on it after the tide has gone out?*

I presume you are worried about your shoes making indentations in the soft sand. The leniency here is the same as mentioned in the answer to question 5 above. You are compressing the earth rather than digging out a hole.

---

5. Rav Dovid Ribiat, *The 39 Melochos*, p. 258; *Orchos Shabbos*, vol. 1, p. 495.
6. *Shulchan Aruch, Orach Chaim* 338:5. See also *Mishnah Berurah* 308:158, who implies that not only games in which the ball rolls are forbidden, but games in which the ball bounces on the ground, like cricket, tennis, and soccer are also forbidden. Some Sephardic authorities forbid all ball games as per *Shulchan Aruch, Orach Chaim* 308:45.
7. *Shulchan Aruch, Orach Chaim* 337:2; *Biur Halachah*, s.v. "veyeish."

However, walking on soft sand or earth in high-heeled shoes is more of a problem because of the deeper, narrow holes you would be making, which are more conducive to protecting a seed than the larger hole created by the wheel or shoe in the previous examples.[8] In a case of real need one could allow it, similar to answer 4 above, but for a walk on the beach one shouldn't wear high heels.

8. *The children's playground has a sandbox. Can the kids play in it on Shabbos?*

A sandbox that has been set aside for playing with has the advantage of not being *muktzeh*, as distinct from sand on the beach, which may not be handled. If the sand is soft and dry and any hole collapses immediately, there is no problem. However, if the sand is wet and a hole would not immediately collapse, making a hole in the sand is not allowed, as mentioned above. To deliberately mix water with the sand is forbidden because of the *melachah* of *lishah* (kneading).

9. *After our Shabbos seudah the floor is rather sticky. Can I give it a wash or at least sweep it?*

Washing a floor is not allowed even inside the house.[9] Sweeping inside a modern home with a soft broom, if necessary, is permitted, especially if one swept the floor before Shabbos.[10] Sweeping outside is usually not permitted even on a solid surface, similar

---

8. See Rav Pesach Eliyahu Falk, *Zochor Veshomor*, "Choresh,"E(i).
9. *Shulchan Aruch, Orach Chaim* 337:3.
10. Ibid. 1, conclusion of *Biur Halachah*, s.v. "veyeish." See *Iggros Moshe, Orach Chaim* 4:74, who only allows sweeping if it is strictly necessary — *kegraf shel re'i*.

to what we said above in our answer to question 6. However, a balcony, even if it has no roof, or a patio that adjoins one's house, is permitted as these are really just extensions of one's home.[11]

However, the use of a carpet sweeper is not allowed because of the *melachah* of *melaben* (cleaning), similar to cleaning clothes, etc., and other reasons.[12]

10. *We're putting up our succah. Can we stand it in the yard?*

If you can avoid it, don't put it up on the grass — it's a halachic minefield. You have possible problems when arranging the table or chairs because the ground might not be straight,[13] their narrow legs might make holes in the ground, water might spill on the ground,[14] etc. If you have no other place, at least build a whole solid floor that the rest of the succah can stand on. Enjoy!

---

11. See *Orchos Shabbos*, vol. 1, ch. 18, note 73; Rav Pesach Eliyahu Falk, *Zochor Veshomor*, "*Choresh*," 2A(iii).
12. *Minchas Yitzchak* 5:39.
13. *Shulchan Aruch, Orach Chaim* 337:4.
14. Ibid. 336:3, *Rama; Mishnah Berurah* 26.

CHAPTER 15

זוֹרֵעַ — SOWING

1. *I only asked Moshe to shake the tablecloth over our backyard and he said it's a shailah. What shailah?*

   If there are some leftover bits of fruit or seeds, they could take root if they are thrown onto earth.¹

2. *Our small vegetable patch needs watering every day in the summer. What can we do?*

   Of course you can't water it on Shabbos. Watering or doing anything that helps something in the ground to grow is not allowed under this *melachah* of sowing. However, if you own a water sprinkler with a timer, it can be set before Shabbos to go on during Shabbos. Just make sure that the system is independent of your domestic water supply so that the pressure is not affected when you turn your taps on and off inside.²

3. *Baruch Hashem it stopped raining. Can we get on with our Succos seudah already?*

---

1. Shulchan Aruch, Orach Chaim 336:4. If it's only bread crumbs, there's no problem.
2. Rav Shimon Eider, *Halachos of Shabbos* (New York: Feldheim Publishers, 2000), "*Zoraya*."

Let first me say that only on the first night (the first two in *chutz laAretz*), would rain cause a delay in a Succos seudah. Otherwise, if it rains, we either go inside or put a cover on the succah and carry on eating the meal. Having said that, this is not a Succos *shailah* but a Shabbos and Yom Tov *shailah*; there is no problem on Chol Hamoed.

In many places where it rains often, usually only in *chutz laAretz*, people have some kind of a roof that they lower onto the succah to keep it dry when it rains. If the roof is flat or soft, a puddle forms when the roof is down. When the roof is raised, there will be a problem on Shabbos or Yom Tov if the water falls onto a garden below. You can avoid a serious *shailah* by either constructing a hard roof that has a good slant so puddles don't form, or building the succah on a properly paved surface.

In an emergency, *poskim*[3] are lenient if the grass is already soaked and a little more water will make no difference, or if the water doesn't go directly onto the grass but via a stone or other solid surface.

4. *Avi can't wait. Can he go behind the bushes?*

Fortunately for Avi (and you) the *Shulchan Aruch*[4] paskens that urine hinders rather than helps growth, so there is no problem of *zorea*. Potential problems of *choresh* and *lishah* are also dismissed by the *poskim*.[5] Although there is a stricter opinion,[6] one can

---

3. Rav Dovid Ribiat, *The 39 Melochos*, p. 269; *Shemiras Shabbos KeHilchasah* 12, note 51.
4. *Orach Chaim* 336:3.
5. Ibid.; *Biur Halachah*; *Orchos Shabbos*, vol. 1, 6:59; Rav Pesach Eliyahu Falk, *Zochor Veshomor*, "Lishah."
6. Rav Shimon Eider, *Halachos of Shabbos*, "Zoraya."

certainly be lenient in an emergency and for a child.

5. *I was hoping to make the kiddush in the yard but the rebbetzin said no. Why not?*

   Your wise *rebbetzin* was obviously aware of the statement of the Rama[7] that it is good to avoid eating and drinking in a yard because of the likelihood of water falling onto earth, leading to questions of *choresh* and *zorea*.

6. *The drips from our air conditioner fall onto the grass. Does this mean we can't use it on Shabbos?*

   If it's on anyway or it's on a Shabbos clock, there is no problem. In Eretz Yisrael it is a common question in the *shemittah* year during which sowing is also forbidden. Clearly during the *shemittah* year, in Eretz Yisrael, one should arrange the system so that it doesn't drip into your yard.

7. *We just noticed that the sewage from the bathroom in our country vacation home comes out at the end of the field. Have we a problem?*

   City dwellers might be taken aback at this arrangement but to the farmer it is simple economics. Why pay for fertilizer when you can get it for free? However, for the Jewish vacation tenant there is indeed a problem. Fertilizing is indeed classic *zorea*. However, if there is no option, one can be lenient.[8]

---

7. 336:3.
8. This is because one has no intention to fertilize, nor an interest in any fertilization; it is only an indirect result of any action.

8. *One neighbor told me that the rav told him not to open his curtains in the room where he has plants growing. Another neighbor told me that the rav told him he can open the curtains even though he also has plants growing. Maybe if I ask him he'll give me a third answer!*

Do I detect a certain scepticism in your question? I'm sure you want to have full *emunas chachamim*, even if they say, "Right is left and left is right."[9] But your problem is, how can he say different things to different people?

Let's see. What could be wrong with opening a curtain in your home on Shabbos? The answer is that opening the curtain allows the sunlight to shine on your plants, which gives them energy to grow. This is *zorea*. Now consider the different situations. Opening the curtain deliberately to enable the plants to grow is certainly forbidden. If you are merely enjoying watching your plants grow and your main intention is just to let light into the room, the custom is to be lenient and to allow opening the curtain.[10] If plants really don't interest you but they are just "part of the furniture" then you can certainly be lenient.[11] Hence the different *pesak* for your different neighbors.

9. *We left the poinsettia just where we like to sit on the patio. Can I move it?*

Moving plants around on Shabbos is another complicated aspect of *zorea* and of the next *melachah*, *kotzer* (uprooting). Lifting a

---

9. See *Rashi, Devarim* 16:11.
10. Although the question is not simple (see Rav Dovid Ribiat, *The 39 Melochos*, p. 274 and note 72), the *poskim* are lenient. See *Orchos Shabbos*, vol. 1, 18:30 and note 48.
11. Since one isn't interested in the plant growing, and for other reasons. See Rav Dovid Ribiat, *The 39 Melochos*, "Zorea," note 72.

plant away from the ground, even inside your home, could reduce the plant's nourishment and constitute a form of *kotzer*. Putting it down again somewhere else could increase its nourishment and is therefore *zorea*.

Besides this, plants might be *muktzeh* and may not be moved at all.[12] So I think you should give your poinsettia the pride of place this week and you sit somewhere else.

10. *It's rather embarrassing. Our Shabbos guests brought flowers. What do I do?*

I'm sure an experienced *kiruv* person could thank the guests profusely, have the flowers moved to the kitchen to be put in an empty vase, and with a winning smile swiftly move on to discussing the weather!

Bottom line is that we are not allowed to put flowers in water if they are going to open up more, and even if they won't, we are not allowed to fill a vase with water.[13] Hence the need for diplomacy in this case.

---

12. Rav Yisroel Pinchos Bodner, *Halachos of Muktza*, p. 86, in the name of Rav Moshe Feinstein.
13. *Shulchan Aruch, Orach Chaim* 336:11, *Rama*; *Mishnah Berurah* 54.

CHAPTER 16

קוצר — UPROOTING

1. *I love going to Grandma's for Shabbos and picking the apples from her tree. Is that allowed?*

   Certainly not. Picking anything from where it is growing, be it in the ground, from a tree, a plant pot, moss from a rock, algae from the side of a pond, even bean sprouts growing in a jar in the fridge falls under the *melachah* of *kotzer*.[1] To lift a whole plant pot from its place on the ground, or even from a solid surface, is also *kotzer*.[2]

2. *Some apples have already fallen off. Can we eat those?*

   The apples that fell off on this Shabbos may not be eaten.[3] This is the halachah even if it is not clear whether they fell off on Shabbos or before Shabbos.[4]

3. *I heard that the berachah over mushrooms is shehakol because they*

---

1. *Shulchan Aruch, Orach Chaim* 336:5–7; *Mishnah Berurah* 34, 35, 39, and 42.
2. *Shulchan Aruch, Orach Chaim* 336:8; *Mishnah Berurah* 43 and 44.
3. *Shulchan Aruch, Orach Chaim* 322:3.
4. Ibid., *Mishnah Berurah* 5.

draw nourishment from the air, not from the ground. Does that mean I can pick them from the ground on Shabbos?

Even though mushrooms are nourished through the air, they grow in the ground; pulling them from the ground is *kotzer*.[5]

4. *The rosemary has a gorgeous scent. Can I say the berachah and smell it?*

   Yes. We are not allowed to smell fruit that is still growing on a tree, in case we might pick it in order to eat it. We may smell a nonedible plant since there is no reason we should pick it.[6] Incidentally, the correct *berachah* on rosemary is *borei atzei besamim*.[7]

5. *Avi loves running through the long grass. Do I have to stop him?*

   Running through long grass will inevitably pull out some grass and is not allowed.[8]

6. *Boys will be boys. Chaim climbed up a tree in the yard. Is he allowed to come down?*

   Boys may be boys but halachah is still halachah. The *Shulchan Aruch*[9] says that we are not allowed to climb a tree in case we break off a twig. The *Mishnah*[10] says that even if the only shofar in the whole town is on top of a tree, we are not allowed to climb

---

5. See *Mishnah Berurah* 336:35; *Chayei Adam, Hilchos Shabbos* 12:1.
6. *Shulchan Aruch, Orach Chaim* 336:10.
7. *Shaarei HaBerachah* 19.
8. *Mishnah Berurah* 336:25.
9. *Orach Chaim* 336:1.
10. *Rosh HaShanah* 32b.

up to get it. The *Shulchan Aruch* continues that if a person deliberately climbed a tree on Shabbos, there is a special rabbinic punishment that he has to stay where he is — in the tree until the end of Shabbos.

If Chaim didn't know that climbing trees is not allowed on Shabbos, he may come down. If he did know, and climbed up on purpose, he has to stay there. If Chaim is a young boy it seems that one cannot apply the strict punishment.[11] Anyway, the *poskim* bring leniencies in cases of severe distress or if one needs to "be excused."[12] But we can see how seriously *Chazal* took this rabbinic prohibition.

7. *Moshe has just come into the yard after Minchah. There's a handy branch to hang his hat on. So why is he still looking for another place?*

Good for Moshe. He is obviously aware of the rabbinic prohibition, similar to the one mentioned just above, to put something on a tree or to take it off.[13] So he's looking for another makeshift hook for his hat (men are experts at it) before relaxing in the yard.

8. *I don't believe it. I left my gold bracelet on the tree trunk. Is there any leniency?*

A few points may be relevant to you recovering your bracelet. First, if the tree trunk is just a stump less than three *tefachim* (nine inches) high, it is considered a raised piece of ground rather than a tree and is permitted.[14] If it is a totally dry, dead tree

---

11. So it seems to me.
12. See Rav Dovid Ribiat, *The 39 Melochos*, p. 297; *Shemiras Shabbos KeHilchasah* 26, note 42.
13. *Mishnah Berurah* 336:3.
14. *Shulchan Aruch, Orach Chaim* 336:2.

trunk, in the summer when there is a clear contrast between a dry, dead tree and a living tree, some are lenient.[15] In the case of a valuable item, which might get lost, one could certainly rely on that view.

One opinion holds that if a tree stump, even if it is still living, and even if it is more than three *tefachim* tall, was cut down for some other reason than to promote growth, the rabbinic prohibition does not apply.[16] If none of these leniencies helps, you might find a non-Jew who may be asked to transgress a rabbinic law to prevent you from suffering a significant loss.[17]

If a Jew keeps this halachah despite great difficulty, he will be in the same category as the Steipler Rav, who, as a soldier in the Russian army, refused to take a fur coat down from a tree where it had been left for him one Friday night. He spent the rest of a freezing Russian winter night on guard duty wearing only thin clothes rather than break this halachah. He was constantly weighing up whether it was a case of *pikuach nefesh*.

9. *There's a hammock hanging between two trees. Isn't that a handy place for a Shabbos shluf?*

If the hammock is tied to the tree itself it is not allowed. If it is tied to hooks that are attached to the tree, it is allowed.[18]

10. *Near the hotel they're offering donkey rides for kiddies free of charge. Is it allowed for oneg Shabbos?*

---

15. *Mishnah Berurah* 336:1.
16. *Aruch HaShulchan* 336:18.
17. *Shulchan Aruch, Orach Chaim* 307:4; *Mishnah Berurah* 22.
18. *Shulchan Aruch, Orach Chaim* 336:13.

No, I'm afraid that riding on a donkey or riding or using any animal is not allowed, similar to the prohibition of using a tree.[19]

---

19. Ibid. 305:18.

CHAPTER 17

מעמר — GATHERING TOGETHER

1. *The grandchildren are coming for Shabbos. They'll enjoy gathering the apples that have fallen off the trees in our backyard. Why did my friend object?*

    Your friend knows this less familiar *melachah* of *me'amer,* which prohibits gathering together produce even after it has been picked from a tree or from the ground.[1] Note that "a good friend" that *Pirkei Avos*[2] advises us to acquire is not merely somebody whom we are happy to spend time with, but someone who is willing to point out, gently and respectfully, when we are making a mistake.

2. *We collected the fruit before Shabbos but the basket got knocked over and all the apples fell out. Can I put them back in the basket on Shabbos?*

    If the basket was knocked over in the same garden or orchard where the apples grew, we are not allowed to collect them again

---

1. Ibid. 340:9, *Mishnah Berurah* 37.
2. 1:6.

to return them to the basket.³ If the basket is now in a different place and the apples are quite close to each other, it is permitted.⁴ If the fruit has been scattered to such an extent that it is quite an effort to collect them, we may only pick up what we intend to eat on Shabbos, without putting them into any container, not even into a pocket of our clothes.⁵ If the fruit, after it fell, became mixed with stones or dirt, we may only pick up fruit to eat right away because of the *melachah* of *borer*.

3. *I'm volunteering on a kibbutz and they asked me to collect the eggs from the chicken coop. Is that a problem?*

   "Is there a problem?" I think the first problem is that you're on a kibbutz that doesn't keep Shabbos. Unless there are special circumstances, it doesn't seem the right place for you to be.⁶ Second, eggs that have just been laid or may have been laid on Shabbos are *muktzeh* for the entire Shabbos, as in our first answer above. Third, to gather the eggs would also be forbidden because of the *melachah* of *me'amer*.⁷

4. *Chaim spilled the salt all over the table. Can we put it back into the saltshaker?*

---

3. Conclusion of the *Eglei Tal*, "*Me'amer*."
4. Ibid.
5. *Shulchan Aruch, Orach Chaim* 335:5; *Mishnah Berurah* 17, 18.
6. After the famous speech of Rav Shach in which he asked what is the Judaism of those who eat rabbit, two members of a secular kibbutz became *baalei teshuvah* and went to Rav Shach for guidance. He said that if they have elderly parents on the kibbutz they must stay there to look after them. When the parents heard what Rav Shach had said, they too became *baalei teshuvah*!
7. *Eglei Tal*, "*Me'amer*"; *Orchos Shabbos*, vol. 1, 18:82.

It seems that Chaim was aware of the great significance of having salt on the table, as mentioned in *Maseches Berachos*,[8] so he poured it over the whole table! Fortunately, you may gather grains of salt as long as it is no longer in the place where it was originally formed.[9]

5. *Avi wanted to help but he tripped and now the peanuts are scattered under the table. Can we rescue them?*

   As mentioned above, if the produce is no longer in the place where it grew, we can collect it again, as long as it is not scattered over a large area.

6. *The kiddush was wonderful but there's popcorn all over the floor of the shul hall. Can we clear up or do we have to leave it until Motzaei Shabbos?*

   You don't say how big your shul hall is or whether you need the space again on Shabbos; these are relevant factors. If you don't need the space until after Shabbos, you may not clean the floor because of *hachanah* (preparing for after Shabbos). If you do need it, we must ask whether this case falls under the rabbinic prohibition against gathering fruit scattered over a large area, in a different place from where the fruit grew. Some say that this halachah applies only outdoors, where there is some resemblance to the classic *me'amer* in a field or orchard, and not inside a house.[10] Others[11] say that the halachah also applies inside a

---

8. 40a *Tosafos*, s.v. "*habah*."
9. *Mishnah Berurah* 340:35.
10. Implication of *Mishnah Berurah*, ibid. See Rav Dovid Ribiat, *The 39 Melochos*, p. 312, and Rav Shimon Eider, *Halachos of Shabbos*, p. 85.
11. *Chayei Adam, Hilchos Shabbos* 13:1.

house. It could be that all opinions would allow you to sweep them to one place, without picking them up, at least if the room is needed again that Shabbos, as mentioned above.¹²

7. *The toys are all over the dining room. Can I tell the children that if they're not cleared up there'll be no ice cream for shalosh seudos?*

   I'm all for tidy rooms and children clearing up after themselves. But let's stick to the halachic issues involved. Even though *me'amer* applies, at least on a rabbinic level, to metals that come from the ground — and let's assume these toys are made from such metals — once its original form has been altered, *me'amer* does not apply.¹³ Tidying toys into different types or groups would not be allowed, however, because of the *melachah* of *borer*, as we discuss in the relevant chapter.

8. *We've got unexpected guests but Moshe's shirts are all over the guest room. Can I quickly hang them up in our wardrobe?*

   No problem. See the previous answer.

9. *If I can just thread on these last few pearls, my necklace will be complete. Can I do it for the bar mitzvah?*

   No, I'm afraid this is not allowed. To assemble pearls to form a necklace is a superior form of assembling and is not allowed even away from the pearls' original place, and even if the pearls had previously been gathered together.¹⁴ It would also fall within

---

12. See *Orchos Shabbos*, vol. 1, 18:85.
13. *Eglei Tal*, "Me'amer"; *Aruch HaShulchan* 340:3.
14. See *Eglei Tal*, "Me'amer," that this could be *me'amer deOraisa*. See also *Mishnah Berurah* 340:38.

the *melachah* of *makeh bepatish* (putting the finishing touches to a new item).

10. *Our toddler loves threading his toy beads, unthreading them, threading them, and so on. What about that?*

Since the beading is very temporary, it is allowed.[15] However, remember that he shouldn't knot the end of the string because of the *melachah* of *kosher*.

---

15. *Shemiras Shabbos KeHilchasah* 16:21.

CHAPTER 18

דש — THRESHING, SQUEEZING

1. *We're down at Uncle Zevulun's farm and he showed us his combine harvester that, he says, does the threshing among other things. I still don't see what this has got to do with our Shabbos in Lakewood.*

   You'd be surprised. Threshing is extracting the edible kernel from the stalk of wheat. This is part of the procedure necessary to bake the bread and cakes we enjoy. The *melachah* of *dash* is the separation of something from its natural source, similar to a kernel from the stalk of wheat, according to the conditions that *Chazal* have taught us. Included in *dash* is squeezing out juice from fruit, squeezing out a liquid from a material in which it is absorbed, and even melting a frozen liquid, as we shall see in this chapter. Milking cows in the ordinary way is also included in *dash*.

2. *Have you ever looked inside a peanut? When you break one in half, you can see the shape of a man's face and his long beard — a talmid chacham waiting to be discovered? But can we shell them on Shabbos?*

   This is a good question and the *poskim* wonder why peeling vegetables, shelling nuts, or taking peas out of a pod are not *dash*. Their conclusion is that in the case of podding peas, it is only permitted when the pod is edible.¹ As for peeling vegetables and shelling nuts, they say that what is normally done in our own homes, rather than in farms or factories, is not included in *dash*.

For example, when nuts are picked from a tree there is an outer green shell that is taken off before they reach the stores and certainly our homes. To take off this outer shell would be *dash*, but to crack and take off the inner shell is not *dash*.² Similarly, we peel our vegetables and, very often, shell our peanuts in our own homes and therefore it is permitted.

Some say that to pick cherry tomatoes off their stalk is a question.³

Having said this, we may only peel vegetables just before we eat them or just before the meal because of the *melachah* of *borer*, as we discuss in the relevant chapter.

3. *We were taught not to squeeze a lemon into a cup of tea, but I've seen the rebbetzin squeezing a lemon onto her salad. What's the difference?*

You're quite right that squeezing a lemon into a cup of tea or into any other drink is not allowed, as we said above. However, squeezing a lemon onto food to improve its taste is permitted⁴ in most cases. The juice, halachically, does not get the status of a liquid, but remains a solid. Because there is an opinion that does not agree with this leniency⁵ we should not squeeze grapes or

---

1. *Mishnah Berurah* 319:21.
2. Rama 319:6; *Mishnah Berurah* 319:24; *Eglei Tal*, "Dash"; *Iggros Moshe, Orach Chaim* 1:125. See, however, *Shevet HaLevi* 1:81.
3. *Orchos Shabbos*, vol.1, ch. 4, note 11.
4. *Shulchan Aruch, Orach Chaim* 320:4.
5. *Rabbeinu Chananel* 320:7.

olives even onto food because squeezing of grapes and olives is at a more serious level of this *melachah*. Someone who avoids squeezing even other fruits onto food will merit a special blessing.⁶ However, to squeeze lemon onto fish or salad, etc., is certainly permitted.⁷

4. *When I cut up my grapefruit, some juice always drips out. Can I drink it?*

Seeing that your real intention is to eat the grapefruit, and the juice has seeped out incidentally, it is permitted to drink the juice.⁸

5. *We've only been sitting down for two minutes and already Chaim spilled his drink on the tablecloth. What am I supposed to do now?*

First of all, if you're thinking of shouting at Chaim, count to ten. If you have children at your Shabbos table, you should either have spare tablecloths or a plastic cover over your tablecloth. Kids spill drinks.

Now to the drink on the tablecloth. There are several issues to be aware of. You have to be careful not to squeeze out the tablecloth and not to squeeze out whatever you are using to wipe up. There is a further question of spreading the spill, which, if we're talking about water or another colorless liquid,⁹ would be *melaben* (bleaching). If it's a colored liquid there is an issue of *tzovea* (coloring). So what do you do?

---

6. *Mishnah Berurah* 320:30.
7. *Biur Halachah*, s.v. "*lischot*," because with lemons there are other reasons why we can be lenient.
8. *Shulchan Aruch, Orach Chaim* 320:1.
9. *Mishnah Berurah* 320:55.

Take some precut[10] paper towels or a plain paper napkin[11] and mop up the liquid. This saves a lot of problems because there is no *melaben* with paper and we are also not afraid that you will squeeze it out because they are made for throwing away after use. Don't press the napkin on the tablecloth to draw out more liquid from the tablecloth.

Some say that if it is a synthetic tablecloth it is questionable whether one may leave a napkin on the area of the spill, as this causes more liquid to be extracted.[12] Don't press down with the edge of a knife or a spoon to clear away some of the liquid, as this will inevitably cause the liquid to be extracted from the cloth.

Even if you use paper, don't squeeze it out to use it again because this would be *dash*.[13] Don't spread the liquid, especially if it is water, because of *melaben*. If it is unavoidable, it is permitted, seeing that it is clear in this case that one has no intention to clean the other part of the tablecloth. If it is a colored liquid and it is unavoidable it would also be permitted because it is *derech lichluch*.[14] Do not use a garment such as a shirt to mop up the spill because there is a danger that a person might forget and squeeze it out, since it is not designed to be used for this purpose, but rather as a garment to wear. A liquid that will stain like wine would not cause this worry because squeezing it out is not going to make any difference. It's going to leave a stain in any case.

---

10. It is not allowed to cut a piece of paper towel or bathroom tissue from a roll on Shabbos for reasons of *korea* (tearing; ch. 33) and *makeh bepatish* (completing the creation of an item; ch. 45).
11. If there is writing or a picture on the napkin, there would be a question of *memachek* (erasing).
12. Rav Pesach Eliyahu Falk, *Zochor Veshomor*, "Dash."
13. On a rabbinic level, if the liquid is being discarded.
14. *Mishnah Berurah* 320:59.

As a practical point, it would be a good idea to lift up the tablecloth, mop up the liquid that is now on the table itself with the paper, and then put the cloth back onto the table.

6. *Moshe says you're supposed to fill up the becher for Kiddush with wine right to the top, even though it's bound to spill. I said okay, but who's going to clean up the floor and how?*

You ask, "Who's going to clean the floor?" Well, with all due respect, Moshe is obviously a *"gelernter* Yid" and is familiar with the opinion of the Rama,[15] who says the *becher* should be full to the brim even if it spills out a little. If Moshe wants to be *mehader* and not rely on the other opinions brought in *Mishnah Berurah*,[16] he should be prepared to clean up what he spills. We don't *mehader* on *yenem's pleitzes*.[17] Even better than that, he should make sure there is a small tray under the *becher* so there's no mess at all.

Now, how will he clean up? In this case there can't be much wine spilled on the floor, so if there's a solid surface where the wine spilled, he can clean it up with precut tissues or paper towels. If the spill landed on a carpet or rug, there's nothing you can do about it until after Shabbos because of *melaben*.

In another case, when a larger amount spilled, the issues are similar to the last question. If possible, use a few paper towels[18] to wipe up without squeezing them out. If you don't have any,

---

15. 183:2.
16. 183:9, that on the contrary, it is better that the cup not be completely full so as not to waste wine, since it invariably spills.
17. This means you can't be extra strict if somebody else is going to suffer as a result.
18. A well-organized Jewish home will always be careful on Erev Shabbos to have precut paper towels, bathroom tissue, aluminium foil, etc., ready for Shabbos use.

you can use a dry *shmatta* or towel, even though they might get colored as above. Don't wet the *shmatta* or towels with water to use them to clean the floor because that implies an intention to squeeze them out as you're cleaning.

7. *I really don't want to ask in public, but sometimes baby needs… cleaning. Can you tell me a method that is efficient, hygienic, and halachically acceptable?*

Here the main issue is squeezing whatever you are using to clean up with. In my opinion, the best way to clean baby is to squirt baby lotion on the dirty area. It should be moist enough to clear up the mess with one or more dry paper towels. If you want to put on a plastic glove to keep your hands clean, do so. Baby wipes are only permitted if the liquid is truly on the surface and therefore you are not extracting it from the wipe, and this is questionable.[19]

8. *Chaya's hair got wet in that sudden rain shower. As soon as I took a towel to dry it, Sarah, who just came back from seminary, gave a shriek. Why?*

Your seminary girl has obviously learned that to extract water from hair is also *dash*. Because of this, it is a well-established custom not to have even a cold shower on Shabbos, in case one comes to squeeze out water from one's hair, among other reasons.[20]

Men sometimes dry their beards or tidy up their *pei'os* in a way that forces out water from the hair — this is not allowed. However, if one is caught in a rain shower or one's hair is wet for

---

19. See Rav Dovid Ribiat, *The 39 Meluchos*, pp. 352–3.
20. *Mishnah Berurah* 326:21.

another reason, the *poskim*[21] allow placing a towel on one's hair so that any liquid is immediately absorbed into the towel.

9. *It's a boiling hot day and we'd all appreciate some ice in our drinks. Is that allowed?*

Yes, to put ice in a drink where it will melt and mix with the existing drink is allowed.[22] What is not allowed is to put ice into an empty glass for it to melt by itself,[23] or even if it is in another liquid, to crush the ice with a spoon, etc.[24] In certain cases of special need there is room to be lenient.[25]

10. *It's a snowy, slushy day and if I go outside, I'm bound to crush and melt the snow. Do I have to stay inside?*

You can go out and walk over the snow or slush even though you might be melting it, since it is unintentional and unavoidable.[26]

What was that about threshing not having anything to do with your Shabbos in Lakewood?

---

21. *Shemiras Shabbos KeHilchasah* 14, note 64, in the name of Rav Shlomo Zalman Auerbach; *Iggros Moshe, Orach Chaim* 1:135.
22. *Shulchan Aruch, Orach Chaim* 320:9.
23. *Rama* 318:16.
24. Ibid., *Mishnah Berurah* 34.
25. See notes 23 and 24.
26. *Shulchan Aruch, Orach Chaim* 320:13; *Mishnah Berurah* 39.

CHAPTER 19

זורה — WINNOWING

1. *We're eating some peanuts in the yard. I just realized that if I hold them up, the wind will blow away the soft brown coverings, leaving just the peanut. That would save us a job, but is it allowed?*

   This is a good question, seeing that this *melachah* is not mentioned in the *Shulchan Aruch*. Using the wind to separate what we don't want from what we do want is the *melachah* of *zoreh*.[1]

2. *This Succos there is intermittent rain, and it's windy and cold. Now some straw has fallen in my soup. Can I blow it out?*

   Using the flow of air from any source, even our own breath, to separate what we don't want from what we do want — as in our case, straw from our soup — is not allowed either.[2]

3. *It's Shabbos Erev Pesach. Can I blow the last few crumbs of chametz into the wind?*

   This involves a slightly different form of *zoreh* — using the wind to scatter just one substance, and not separating two different

---

1. *Eglei Tal*, "Zoreh."
2. Ibid.

substances. Although not every *posek* agrees on this form of *zoreh*, we avoid it, especially with a product of the ground like chametz.[3]

4. *I haven't used this sefer in years. Can I blow off the dust and learn from it?*

   No, leave it until after Shabbos. See the previous answer.

5. *I had a feeling that he wouldn't control himself; Chaim is squirting his water pistol at his little sister. How many times should I tell him off?*

   Well, one telling off is certainly in order. Squirting his little sister may be Chaim's *oneg Shabbos*, but it's probably not hers. A second telling off for breaking Shabbos is probably not required. Since water is not regarded as a product of the ground, it is not included in *zoreh*.[4] If Chaim squirted into the wind deliberately so the water scatters, it could be prohibited,[5] but in this case he was probably aiming at her, not into the wind!

6. *The sink is blocked. Can I throw the negel vasser out the window?*

   Here your primary intention is to get rid of the water, not to scatter it in the wind. As it is only water, it would be allowed. Of course, you may not pour the water over grass or plants because of *zorea* and *choresh*. I would also make sure nobody is sitting

---

3. See *Magen Avraham* 446:2; *Rama* 319:17; *Biur Halachah*, s.v. "*mefazer*"; *Minchas Yitzchak* 6:26.
4. *Biur Halachah*, s.v. "*mefazer.*"
5. According to the second answer of Reb Akiva Eiger brought in the *Biur Halachah*, ibid.

under the window — just to avoid any ill feeling!

7. *It's Shabbos sheva berachos. Can we throw confetti over the chassan and kallah as they come through the yard?*

Throwing confetti into the wind, which scatters it over the *chassan* and *kallah*, is not permitted.[6] Inside or even outside on a day without any wind it is permitted.[7]

8. *My neighbor says you can't spray air freshener on Shabbos. Is she right?*

Air fresheners are permitted. Although air pressure pushes the liquid to the top, the liquid is not scattered as a result of the air pressure but because of the tiny hole at the top that breaks down the liquid into tiny particles, and our leading authorities[8] have deemed it not *zoreh*.

9. *Can I politely suggest to Moshe that he put some deodorant on before we go to the bar mitzvah?*

A spray deodorant is permitted, as we have just explained, as long

---

6. Rav Dovid Ribiat, *The 39 Melochos*, p. 376, in the name of the *Ketzos HaShulchan*.
7. Although throwing confetti is based on our old custom of showering the *chassan* and *kallah* with wheat, seeds, etc., as a *segulah* to be fruitful (*Berachos* 50b), it is now a non-Jewish custom and might be incorrect because of *chukas hagoy*.
8. *Minchas Yitzchak* 6:26; Reb Moshe Feinstein brought by Rav Shimon Eider, *Halachos of Shabbos*.

as the spray goes over the body and not over the clothes.⁹ Over the clothes is definitely not permitted because of *molid rei'ach*.¹⁰ If some of the spray affects the clothes by accident, it is still permitted.¹¹ Women who use a scented deodorant should be particularly careful that the spray does not go on their clothes even inadvertently.¹² Roll-on deodorants are permitted but deodorant sticks are not allowed because of *memachek* (smoothing down).

10. *Can I politely suggest to Malka to use some hairspray to tidy up her sheitel before we go to the sheva berachos?*

No, 'fraid not.¹³ But this is not because of *zoreh* but because of *makeh bepatish*.

---

9. Some are *machmir* even over the body, see *Piskei Teshuvos* 322:7. However, Rav Eliyahu Falk and others have told me that the main halachah is to be lenient.
10. *Mishnah Berurah* 322:18.
11. Rav Dovid Ribiat, *The 39 Melochos*, p. 1193.
12. Heard in the name of Rav Moshe Feinstein because for them it would be *nicha lei*.
13. *Shemiras Shabbos KeHilchasah* 14:50.

CHAPTER 20

בורר — SEPARATING

1. *I don't see what's so difficult about borer. All you have to remember is that you separate what you do want from what you don't want and to do it beyad and miyad (by hand and for immediate use).*[1]

   I agree that if you've got this principle straight you're over halfway there. However there are still some details you need to learn. Read on.

2. *I get up later on Shabbos morning. Can I get Chaim's Shabbos clothes ready on Friday night so he can dress himself and go to shul?*

   If his clothes are in a pile or hanging up with his other clothes, you can't separate them on Friday night because, as you said, we're only allowed to separate even what we want from what we don't want for immediate use.

   However, if there are two identical shirts, for instance, you could separate one from the other in advance, since the prohibition of *borer* applies only to two items that differ in some way.[2] If the clothes you want to take out are not hanging closely

---

1. *Shulchan Aruch, Orach Chaim* 319:1 and the introduction of the *Mishnah Berurah*.
2. *Shulchan Aruch, Orach Chaim* 319:2; *Mishnah Berurah* 15.

together with the others you don't want, it isn't a mixture and there wouldn't be a problem.

3. *Wait a minute. We're not supposed to leave eggs overnight without the shell,[3] but you can't take away what you don't want from what you want. So how can I shell the hard-boiled eggs for shalosh seudos?*

   We're allowed to remove an eggshell that is preventing us from eating the inside as long as it is just before we eat the food or just before the meal. The *Biur Halachah*[4] says that since this is the only way we can get at the inside, it is not called *borer*, but eating. Of course it goes without saying that the eggs were cooked before Shabbos.

4. *This week is the bar mitzvah and the whole family is coming for Shabbos dinner. We can't keep all the guests waiting while we set the table. On the other hand I can't do it two hours in advance. So what do I do?*

   First of all, mazal tov on the bar mitzvah. Now, a well-organized *balabusteh*, as I'm sure you are, will keep all the cutlery in separate compartments of her kitchen drawer. There is no mixture from which you are doing *borer* so there is no problem in setting the table before you go to shul. The glasses for dinner should not be mixed with other types of glasses.

   The problem is more relevant if you used the same cutlery and dishes on Friday night that you were planning to use on Shabbos day, and after they were washed, everything was mixed up. Some

---

3. *Niddah* 17a. See, however, ch. 23, answer 6, that if the egg is hard-boiled, the general custom is to allow it to be shelled and left overnight.
4. 321:19, s.v. "*liklof.*"

forethought will help you. As you wash by hand, you usually take a bunch of cutlery in one go. You then separate items of cutlery from the bunch, one by one, without paying attention to what item of cutlery it is,[5] to wipe them individually. At that point, as you finish with each item, you can put it in a separate compartment. The same applies to plates; when you've finished wiping each one, put each big plate with the big plates and each small plate with the small plates, etc. This is not called *borer* because you are separating each item for an immediate use, i.e., to wipe it. In this way, you will be able to put all the plates, knives, and forks, etc., in their right places on the table before you go to shul because now they aren't mixed.

5. *I wish your sefer had come out earlier. Avi had a tantrum last Friday night. He likes chicken soup but hates carrots. By mistake I put a carrot in his soup and nobody knew what to do.*

The problem could have been solved quite simply. First of all, assuming that other people like carrots and would have been happy with another one, you or they could have taken out the carrot from Avi's soup dish and put it into theirs. They are taking what they want from what they don't want, which is permitted. In fact, even Avi could have taken out the carrot since he would have been extracting it for someone who wanted it.[6] Further, only a bowl of soup with small pieces of carrot is considered a mixture, but not if the pieces of carrot are relatively large.[7] Another solution would have been to make sure that as you took out the carrot

---

5. See *Orchos Shabbos* 3:121.
6. *Mishnah Berurah* 319:6, 321:43; Rav Dovid Ribiat, *The 39 Melochos*, p. 415.
7. Rav Dovid Ribiat, *The 39 Melochos*, p. 388.

you also took the soup immediately around it.⁸

6. *Before I learn, I like to take out all the sefarim I'm going to be using. Is that allowed or should I go to the bookcase every time I need a new sefer?*

Just as you can prepare for a whole meal before you start,⁹ you can take out *sefarim* before you start a learning session.¹⁰ Anyway, if the *sefarim* are in a bookcase, each one clearly different from the others, it is not considered a mixture.¹¹

7. *I was handing around a tray of assorted meats last Shabbos and one guest surprised me by ignoring the fork and taking his pieces by hand. He said you can't use an implement because of borer. Is he right?*

He's not right in this case. Where the implement helps to separate one thing from another in a way better than one can do by hand, it would not be allowed. But where it doesn't, but one is using an implement such as a knife or fork because the food is hot or so as not to get one's hands dirty, it is allowed.¹²

8. *It's a mitzvah to eat fish on Shabbos.¹³ Yet fish have bones. How can you take out the bones to eat the fish safely?*

---

8. *Taz, Orach Chaim* 319:13. This way you have removed the whole mixture. The rest of the soup is not regarded as being part of the mixture. This is the way the *Chazon Ish* 53 explains the *Taz*.
9. *Rama* 319:1.
10. *Orchos Shabbos*, vol. 1, 3:53.
11. Ibid., 23.
12. *Iggros Moshe, Orach Chaim* 1:124.
13. *Mishnah Berurah* 242:2.

The easiest solution is to prepare fish before Shabbos with the bones taken out, like our traditional gefilte fish.[14] If you haven't done that, it is a challenge. One solution is to lick every bone as you extract it so you are separating what you do want.[15] Or you can put the fish in your mouth with the bones and extract the bones as you are eating.[16] When there is no alternative, for instance, with a child or sick adult, one may remove the bone from a piece of fish immediately before feeding him that piece of fish.[17]

9. *The chicken soup smells delicious but my dietician told me I musn't have the fat from the top of the soup. Is there a way to take it off?*

As we said at the end of answer 5, you can take all the fat with the soup around it, thus removing the whole mixture.

10. *In our shul in the winter, there can be five coats on each peg. Can I take away the top coats to get at mine?*

If the coats are clearly distinguishable and you are just removing the top coats to get to your coat, it is permitted.[18] If the coats are very similar and are lying or hanging right next to each other,

---

14. It is said in the name of the *Beis HaLevi* that the source for the Jewish tradition to eat gefilte fish is avoiding *borer*.
15. *Biur Halachah* 319, s.v. "*mitoch, besof devarav.*"
16. *Chazon Ish* 54:1; Rav Dovid Ribiat, *The 39 Melochos*, p. 422. It is considered *derech achilah* and not *derech borer*.
17. *Shaar HaTziyun* 321:89; *Iggros Moshe, Orach Chaim* 4:74, "Borer" 7. Rav Pesach Eliyahu Falk in *Zochor Veshomor*, "Borer," advises that one should first give the child a boneless piece of fish so one has another possible opinion to rely on, that after one has started eating it is even permitted to separate *pesoles* from *ochel*.
18. *Biur Halachah* 319:3, s.v. "*le'echol.*"

this is a mixture and you can only remove yours if you intend to wear your coat right away.[19] If you don't know which is yours and you are looking through all of them to find it, it is questionable whether you can take away the ones that are not yours as you are searching.[20] Therefore in such a case it is preferable to hold them all together while you look for your coat, remove your coat to wear it, and put the others back on the peg together.[21]

---

19. *Orchos Shabbos*, vol. 1, 3:126 and note 142.
20. See *Shevisas Shabbos*, "*Borer*" 13.
21. See *Orchos Shabbos*, vol. 1, ch. 3, note 145.

CHAPTER 21

טוחן — GRINDING

1. *To wake up properly in the morning, I make myself a strong cup of coffee from beans that I grind fresh every morning. I understand this is not allowed on Shabbos. Why?*

   Grinding is one of the thirty-nine *melachos* on Shabbos, so grinding your coffee beans is definitely not allowed.

2. *Our Avi loves a cracker with mashed banana for breakfast. Is there a way I can give it to him on Shabbos as well?*

   Yes, Avi can certainly enjoy his mashed banana on cracker on Shabbos as well. The best way to prepare the banana, which fulfils all opinions, is to mash it with the handle of a spoon, fork, or knife and then spread it on the cracker.[1] Another way of mashing the banana is by pressing down on it with the underside of a cup or plate.[2] All this would apply equally to mashing a ripe avocado to make an avocado spread for adults or children.[3]

---

1. See the *teshuvah* of Rav Moshe Feinstein at the back of *Halachos of Shabbos* by Rav Shimon Eider.
2. Rav Dovid Ribiat, *The 39 Melachos*, p. 461, in the name of Rav Pesach Eliyahu Falk.
3. *Chazon Ish* 57.

3. *One of my favorite treats on Shabbos is mashing the potatoes from the cholent into the gravy. It is allowed, isn't it?*

It certainly sounds delicious and I'm sure you eat it *lekedushas Shabbos kodesh*.[4] Furthermore, many *poskim*[5] would agree that once a vegetable has been fully cooked, it is soft enough to be regarded as "ground." However, if you wanted to fulfill all opinions,[6] I would make sure the potatoes are cut up into small pieces before Shabbos[7] and that you intend to eat it immediately.[8] This is if you want to mash the potatoes with a fork. If you mash them with the handle of spoon, fork, or knife it is allowed anyway, as we said in the previous answer.

4. *Our new son-in-law wants to cut up an onion at the Shabbos table to mix with hard-boiled eggs. He assures me his father did it and his grandfather before him. What do you say?*

It's good that you ask. Many people who have seen only one community or one custom think theirs is the only correct way and any other way is wrong. This is especially important when it concerns a new in-law or spouse.

There is indeed a longstanding custom to rely on those opinions that allow cutting up vegetables just before a meal, just as we are allowed, subject to certain conditions, to do *borer* just before a meal as we saw in the previous chapter.[9] The *Mishnah Berurah*[10]

---

4. See *Mishnah Berurah* 250:2.
5. *Chazon Ish* 58:9. *Orchos Shabbos*, vol. 1, 5:9, *paskens* like this *Chazon Ish*.
6. *Kalkeles HaShabbos*, "Tochen."
7. *Iggros Moshe, Orach Chaim* 4:74, "Tochen" 5.
8. See Rav Dovid Ribiat, *The 39 Melochos*, p. 470.
9. *Rama* 321:12.
10. 321:45.

says explicitly that one should not rebuke anyone who follows this custom. Nevertheless, the *Mishnah Berurah* does advise that it is better to be careful to cut the vegetables up into slightly bigger pieces than usual. It could well be that your son-in-law does this.

Aren't you glad you asked before making a negative comment? You certainly helped your daughter's *shalom bayis*! If he mixes mayonnaise into the egg and onion, that's another obstacle course. But we'll leave that to the *melachah* of *lash* (kneading).

5. *I know you can't chop vegetables into small pieces but what about slicing them thinly?*

Many authorities consider cutting vegetables into thin slices to be *tochen*.[11] Therefore if you want to enjoy freshly sliced tomato, cucumber, carrot, etc., on Shabbos, and it wasn't prepared before Shabbos, slice these vegetables thicker than usual, just before the meal.[12] The slicing should be done with an ordinary kitchen knife, not a specialized knife and certainly not a slicer.[13]

6. *I just asked my new mother-in-law if there's anything I can do for shalosh seudos and she handed me the egg slicer. Help!*

Calm down. First of all we may cut up or mash eggs on Shabbos as they do not come from the ground. The only potential problem

---

11. See a list of those authorities in Rav Shimon Eider, *Halachos of Shabbos*, "Tochen," note 102. Interestingly, Rav Moshe Feinstein held that slicing is not *tochen*. However, since others held that it can be *chayav*, it is correct to be stringent unless you follow Rav Moshe in all his *pesakim*, both strict and lenient. See note 28 below.
12. *Biur Halachah* 321:12, s.v. "hamechatech."
13. *Mishnah Berurah* 321:36.

is using a utensil, which could be *uvdin dechol*. Since an egg slicer is used only in a domestic setting, the *poskim* allow it.[14] A domestic tomato slicer is not allowed as it is an instrument of *tochen*.

7. *Our Friday night guest just asked if he can break up some matzah into the chicken soup. I had to admit that I didn't know.*

Breaking up the matzah is explicitly allowed by the Rama[15] without any disagreement. The reason is that we may grind and certainly break up by hand any food that has already been ground, like bread or matzah. "*Ein tochen achar tochen* — There is no prohibition of grinding something which has already been ground."

However, there could be a question of *bishul* (cooking). The Rama says that we should not put something that has merely been baked, as distinct from boiled, in a liquid into a *kli sheini*.[16] The *Mishnah Berurah*[17] says that if one used a ladle to take soup from the *kli rishon*, the soup plate is counted as a *kli shelishi* and it is allowed.

8. *Chaim has just appeared with mud all over his Shabbos shoes. He gave one of his smiles and said his teacher said he can't clean the mud off on Shabbos. I gave him one of my smiles and told him he's*

---

14. *Shemiras Shabbos KeHilchasah* 6:3 in the names of Rav Shlomo Zalman Auerbach and Rav Moshe Feinstein at the back of Rav Shimon Eider's *Halachos of Shabbos*.
15. 321:12.
16. *Shulchan Aruch, Orach Chaim* 318:5.
17. 318:45. This is assuming the ladle was not left in the *kli rishon* long enough to acquire the status of a *kli rishon*, which would make the soup plate a *kli sheini*. It would then not be permitted to put bread or matzah into the soup.

not coming into the dining room wearing those shoes. Where do we go from here?

You're both right! If the mud on Chaim's shoes is dry, he can't clean them. The mud would break up into small pieces, which is not allowed to be cleaned off because of the *melachah* of *tochen*.[18] If the mud is wet, he can't clean them because of the *melachah* of *melaben*.

At the same time, he doesn't have to dirty your dining room floor. So it's a case of "Off with his shoes — on with his slippers." But after Shabbos, Chaim will have to roll his sleeves up and get those shoes sparkling!

9. *This is a new one on me. Moshe said the rabbi said we can't put our washing machine on just before Shabbos because of tochen! Did he mishear?*

No, he didn't mishear. Let me explain. In chapter 2, "Erev Shabbos," we discussed starting a *melachah* before Shabbos that will continue on Shabbos. Many things are permitted, like starting a water sprinkler before Shabbos even though it will continue over Shabbos. However, the Rama[19] says that we may not work a mill that grinds wheat noisily even if it started before Shabbos because people will hear the noise and come to the (wrong) conclusion that a Jew is grinding wheat on Shabbos. Therefore, we have a rabbinic prohibition of *mashmaas kol* (producing a noise) an offshoot of this *melachah* of *tochen*, which says that we may not, even before Shabbos, start any machine that will make a noise on Shabbos that people outside or even in another room

---

18. *Shulchan Aruch, Orach Chaim* 302:7; *Mishnah Berurah* 36.
19. 252:5.

can hear. A washing machine is certainly included in this category, as is a dishwasher and many gadgets found in a modern home. A dryer does not usually make much noise, but perhaps some models do.

In a case of potential loss or extreme need, for instance, someone has to leave right after Shabbos, one can be lenient.[20] An alarm clock that is required to wake up someone for *tefillah betzibbur* or a *shiur* is also permitted for the same reason.[21] Of course it has to be set before Shabbos. It is preferable that only *you* hear the alarm and not your neighbor, for more than one reason.[22]

10. *This I find very difficult to understand. Apparently if you've got a headache or toothache on Shabbos you can't take a painkiller, also because of tochen. Is this right?*

Yes, there is a rabbinic ruling, subject to a number of conditions, that says we may not take medicines to relieve headaches, toothaches, etc., unless we feel so weak that we need to lie down. The reason given is that the production of pills and other medications often involve the *melachah* of *tochen*. A person, precisely because he is in pain,[23] might forget or be tempted to prepare a medication on Shabbos. Actually, it is not only *tochen* but other *melachos* that are at risk.[24] Therefore this halachah protects us from transgressing a *melachah* of the Torah.

---

20. *Piskei Teshuvos* 252:5.
21. *Shemiras Shabbos KeHilchasah* 28:29. See note 65 that it is also just *grama lehashmaas kol*.
22. Stealing someone's sleep is a serious form of theft — you can't it pay back!
23. See *Shemiras Shabbos KeHilchasah* 34, note 7, in the name of Rav Shlomo Zalman Auerbach.
24. That is why these halachos of *refuah* apply on Yom Tov as well, even though, subject to certain conditions, *tochen* is permitted on Yom Tov.

There are many details of this halachah that are beyond the scope of this *sefer*. Sometimes what appears to be a minor problem can be in fact serious, especially for elderly people. Babies and children under the age of four are excluded from this ruling.[25] One can also be lenient for a particularly weak child under the age of ten;[26] some even allow up to bar mitzvah.[27] Those in the middle of a course of treatment can sometimes be lenient.[28]

If one anticipates the problem before Shabbos one can prepare the medication in a way that will make it permitted to take. There can be other leniencies; one also needs to know which illnesses are considered serious enough to warrant medical treatment, even if the person doesn't feel so ill. An acute localized pain can also be regarded as the same as needing to lie down.[29] Therefore, one needs to properly study the subject. The reader is recommended to *Halachos of Refuah on Shabbos*,[30] which is authored jointly by a rabbi and a doctor, or other more exhaustive *sefarim* on *hilchos Shabbos*.

---

25. Rav Yisroel Pinchos Bodner and Rav Daniel B. Roth, *Halachos of Refuah on Shabbos*, pp. 46–47.
26. Rav Pesach Eliyahu Falk, *Zochor Veshomor*, "Hilchos Refuah BeShabbos" 2:5.
27. Ibid., note 13.
28. On this point Rav Moshe Feinstein was *machmir* (*Iggros Moshe, Orach Chaim* 3:53). See note 11 above.
29. Rav Pesach Eliyahu Falk, *Zochor Veshomor*, "Hilchos Refuah BeShabbos" 2:5.
30. By Rav Yisroel Pinchos Bodner and Rav Daniel B. Roth (New York: Feldheim Publishers, 2008).

CHAPTER 22

מרקד — SIFTING

1. *I know a rekidah is a dance. So why does meraked mean "sifting"?*

   Classic *meraked* is sifting flour with a sieve.[1] As a person sieves, the flour "jumps" up and down as if it were dancing. That is why the same word is used for sifting and dancing.

2. *We're not allowed to bake on Shabbos, so are there practical questions about meraked for us?*

   You'd be surprised. *Meraked* can be relevant on Shabbos — pouring a cup of tea, turning on the tap, giving a baby a bottle of milk, sprinkling salt on food, and many other ordinary situations.

3. *We prepared our tea before Shabbos but there are quite a few tea leaves in the tea essence. What shall we do?*

   If there are enough tea leaves in your essence to spoil your enjoyable cup of tea, straining the tea in a strainer is not allowed. If your teapot has a built-in strainer at the base of the spout (have a look, you might get a surprise), it is similarly not allowed. If the tea leaves have settled at the bottom of the teapot and above

---

1. *Eglei Tal*, "Zoreh."

them is more or less clear tea, you could pour that bit just prior to drinking it[2] but as soon as the tea leaves begin approaching the spout, you have to stop.

If you left your tea bags inside the essence, or in a glass of tea,[3] you also have to be careful not to pull them out by the string since this also causes the liquid tea to be strained as it comes out of the tea bag. Rather, take the tea bag out with a spoon without putting any pressure on the bag. Bottom line is that we should remember to prepare clear tea essence before Shabbos to avoid these problems.

4. *Our tap water is basically clean but I do prefer to use a filter for added cleanliness. Can I use it on Shabbos?*

Seeing that you only *prefer* to strain the water but if the water were not strained you would also drink it, you may strain it. This assumes that you are not an exception but you are like the majority in this regard. The water in developed countries, which is pure enough for the average person to drink safely, is in this category.

5. *We've got a guest for Shabbos who usually only drinks bottled water. She says that if we use our filter she'll drink it. Would that be okay?*

Your guest is in a special category of people called "*istanis.*" For her, normal water is undrinkable; she is not allowed to use a strainer.[4] Whether you can do it for her is questionable.[5] In fact,

---

2. To avoid *borer*.
3. According to those *poskim* who allow making tea in a *kli shelishi*.
4. Shulchan Aruch, Orach Chaim 319:10; Biur Halachah, s.v. "*ho'il.*"
5. See Shulchan Aruch, Orach Chaim 302:1; Biur Halachah, s.v. "*vehu.*"

she won't even be allowed to turn on her own cold tap for drinking water because of the strainer built into the tap itself. She may turn on the tap to wash her hands, since she doesn't mind tap water for washing.[6]

6. *Now I heard there's a real problem of mites in the water supply. Is there anything we can do?*

To strain water through a strainer to remove mites is certainly forbidden. What might be permitted is to attach to the tap a clean cloth,[7] designated for this purpose,[8] which will filter the water as it comes out. It should be fixed tightly, touching the mouth of the tap.[9]

However, this is only permitted if the water is halachically permitted as it is and this is just an extra precaution beyond the strict requirements of halachah. If there is a real danger of mites in the water, which means that the water is now halachically forbidden for drinking, this method is not allowed.[10]

---

6. Rav Dovid Ribiat, *The 39 Melochos*, "Meraked," note 54.
7. To avoid a question of *melaben*.
8. To avoid any temptation to squeeze out the cloth.
9. This constitutes a change from the normal way one would strain through a cloth.
10. Implication of *Shulchan Aruch, Orach Chaim* 319:16. Although the *Nishmas Adam, Hilchos Shabbos* 16:5 gives a possible reason to be lenient because the water really is drinkable, the proof being that non-Jews drink it, in a nonemergency situation one should not rely on it. Nowadays there is no shortage of bottled water and other beverages we can drink over Shabbos. And of course we can strain water before Shabbos. Hot water is prepared in advance anyway. The *Minchas Yitzchak* 7:23, who was more lenient because of the extreme inconvenience, was writing when there were not so many alternative drinks available.

7. *This is serious. My wedding ring has fallen into the sand. Please let me sieve the sand to find it.*

   No, I'm afraid there is no leniency here. Besides the halachah of sifting, the sand is *muktzeh*.[11] Crumbling solid sand will be *tochen*. In the *zechus* of keeping Shabbos, I think you'll probably find it tomorrow.

8. *I've just realized that the saltshaker has a small sieve under the hole where the salt comes out. What about that?*

   If there is only salt in the saltshaker, there is no problem. The sieve by the hole is just to prevent too much salt from coming out at once. If there are grains of rice in the salt to absorb moisture there is a problem according to some *poskim*.[12] Therefore I advise you to get a special saltshaker for Shabbos without a little sieve and leave out the rice to fulfill all opinions.

9. *It's Chaya's birthday and I want to sprinkle confectioners' sugar over her birthday cake. Can I use a sieve?*

   This is not *meraked* because you are not using it to keep one item back while another item goes through, but merely to scatter the sugar evenly.

   If there are solid clumps of sugar that will be held back by the sieve, it will not be allowed. However, since the sieve is normally used for sifting, it is *muktzeh* and may only be used if there is no

---

11. Unless it is designated for use before Shabbos, like a children's sandbox.
12. Rav Shimon Eider, *Halachos of Shabbos*, in the name of Rav Moshe Feinstein. *Orchos Shabbos*, vol. 1, 3:82 says that Rav Yosef Shalom Elyashiv is lenient since the sieve is not designed to sift out the rice and the person is also not using it for this purpose.

other way of scattering the sugar evenly.

10. *Baby's bottle has a built-in strainer at the top to catch bits of cream that sometimes form. Do we need to have a special bottle for Shabbos without the strainer?*

    No, you don't need a different bottle because the *Shulchan Aruch*[13] specifically says that if one is eating or drinking through the strainer or cloth it is permitted. Having said that, it is a good idea for babies to have special items for Shabbos, as a reminder that it is a special day.

---

13. *Orach Chaim* 319:16.

CHAPTER 23

לש — KNEADING

1. *Chaim says he can't build sandcastles in his sandbox because the sand is too dry. Can he pour some water on the sand?*

   Anyone who bakes knows that kneading is the mixing of water with flour to form dough. This is not allowed on Shabbos. It doesn't have to be water and it doesn't have to be flour; the mixing of any liquid with any solid (including sand) to form a dough-like mixture is not allowed under this *melachah*. So, no sandcastles for Chaim today.

2. *Someone told me that mixing hot water with instant coffee on Shabbos is not allowed because of lash. Is he right?*

   No, he is wrong. Although you are mixing a liquid with a solid, the net result is not a doughy mixture, not even a semi-doughy mixture, but a liquid, and therefore has no connection to *lash*. We do have to be careful about *bishul*, however, and even assuming this is instant coffee, which is precooked, we can only pour in hot water from a *kli sheini*, not a *kli rishon*.

3. *How can I prepare Avi's breakfast?*

   You're right to ask this question, as children's breakfast on Shabbos is one of the real danger zones for *lash*. As we implied in the previous answer, *lash* includes making a thick doughy mixture and even a semi-doughy mixture. However, as we have seen in some previous *melachos* like *borer* and *tochen*, *Chazal*[1] allowed certain *melachos* that would otherwise be forbidden by rabbinic law to be done if we do them in an unusual way. With *lash* however, there are a number of details that make things more complex, as follows:

Kneading has two parts: the initial combining of the liquid and the solid, and the mixing of the liquid and the solid. There are two opinions about which is the main part of the process. Furthermore, there is a dispute about whose opinion is the accepted halachah. Therefore we have to make a change in both parts of the process.

We have to change the way the liquid and the solid are combined; if the liquid is usually poured into the solid, on Shabbos the solid should be put into the liquid or vice versa. Also, instead of mixing in the usual way, we have to mix the solid and liquid with a criss-cross action. A minority opinion holds that we have to take the spoon or other implement out of the mixture after every criss and cross.

Another point is that although usually we can be lenient to do *lash* if we make these two changes, it is ordinarily only allowed if the mixture is liquidy to the extent that it could pour from one plate to another. If it is too thick to pour smoothly, it is only allowed if there is a special need.

Having said all this, there is a major problem with some cereals, particularly baby cereals. Some cereals are manufactured in such a way that the milk immediately spreads around the cereal, making it into a doughy mixture without any stirring. We can't

---

1. Short for "our *chachamim* (sages) *zichronam livracha*."

mix it in an unusual way because it mixes by itself. Such cereals can be used only if one puts enough milk in to ensure that the mixture remains liquidy enough to pour from one vessel to another as explained above.

Now on to Avi's breakfast. If it's a baby cereal, it almost certainly has to be made into a runny mixture for the reason we just mentioned. Even so, the solid and the liquid should not be mixed in the usual order. And one has to be sure, or at least plan, that the mixture will remain runny until it is all eaten.[2] Other cereals, e.g., matzah meal, can be made according to the rules we mentioned earlier.

A thick mixture, even with the two changes, is only permitted in a case of special need, e.g., a baby who needs or will only eat such a thick mixture. If it is not strictly necessary, make a more liquidy mixture as explained before. Is the milk usually put into the solid or vice versa? Do it on Shabbos in the opposite way. If there is no usual way, there is a dispute.[3] In a case of need, as for a baby, when there is no regular order, put the solid in first and then the liquid.[4] Now mix it with criss-cross strokes as explained above. Many other cereals, like cornflakes, shredded wheat, Cheerios, and Rice Krispies, etc., do not stick together unless left for some time, and these could be your child's Shabbos treat.

4. *I heard that Weetabix is a particular problem. Why?*

---

2. See Rav Pesach Eliyahu Falk, *Zochor Veshomor*, "*Losh.*" If under normal circumstances the cereal would all be eaten while it is still runny, but just this time the baby decided not to have any more and it became a thick mixture, one would not have been *mechallel Shabbos*.
3. *Shulchan Aruch, Orach Chaim* 321; *Mishnah Berurah* 57.
4. *Iggros Moshe* 4:74, *Orach Chaim*, "*Lash*" 3.

ל — Kneading   **151**

Weetabix and similar cereals are a problem because, like the baby cereals we mentioned above, as soon as you add the milk or put the Weetabix into milk, it mixes by itself and there is no possibility of mixing it in an unusual way. As we said, if you make sure it is runny you can prepare it as we described in the previous answer, but it is not so practical, as implied in note 2. If your child or baby really wants such a cereal, you can prepare it before Shabbos and leave it in the fridge. If it is too thick by Shabbos morning, you can add milk and mix it normally. Thinning a mixture with a liquid is the opposite of *lash* and is permitted.

5. *Do you think that cornflakes are a good idea?*

   Yes, as mentioned in our answer above.[5]

6. *I told you[6] that our new son-in-law prepares his egg-and-onion salad at the Shabbos table. You explained about tochen but what about lash?*

   Anyone who makes an egg-and-onion salad on Shabbos certainly has to be very careful about *lash*. So why not make it before Shabbos? Indeed that is how many people prepare it, including, according to testimony, in the house of the Chazon Ish.[7]

   So why does your new son-in-law prepare it on Shabbos? The answer is that in his father's house and probably in all his ancestors' houses for hundreds of years, they were worried about

---

5. In terms of the correct *berachah* for cornflakes, if it is made from unground corn, like the Kellogg's brand, the *berachah* is *ha'adamah*. If it is made from ground corn (like most other brands), the *berachah* is *shehakol*. See my *sefer Do You Know Hilchos Brachos?*
6. See ch. 21, question 4.
7. Rav Dovid Ribiat, *The 39 Melochos*, "Losh," note 87b.

leaving an unshelled egg overnight, which is said to be a danger.[8] Although the general custom is only to be concerned about a raw egg,[9] this isn't your son-in-law's custom, so don't try to change him.

If it is made on Shabbos, how should it be done? If you use oil or runny mayonnaise, it can be done by changing the order of the initial contact and mixing it in a criss-cross way, as mentioned above. Even though we said that even with these changes, we should only make a liquidy mixture, in the case of a food that is really desired and cannot be made before Shabbos,[10] we can be lenient.[11] There are some people who are more lenient and if that is their family custom, don't criticize them.[12]

If one uses thick mayonnaise that doesn't mix at all with the eggs unless it is stirred in, there is no need to change the order, as placing the mayonnaise on top of the eggs is of no significance at all. The mixing will, of course, still need to be done in the unusual way of criss-crossing. Enjoy!

7. *Moshe likes to add mayonnaise to the chopped liver. I told him to ask a shailah.*

It is a *shailah*, but if done in the right way it is permitted. He should use the thick mayonnaise as in the previous answer and mix it criss-cross. The runny mayonnaise would be a problem even if Moshe would make the two changes because it is going to be a thick mixture and this is not normally allowed unless

---

8. *Niddah* 17a. Also see *Minchas Yitzchak* 9:28.
9. *Darchei Teshuvah* 116:74.
10. Because of the problem of leaving a shelled egg overnight.
11. *Shaar HaTziyun* 321:84.
12. See *Orchos Shabbos*, vol. 1, 6:40 and note 77.

there is a special need, as for a baby or if it cannot be made before Shabbos as above.

8. *I'm really running late. Can we have instant mashed potatoes on Shabbos?*

   Only if you prepare them before Shabbos. The potatoes will be a thick mixture that, as we have said, even with the changes is only permitted in cases of special need, such as for a baby. Sometimes the potato flakes will mix by themselves without any effort, which, as we mentioned above, is not allowed. Also there are questions of *bishul* (cooking) seeing that the potato flakes are inedible before the hot water is poured in.[13]

9. *What about Jell–O?*

   No, Jell–O cannot be prepared on Shabbos because of *lash* and other reasons.[14]

10. *Can you give me some easy rules to make sure I keep hilchos lash?*

    If you remember only to make a loose mixture, change the order, and mix criss-cross, you won't transgress *lash*.

---

13. Rav Pesach Eliyahu Falk, *Zochor Veshomor*, "Losh."
14. Rav Dovid Ribiat, *The 39 Melochos*, p. 547.

CHAPTER 24

בישול — COOKING, Part I

1. *I'm sure I heard the rav saying that he fried an egg last Shabbos. Did I mishear?*

   Assuming your shul is Orthodox, there must be an explanation. In terms of *hilchos bishul*, the only possible explanation is that he fried it in the sun. To cook with fire or something heated by fire or something heated by the sun is not allowed. But cooking using the direct heat of the sun alone is permitted.[1]

   This does not mean that one can use a *dud shemesh*, which heats water by the hot sun, because hot water leaving the *dud* is replaced by new cold water, which is then heated up by the rest of the hot water in the *dud*.[2]

2. *The guests have arrived early. Can I check if the chicken is cooked?*

   This can be a problem. If it's cooked, that's fine. But if it's not fully cooked you're not allowed to put the lid back on the pan, as this

---

1. *Shulchan Aruch, Orach Chaim* 318:3.
2. *Shemiras Shabbos KeHilchasah* 1:45. Other *poskim* have other concerns about a *dud shemesh*. See *Minchas Yitzchak* 4:44. See also *Orchos Shabbos*, vol. 1, 1:103.

would speed up the cooking process.³ It is better to make sure all foods and liquids are fully cooked before Shabbos to avoid this and similar problems.

3. *Rivky will be back a little later than the rest of the family. Can I put her soup on the top of our cholent pot to keep hot?*

I assume the soup was boiling hot, having been on the *blech* or Shabbos hotplate since Shabbos came in. Now everyone has enjoyed it but you want to keep some hot soup for Rivky. Now it is obviously not bubbling hot anymore, which means that according to the Sephardic custom it may not be put back on any source of heat.⁴ However, the Ashkenazic custom is to allow it as long as it is hot enough to be enjoyed, even though it's not piping hot.⁵ But this can only be done in a place that is not usually used for cooking, like the top of another pan.⁶ A solid piece of food that was fully cooked but has now gone cold may be heated up on top of another pan according to all opinions. But see also *"Bishul,"* part II, question and answer 4.

4. *Avi likes his milk warm, but not hot. Can I put his bottle next to the stove to heat up a little?*

If the milk would not get hot, even if it were left there the whole day, it is allowed. However, we may not put uncooked food or

---

3. *Shulchan Aruch, Orach Chaim* 254:5.
4. Ibid. 253:2. See *Mishnah Berurah* 54.
5. *Shulchan Aruch, Orach Chaim* 318:15, *Rama*.
6. *Shulchan Aruch, Orach Chaim* 318:15; *Mishnah Berurah* 92.

drink in a place where it would eventually cook[7] if it were left there. Even though we intend to take it away before it is cooked, there is a risk of forgetting.[8]

5. *It's very cold and I'd like a hot-water bottle to keep me warm in bed. Perhaps there are drops of cold water left inside the bottle that will get very hot when I pour in the hot water. What do I do?*

There are possible grounds to ignore what could amount to reboiling these drops,[9] but it is better to avoid the question by pouring from a *kli sheini*, i.e., first pour the hot water from the Shabbos urn into a dry jug and from there into the bottle. If there is no dry jug available, it is permitted to pour directly into the bottle if you have shaken out as much of the old cold water as possible.[10]

6. *This cholent is delicious. Do I have to wipe the plate before taking seconds?*

As we mentioned in answer 4 above, if there is only a cooked solid like potatoes, there is no prohibition in reheating it and therefore no problem in putting hot cholent straight from the pan on top of it. But if there is still cooled gravy on the plate, you do have a problem. I take some challah and wipe up the gravy to avoid the *shailah*. It tastes great! If there are only a few drops left, you don't need to worry.[11]

---

7. That is, reach *yad soledes bo*, which, according to some *poskim*, is 104 degrees Fahrenheit (49 degrees Celsius) — about the temperature of the water in a hot bath (Rav Dovid Ribiat, *The 39 Melochos*).
8. *Shulchan Aruch, Orach Chaim* 318:14.
9. See *Iggros Moshe, Orach Chaim* 4:74, para. 19.
10. Ibid.
11. As in note 9.

7. *I've always wondered about this: Can I eat the hot meat with the cold carrot salad together?*

   A number of factors in this situation could result in a lenient conclusion. It is doubtful that hot meat, if it is no longer in a *kli rishon*, can cook anything else.[12] You don't intend to cook the carrot salad and even if it happened, it would spoil rather than improve the taste of the carrot.[13] For these reasons, we cannot say that somebody who is lenient has done wrong. Even so, some say that *lechatchilah* we should try to avoid allowing hot meat to touch raw vegetables.[14]

8. *What about ketchup on the hot chicken?*

   I am sure ketchup fans are glancing anxiously at the answer to this question. Well, they can relax. Ketchup is certainly precooked. The only question is whether it is a solid or a liquid. Most opinions consider ketchup to be a solid in this context, so it may be reheated.[15]

   Also, we mentioned above, that it is not so clear that hot meat, once it has been removed from the pan where it was cooking, can cook something else.

   So, bottom line — you can enjoy your hot chicken with ketchup.[16] Just don't forget to say "*lekavod Shabbos kodesh*"!

---

12. See the various opinions brought in Rav Dovid Ribiat, *The 39 Melochos*, "Bishul," note 105.
13. *Maor Shabbos* in the name of Rav Shlomo Zalman Auerbach.
14. Ibid. in the name of other *poskim*.
15. *Orchos Shabbos*, vol. 1, ch.1, note 47, in the name of Rav Yosef Shalom Elyashiv and Rav Shlomo Zalman Auerbach.
16. *Iggros Moshe, Orach Chaim* 4:74, "Bishul" 5.

9. *The cholent is getting too dry. Is there any way I can add hot water to it?*

Join the millions of Jews, especially young couples, who have had this question over the centuries. What do I do if the cholent dries out? How many young (and not so young) *balabustehs* nervously lift up the lid of the cholent pot to see if the cholent has gone dry? Several questions are involved.

Can we take water from one *kli rishon*[17] to another *kli rishon*? Does pouring water into the cholent constitute *hagasah* (stirring)? *Hagasah* is not allowed in a *kli rishon al ha'eish*[18] even if it is fully cooked.[19] What are the implications if steam from the meaty cholent goes onto the pareve Shabbos urn? Are we allowed to pour from the urn into a cup and from there into the cholent?

It is difficult to fulfill all the opinions, but according to the Shaar HaTziyun,[20] the best method is:

Take the cholent off the fire with the intention of returning it to the fire. Do not let go of it even if you put it on a surface near the stove. Take off the lid. Now pour water from the Shabbos urn into a new disposable cup, then pour that water into the cholent. This can be done as many times as necessary. Replace the lid and return the cholent to the fire, making sure that it is covered by a *blech*.

This avoids the otherwise inevitable question of meaty steam touching the pareve urn and conforms with the rules of

---

17. A vessel in which food or liquid was cooked on the fire (gas or electric).
18. When it is actually on the fire.
19. *Shulchan Aruch, Orach Chaim* 318:18; *Mishnah Berurah* 113, 117.
20. *Shaar HaTziyun* 253:47. See there that he writes "*Pashut deyesh lismoch al hameikilim.*" See *Orchos Shabbos*, vol. 1, 2:72, who allows this method *lechatchilah*.

*chazarah*²¹ (see next chapter) according to the *pesak* of the Shaar HaTziyun.²² It also avoids the question of *hagasah*, which only applies to cooked food if the pot is on the fire.²³

The Sephardic *pesak* does not allow transferring water even from one *kli rishon al ha'eish* to another.²⁴ Many Sephardim, for this reason, put a bag of water with the other ingredients in the cholent. If the cholent becomes dry, they tear the bag open²⁵ and let the boiling water out into the cholent.

10. **My cup of tea is too hot. Can I pour in some cold water?**

If your cup is a *kli shelishi* there is no question. Even if it's a *kli sheini*,²⁶ it is still permitted.²⁷ We may not put most uncooked foods or liquids into a *kli sheini*, but water is an exception because it definitely does not cook in a *kli sheini*. Some authorities say that water that is *yad nichvas bo* (hot enough to burn a person's hand), since it has just come from a Shabbos urn, has the same halachah as a *kli rishon*.²⁸ A drinking cup holds a relatively small amount of water, so it will be less than boiling as soon as you put in some cold water. This is permitted according to all opinions.²⁹

---

21. Returning a pan to the fire.
22. As in note 20.
23. *Mishnah Berurah* 318:117.
24. *Shulchan Aruch, Orach Chaim* 253:2; *Kaf HaChaim* 253:38.
25. Seeing that it is done in a nonconstructive way for consuming, it is certainly not prohibited because of *korea*. See ch. 33.
26. A second vessel, i.e., the vessel into which the contents of the first vessel were poured. If these contents are now poured into a third vessel, this is the *kli shelishi* refered to just before.
27. *Mishnah Berurah* 253:42, *Shaar HaTziyun* 68.
28. *Chayei Adam* 20:4; *Mishnah Berurah* 318:48.
29. Rav Pesach Eliyahu Falk, *Zochor Veshomor*, "*Bishul*" 6D(ii).

CHAPTER 25

בישול, Part II

1. *The car broke down and I arrived home just twenty minutes before Shabbos. Can I still put on the raw cholent for tomorrow morning?*

   Although the cholent will not be cooked before Shabbos, all is not lost. Although it is far from ideal because of possible mistakes, the halachah does allow us to put uncooked food on the stove under certain conditions. The danger is, according to rabbinic law, that a person might forget and try to speed up the cooking process on Shabbos by "stoking the coals" under the pan. In order for the cooking to be allowed, we have to cover the burning coals or sweep them away.[1]

   In the context of our modern stoves, we must cover the source of heat and ideally also the knobs or buttons that alter the flow of gas or electricity.[2] Traditionally we have used a metal cover, called a *blech*, to do this. Some *blechs* have a panel that covers the knobs too. Any covering that covers at least the flame is acceptable. If we put even raw food in a pan over a *blech* to cook, it is permitted.

   Of course, once Shabbos begins, we can't alter any settings.

---

1. *Shulchan Aruch, Orach Chaim* 253:1.
2. *Iggros Moshe, Orach Chaim* 1:93.

In fact, even before Shabbos comes in, having put the pan on the *blech*, we are not allowed to lift up the *blech* and alter the settings as this would defeat the whole idea of using a *blech*.³ We also have to remember that until we are sure that the food is completely cooked, we may not take off the lid of the pan, as replacing the lid would quicken the cooking process.

As I said, doing things in this way is not ideal, but in an emergency, with special attention to the points mentioned, your Shabbos can be salvaged.⁴

2. *Help! Moshe brought out the cholent instead of the chicken soup. Unless I can put it back we'll have nothing hot tomorrow. What's the halachah?*

This is probably the most common *shailah* in all the halachos of *chazarah*. A well-meaning husband gets mixed up between the soup for Friday night and the cholent for Shabbos morning — with the ensuing risks to *shalom bayis*. Let's answer the *shalom bayis* issue first. So, your husband made a mistake. And you never make mistakes? You've got a husband and a well-meaning one to boot. Be thankful for that. Bite your tongue (figuratively) and move on.

Now the question of *chazarah*. The halachah does not allow food that was taken off a stove to be returned unless a number of conditions are fulfilled:

---

3. *Shemiras Shabbos KeHilchasah* 1, note 54.
4. According to the strict halachah, if the food is edible (half-cooked, in an emergency one-third cooked) a *blech* is not required but the *poskim* recommend us always to use a *blech* even if the food is completely cooked to avoid mistakes. See *Biur Halachah* 253:1, s.v. "venahagu." See also ch. 44, "Mechabeh," answer 5.

a. The food has to be fully cooked.
b. The flame has to covered with a *blech* or something similar.
c. When we take the food off the stove our intention must be to return it before it goes cold.[5]
d. If we put the pan down, we must continue to hold it with at least one hand.[6]

In this case there may be room for leniency. Moshe might well not have put the cholent down yet and most of the other conditions were also fulfilled. The only missing condition was his intention to return it, since he thought it was the soup. The *Mishnah Berurah*[7] holds that if one of the last two conditions was not fulfilled, we may be lenient in a case of need. And even if neither of these conditions was observed, there are good grounds to be lenient to prevent a "ruined" Shabbos lunch, as long as the food was fully cooked, the heat source is covered, and the main course of the Shabbos meal would be lost if this pan was not kept hot.

Further, if this would be a way of avoiding the risk to *shalom bayis*, that would also be good grounds for leniency. The Sephardic custom, as mentioned in the previous chapter, is to be strict if there is liquid in the pan that was taken off the stove, even if it was fully cooked. So they will have to be especially careful. No "well-meaning husbands" allowed in the kitchen!

3. *Our Shabbos hotplate just turned itself off. While the food is hot, can I take it to a neighbor?*

I like this question. Who else but Jews would be seen scurrying with hot pans in their hands, knocking on their neighbors' doors

---

5. *Shaar HaTziyun* 253:49.
6. *Shulchan Aruch, Orach Chaim* 253:2.
7. 253:56.

on a Friday evening? The question is interesting because since the hotplate is off, the food is not on the fire anymore. No one took it off the fire with the intention of putting it back, which is usually one of the conditions for *chazarah*.

However it could be argued that what the halachah is really concerned about is if someone took the food off with the intention of not returning it. That didn't happen in this case because it came off "by itself." In practice most *poskim*[8] are lenient if the food was fully cooked and is still pleasantly hot. Also your neighbor's stove needs to have a *blech* over it. And of course, we're talking about a place with a kosher eiruv.

4. *We like hot kugel with our shalosh seudos. Can I put it on the Shabbos urn to heat up?*

First of all, *yasher kochacha* on having hot food even for *shalosh seudos*, which is definitely *kavod Shabbos*. You must just make sure it is done in a permitted way. Reheating the kugel that is fully cooked and dry is not a problem. Putting it on the top of the Shabbos urn or another pan that contains hot food or water is also permitted from the point of view of *chazarah*, as it is not a place where we normally cook. If we do not have a vessel on the stove with hot food or liquid in it, some *poskim*[9] also allow putting dry, cooked food on top of an upturned empty pan on the stove, although other important *poskim* do not approve.[10]

A compromise opinion[11] is to allow putting cooked food

---

8. *Iggros Moshe, Orach Chaim* 4:74; *Shemiras Shabbos KeHilchasah* 1:69 in the name of Rav Shlomo Zalman Auerbach.
9. See *Shemiras Shabbos KeHilchasah* 1:38.
10. *Az Nidberu* 3:14.
11. Rav Pesach Eliyahu Falk.

onto an empty, upturned vessel on top of a Shabbos hotplate that is not designed for cooking, but not on an empty, upturned vessel over a stove. The top of the upturned vessel should be at least 1.5 inches (4.5 cm) above the surface of the hotplate.[12]

There could be a question of *hatmanah* (wrapping food as a way of increasing or maintaining heat), which is not allowed on Shabbos. If this is done in a place where there is a constant source of heat we may not do it even before Shabbos. To wrap up your kugel in a towel would not be allowed. To wrap it in a piece of aluminium foil is not regarded as *hatmanah*, as one layer of foil protects the food from insects, etc., and prevents the food from drying out. Even a larger piece of foil folded into what amounts to a thick layer is also permitted since it is still called one covering.[13] Using two separate pieces is not allowed.

5. *I was warming up Avi's milk bottle in some hot water when Chani told me she heard that it's not allowed. Is she right?*

You could both be right. Indeed, to submerge Avi's bottle totally in hot water, even in a *kli sheini*, is not allowed because of *hatmanah*.[14] If it is only partially submerged, that is not *hatmanah* and is permitted.

6. *I live alone and have to work on Erev Shabbos. Is there any shailah in putting everything in a slow cooker in the morning so that by Friday night it will be ready for my seudah?*

This is a controversial question. As we have just said, if a pan is

---

12. Ibid.
13. *Machazeh Eliyahu* 32.
14. *Mishnah Berurah* 258:2.

only partially surrounded, it is not called *hatmanah*. This is why some *poskim*[15] see no problem in a slow cooker or crockpot even though the inner pan is surrounded on three sides, leaving the top open. Rav Shlomo Zalman Auerbach famously considered using a crockpot to be *hatmanah* because it is designed to keep food hot, notwithstanding the open top.

Some *poskim* say that a layer of foil over the base and sides of the inner pan solves the halachic problem.[16] Some say[17] one should put balls of crushed foil under the base of the inner pan so that it sits partially above the sides. *Lechatchilah* we try to fulfill all opinions when there is a halachic dispute, especially in the case of *kedushas Shabbos*. I would say that if you can, try to incorporate the halachic improvements mentioned and this will be a source of *berachah*. If your slow cooker is just a base without the walls around the sides, it is certainly permitted.

7. *A neighbor said that thermos flasks are definitely not allowed on Shabbos. I told him that I've never heard that from our rav. Who is right?*

Although I just said that *lechatchilah* we try to fulfill all opinions, in this case all the main *poskim* hold that, even though a thermos flask is designed to keep its contents hot, it does not constitute *hatmanah* for various halachic reasons.[18] So, as always, listen to your *rav* rather than a neighbor.

---

15. Rav Moshe Feinstein quoted by Rav Dovid Ribiat, *The 39 Melochos*, p. 633.
16. Rav Dovid Ribiat, *The 39 Melochos*, p. 633.
17. Ibid., "Bishul," note 186.
18. See *Iggros Moshe, Orach Chaim* 1:95 that here even a *baal nefesh* (one on an elevated spiritual level) has no reason to be *machmir*.

8. *I know everything should be ready before Shabbos but sometimes I find it very difficult. Can I prepare the baby's bath before candlelighting and then bathe him afterward?*

I appreciate your admission that you should be ready before Shabbos and also your situation that can make the ideal "easier said than done."

So let's look into the precise halachah. There is a longstanding rabbinic prohibition of immersing in hot water even if the water was prepared before Shabbos.[19] The halachah does allow a partial washing, as long as one doesn't wash most of the body. There are also leniencies for someone who is ill or a baby who needs bathing thoroughly.[20] So if your baby is dirty and needs a bath to get properly clean, *bediveved* you can bathe him in water prepared before Shabbos.

However, if the baby is basically clean and you just want him to have his "Shabbos bath," it would not be allowed. From another angle, it might be possible to be more lenient. At least according to one major opinion, if the water is cooler than the usual bathing temperature, the prohibition does not apply.[21] If you can make sure your baby's bath is at a temperature that an adult would not normally bathe in, certainly if it is lukewarm,[22] it would be allowed according to the strict halachah.

However I would not be happy for you to take advantage of this in practice because of the numerous halachic issues involved.

---

19. See *Shabbos* 40a that some of the bathhouse attendants heated the water on Shabbos but claimed they did it before Shabbos.
20. *Shemiras Shabbos KeHilchasah* 14, note 8.
21. *Iggros Moshe, Orach Chaim* 4:74, "Rechitzah."
22. Which would fulfill the opinion that if it feels at all hot, it is not allowed. See *Orchos Shabbos*, vol. 2, 21:3.

Using a bar of soap is definitely not allowed. The same applies to a washcloth and to shampooing baby's hair. Drying baby's hair risks *sechitah* (squeezing). Almost instinctively you would want to brush baby's hair, which may only be done using a soft brush set aside for Shabbos. In a moment of forgetfulness you may add hot water — the list goes on and on. In fact, precisely because of these pitfalls[23] the custom is not to immerse oneself even in cold water unless one is in distress.[24]

I appreciate the pressures of caring for little children. Sometimes twenty-four hours a day are not enough. But in practice, if baby is in distress, you can give him a bath in water prepared before Shabbos, being careful about the various possible pitfalls, but not just for a Shabbos bath. Maybe try first thing on Friday morning. *Hatzlachah!*

9. *Chaim has been playing in the yard. He needs to wash his hands and face with hot water. He says that his teacher said you can't wash with hot water on Shabbos. How are we going to resolve this one?*

No problem. You explain to Chaim that his teacher only said we are not allowed to wash in hot water if we are washing most of our body or even a small part of the body, if the water was heated (even in a permitted way) on Shabbos. If the water was heated before Shabbos or even if we have poured hot water into a *kli sheini* and added cold water to it, to cool down the hot water,[25] we may wash our hands and face.

10. *Our newly married daughter has confided to us that her husband*

---

23. Particularly because of the danger of *sechitah*.
24. *Iggros Moshe, Orach Chaim* 4:75.
25. *Eglei Tal*, "*Ofeh*" 66.

immerses in a hot mikveh every day including Shabbos. Shall we say anything to him?

No. Repeat three times: No, no, no.

First of all, perhaps your daughter should not have confided in you at all. If she has a question, she should have asked her husband. Second, your son-in-law may take exception to this breach of privacy. When a man goes to the mikveh has nothing to do with his parents-in-law. Third, if you made your own inquiries, you would find that many very pious men go the mikveh every day and some indeed go into a hot mikveh although not all the *poskim* approve. Those who are lenient rely on a well-known, if minority, opinion[26] that the prohibition of immersing in hot water does not apply to immersing in a mikveh. Others make sure that the water is below the usual temperature and rely on the opinion mentioned in answer 8 above.

We have already mentioned[27] that sometimes different communities have different customs based on their rabbanim and we have to respect that, especially where it concerns *shalom bayis*.

---

26. *Korban Nesanel* brought in *Mishnah Berurah* 326:7.
27. Ch. 21, "*Tochen;*" ch. 23, "*Lash.*"

CHAPTER 26

גוזז — SHEARING

1. *If the rabbi wants to give a shiur on shearing, let him go to the local farm. What's it got to do with us?*

   As with all the *melachos,* the activity was done in a certain way in the Beis HaMikdash but it can also be done in a domestic setting. Shearing wool from a sheep is an example of uprooting something that is growing on a living creature. Therefore, cutting our hair or nails or removing loose skin, etc., are forbidden under the *melachah* of *gozez* (shearing).

2. *My daughter's hair is a mess. What can we do about it?*

   Gozez is an area of Shabbos observance in which our *yiras Shamayim* (fear of Heaven) can be tested more than many others. Our personal appearance is important to us and we can be tempted to cut halachic corners to this end. Of course the reward for avoiding these temptations will be all the greater.

   In the case of brushing hair, although we may not really mean to uproot any hair, we might well end up doing just that and transgressing *gozez* unless we are very careful and follow the halachah. Combing is out of the question.[1] When the teeth of

---

1. Shulchan Aruch, Orach Chaim 303:27.

a comb meet a knot that is tying two or more strands of hair together, it doesn't undo the knot, but pulls out some of the hair. Some brushes with strong bristles fixed fairly far apart act in the same way as combs and are equally forbidden. Other brushes will also inevitably pull out hairs and are not allowed[2] under the principle of "*Psik reisha velo yamus?* — Can you cut off the head of a chicken and the chicken won't die?"[3]

Only a soft brush, ideally one designed for babies, which shapes the hair rather than separates hairs, may be used. Even with this type, we should brush gently.[4] The *poskim* say that we should designate this soft brush for Shabbos only.[5]

We are allowed to "brush" our hair by hand as long as we are careful to stop if our fingers come across a knot or any other obstruction in the hair.[6]

3. *I've got some loose skin on my lip. Please let me pick it off.*

How uncomfortable you must be feeling to ask me to allow you to pick the loose skin off your lip! Halachically this would be more serious than other forms of *gozez*, like cutting nails. We normally trim our nails with scissors, a nail file or a clipper, so breaking off a nail by hand would be prohibited on a rabbinic level. We never use scissors, etc., to remove loose skin from our lips, so to pick off loose skin by hand would be the normal way of

---

2.   *Mishnah Berurah* 303:86.
3.   In other words, even if you don't intend for the chicken to die, seeing that it's inevitable that it will die if you cut the head off, it is forbidden. Here also, even though you don't want to uproot hairs, seeing that using a brush will inevitably uproot hairs, it is not allowed.
4.   *Mishnah Berurah* 303:87.
5.   Ibid.
6.   Ibid. 88.

doing it and be prohibited on a Biblical level (*deOraisa*).[7]

Maybe I can make a more general point. Many people have habits such as picking lips, biting nails, picking off loose cuticles, etc. They will find it very hard not to do these things on Shabbos. To make life easier, therefore, and to help us enjoy Shabbos and keep Shabbos on a higher level, we should make every effort to stop these habits during the week. It may be difficult, but with willpower and private incentives we can be successful. Needless to say, "according to the effort is the reward"[8] and if we can work on breaking these habits during the week with the intention of enhancing our Shabbos observance, we will be fulfilling the mitzvah of "remembering the Shabbos day to keep it holy" on a constant basis.

4. *I caught my nail on something and now it is almost off. Can I bite off the rest?*

Ordinarily, cutting off a nail, even a small part of a nail, is strictly forbidden as we have said. There may be a leniency here if the nail is causing pain — not inconvenience, but actual pain if, say, the nail is catching on things. It may be scratching against the next finger and causing pain. In such cases, seeing that the majority of the nail is not attached, you can remove that part, but only with your hand or teeth, not with an instrument.[9]

Just as in this case there is room to be lenient, there may be a possibility of leniency in other questions of *gozez* that arise with

---

7. *Biur Halachah* 340:2, s.v. "*yevoles.*"
8. *Pirkei Avos* 5:26.
9. *Shulchan Aruch, Orach Chaim* 328:31. See *Orchos Shabbos*, vol. 1, 17:5 and note 8. The controversy mentioned in the *Shulchan Aruch* concerns pieces of skin next to the nails, not the nails themselves.

certain medical conditions and certain emergency situations. In such cases a competent *rav* should be consulted.

5. *I thought this was a first-class hotel but the roast chicken still has bits of feather attached. Can I pull them out?*

There is a dispute whether removing feathers from a cooked chicken transgresses *gozez*.[10] To avoid the question and also the question of *borer*, take off the skin with the feathers still attached and discard both together. If you were faced with a feathery chicken at home, do the same thing but just before you are ready to eat. In the hotel, presumably, you are already in the middle of your meal when you were served this chicken. However, I would certainly complain to the head waiter!

---

10. *Orchos Shabbos*, vol. 1, 17:9.

CHAPTER 27

מלבן — LAUNDERING

1. *Oh no, not again. Some cholent fell on my Shabbos suit. Do I have to go around like this for the rest of Shabbos?*

    The *Mishnah Berurah*[1] specifically warns us to take precautions so that we don't get into situations like yours. "Cover yourself with a cloth before picking up a baby; don't hang your coat or hat where it's liable to fall off and get dusty," etc. This is because cleaning clothes is a classic example of *melaben*.

    Bedieved, if there are traces of cholent on your suit, there are ways to improve its appearance, but you're not going to come away with a clean suit.

    Solid pieces of food that have not been absorbed by the fabric may be removed. The question is: When you are lifting cholent from the surface, how can you be sure that you're not going too far and extracting cholent from the fabric as well? The *poskim* allow us to use a spoon or the blunt side of a knife[2] to gently take off what's on the surface. A stain will remain; it can't be helped. If

---

1. 302:6.
2. *Mishnah Berurah* 302:34, *Shaar HaTziyun* 42; *Shemiras Shabbos KeHilchasah* 15:27.

the food has dried, we can't even remove what is on the surface[3] because there is another potential problem of *tochen* (grinding).

On the one hand, wearing a suit with a stain is not *kavod Shabbos*; on the other hand, the fact that you have left it because the halachah does not allow cleaning it is a form of *kavod Shabbos* in itself. Best of all, be more careful!

2. *My hat fell on the floor. Can I just brush off the dust?*

If it is very dusty, I'm afraid you can't rub it clean.[4] If it is the only suitable hat you have and you would be embarrassed to walk around in it, you can ask a non-Jew to clean it for you.[5] If there is only a small amount of dust and it really wouldn't worry you to go out like this during the week, but *lekavod Shabbos* you want the hat to be completely clean, you may brush it with your hand or a cloth.[6] Even when it is permitted, the custom is not to use a clothes brush or hat brush.[7]

These same halachos apply to removing dust from a couch or armchair, which sometimes get dusty when children stand on them, and even removing footprints from our clothes when our beloved toddler decides to "walk all over us."

3. *This always happens. Cola spilled onto the tablecloth. Can I wipe it up with a paper napkin?*

---

3. Even if *tochen* is not relevant, for instance with meat, dried food tend to become embedded in the garment. Removing it will be forbidden because of *melaben* (Rav Pesach Eliyahu Falk, *Zochor Veshomor*, Melaben 1D).
4. *Mishnah Berurah* 302:6.
5. Ibid.
6. Ibid. 5.
7. *Biur Halachah* 337:2, s.v. "hakalim."

When there are children sitting at a table, it's a question of "when" rather than "if" there will be a spill, so it may well be advisable to use thin plastic tablecloth covers to avoid this kind of situation on Shabbos. Lack of due care can lead to getting annoyed and tense with children, and even the risk of transgressing Shabbos. When the children have "flown the nest" parents can enjoy their beautiful Shabbos tablecloths, at least until the children return with their own little broods, *be'ezras Hashem*.

But now to the question itself. A plain paper napkin is indeed the best idea. To use a cloth napkin would not be *melaben* since the cola would dirty it. Since it is made to clean up messes we aren't afraid that you will squeeze it out[8] unless it's too small to absorb all the liquid. It may raise the question of *tzovea* (coloring).[9] We still have to be careful not to squeeze out our paper napkin. Squeezing liquid from anything is forbidden since it is part of rinsing, which in turn is one of the essential stages of washing a garment.[10] We may not squeeze paper either, so use plenty of paper napkins and throw them away. If the napkins are printed with lettering or pictures, we may not use them to mop up spills that would inevitably cause the words or pictures to be erased.

Another point to remember is not to leave even a paper napkin pressed against a wet fabric tablecloth as this causes the liquid or at least some of the liquid to be extracted from the cloth and absorbed into the paper, which is a form of squeezing.

4. *Mom told me I'm not allowed to come inside with dirty shoes. Can I rinse them in a puddle?*

---

8. This might not be the case with more fancy cloth napkins.
9. *Mishnah Berurah* 320:59.
10. Rambam, *Hilchos Shabbos* 9:11.

That's a good question from what sounds like a well-behaved young man! There are three types of materials relevant to this *melachah*:

a. Cloth that absorbs water freely. We may not soak this in water as this will clean it to some extent.

b. Materials like leather, which are partially absorbent. We may soak these, but not rub them in any way in order to clean them.

c. Nonabsorbent materials like kitchen utensils, which we can wash if we're going to need them during Shabbos.

According to this, muddy shoes fall into the middle category, so you could just rinse them in a puddle without rubbing them to make them clean. However, if your shoelaces are made of cloth, they are in the first category, and can't even be put in water.

Having said all this, soaking your shoes in a puddle is not going to clean them thoroughly, so it might be an idea to just take them off as soon as you go inside, and put on your slippers. *Hatzlachah*!

5. *My wife's crying. Her new Shabbos jacket has fallen into the negel vasser, and nothing else matches her skirt. Is there any solution?*

We certainly need to try to find a solution. As it happens, the halachah is very understanding of the person whose Shabbos clothes have gotten wet. Although normally, wet clothes are considered *muktzeh* as a safeguard against being tempted to wring them out, the clothes are not *muktzeh* and may be worn if they are one's only suitable clothes for Shabbos.[11]

The question now is how wet they are. Your wife cannot go to shul or even walk around in a dripping wet jacket. Can she

---

11. *Mishnah Berurah* 301:162, *Shaar HaTziyun* 203.

put it over a radiator? No. That is forbidden because of both *melaben*[12] and *bishul*.[13] If it's sunny, can she hang it up outside? No. This is not allowed because the halachah says that we may not hang wet clothes up even in the privacy of our own homes because people may think we have washed them on Shabbos.[14] However, you can hang the jacket in a place where you normally hang clothes after use. After it has stopped dripping, your wife could put it on and walk around outside in the sunshine. So it seems that if she has half an hour to an hour to spare, the crisis can be managed.

PS. If the jacket is damaged by the water, I hope you'll be able to buy your wife another one soon!

PPS. *Negel vasser* is not *muktzeh*[15] so I suggest being careful to pour it out as soon as possible in the future.

6. *I forgot to bring in the clothes from the washing line before Shabbos. Can I do it now?*

If the clothes were dry before Shabbos, there is no problem about bringing them in on Shabbos. If they were still wet when Shabbos began, you can also bring them in if you need them for Shabbos, meaning you have nothing else suitable to wear, as we mentioned earlier.[16] If they were wet when Shabbos came in,

---

12. *Mishnah Berurah* 301:169.
13. *Mishnah Berurah* 301:170.
14. *Shulchan Aruch, Orach Chaim* 301:45. Some *poskim* hold that since such clothes are normally dry-cleaned and not washed in water, the *gezeirah* does not apply. Others disagree. See the lengthy discussion in Rav Dovid Ribiat, *The 39 Melochos*, "Melaben," note 17. One who is lenient has a basis for it.
15. *Shulchan Aruch, Orach Chaim* 338:8; *Biur Halachah*, s.v. "assur."
16. See note 11.

and they are not needed for Shabbos, leave them there till after Shabbos in order to avoid the question of *muktzeh*.[17]

7. *This is a sight I thought I'd never see. The Chassidim are wading through the river on the way to see the Rebbe. I understand why they're allowed to go, but can they come back?*

We can certainly learn from Chassidim the importance of being close to one's rebbe or *rav*, even to the extent of wading through a river (where there is no suitable bridge) to see him; this is even allowed on Shabbos.[18]

The same halachah applies to anyone who is on the way to do a mitzvah like visiting the sick. And yes, they may even come back.[19]

The *rishonim* are troubled by the question of why the immersion of one's clothes in the river is not in itself forbidden because of *melaben* since, as we mentioned above, even soaking cloth is not allowed. The *Tosafos Yeshanim*[20] in one answer says that it is permitted because the river will probably dirty the clothes rather than clean them. This is also why we may dry our hands on a towel on Shabbos, since we don't consider it to be cleaning the towel.

The question still remains why it is not forbidden because of the risk of wringing out the wet clothes. The *Shulchan Aruch*[21]

---

17. *Mishnah Berurah* 308:63. I say it's a question of *muktzeh* because there are other opinions on the subject. See *Orchos Shabbos*, vol. 2, ch. 19, note 563 and *Miluim* 24.
18. *Shulchan Aruch, Orach Chaim* 301:4.
19. Ibid. 301:5. This is based on *Yoma* 77b.
20. S.v. "oveir."
21. *Orach Chaim* 301:4.

says that indeed in order to remember not to wring out his clothes, he has to cross the river in an unusual manner, such as with his hands inside his garment, as a reminder.[22]

There is one more point to bear in mind when considering crossing a river: Whether it is Shabbos or a weekday we may not wade through a river deeper than waist height if there is a strong current because of possible danger.[23]

8. *It's the first day of Pesach and the carpet is full of matzah crumbs. Can I use the carpet sweeper?*

Matzah crumbs on the carpet are certainly a problem. No one likes to live in an untidy room, yet when you've had a Seder with young and old eating their matzah reclining as per the halachah, you can't avoid matzah falling on the floor. You can pick up bigger pieces of matzah by hand. Some allow using a brush since it is not the usual way we clean a carpet,[24] but not a carpet cleaner.

If it really is bad, especially if ants or mice think they've been invited for lunch, you could ask a non-Jew to clean the carpet even with a manual carpet sweeper.[25] I would suggest asking people to be as careful as possible during the Seder, and putting some form of covering on the carpet under the chairs that can be removed later, taking the mess with it.

9. *I got caught in a snowstorm. Can I shake the snowflakes off my coat?*

---

22. See *Aruch Hashulchan* 301:46 who explains the Gemara differently and in effect does not require the *shinui* of the *Shulchan Aruch*.
23. *Yoma* 77b.
24. Rav Pesach Eliyahu Falk, *Zochor Veshomor*, "Melaben."
25. *Mishum kavod habriyos*. See *Orchos Shabbos*, vol. 2, ch. 23, note 125.

If your raincoat is made of plastic or rubber, there are no restrictions.[26]

If it is made of a material that does absorb moisture, the rules are as follows: If the snowflakes are definitely only on the surface and they have not begun to melt, you may shake the coat gently so that the snowflakes fall off.[27] Since they have not been absorbed into the material, it is permitted, as in answer 1 above. If the coat is wet or the snowflakes have begun to melt, we may not shake it at all[28] if the coat is dark colored and looks reasonably new, which is likely with a "Shabbos coat." If it is light colored or an older dark coat we may shake it gently.[29] Shaking it vigorously is not allowed as this could extract water that was absorbed into the material. This would be like squeezing water out of a garment, which is definitely not allowed, as in answers 1 and 3 above.

10. *Are we allowed to fold our tallis on Shabbos morning?*

To fold up a tallis or any other garment in its folds is not usually[30] allowed, since this prevents unwanted creasing and is regarded as part of the washing process.[31] Folding in a different way from the original folds is allowed.[32] However, some are *mehader* not to fold up a garment even not in its folds.[33]

---

26. Rav Dovid Ribiat, *The 39 Melochos*, "Melaben," note 107; *Shemiras Shabbos KeHilchasah* 15, note 117.
27. *Biur Halachah* 302:1, s.v. "*min.*"
28. *Shulchan Aruch, Orach Chaim* 302:1.
29. See note 27.
30. See *Shulchan Aruch* 302:3 for a list of conditions which, if fulfilled, would allow folding.
31. *Mishnah Berurah* 302:12.
32. Ibid. 19.
33. Ibid.

The *Mishnah Berurah*[34] says that it was the custom of the Maharil to fold up his tallis right after Shabbos in order to start the week with a mitzvah.[35] The *Taamei HaMinhagim*[36] brings that the custom of folding one's tallis on Motzaei Shabbos is a *segulah* for *arichus yamim* for one's wife.[37] This is the source of the well-known comment that folding up one's tallis on Motzaei Shabbos is good for one's *shalom bayis*. It's also known that rolling up one's sleeves (to help clean up) also helps!

---

34. 299:40.
35. See *Taamei HaMinhagim* 424, who brings, *al pi kabbalah*, the serious consequences of not folding up one's tallis on Motzaei Shabbos.
36. *Inyanei Ishus, Kuntres Acharon* 547.
37. Because usually the *kallah* buys the tallis for her *chassan*. Therefore by looking after the tallis, he is indicating his hope that he won't lose his wife and have another *kallah* buy him a new one.

CHAPTER 28

מנפץ, צובע — COMBING RAW FIBER AND DYEING

1. *It was quite windy on the way home from shul and my sheitel is a mess. How can I make it respectable?*

We have explained[1] that we may not comb our natural hair. Combing a sheitel, whether natural or synthetic, is certainly not *gozez*, which applies only to hair attached to its source. However, some *poskim*[2] hold that it might be forbidden because of the *melachah* of *menapetz*. This *melachah* involves combing wool or certain other fibers into individual strands with a view to spinning and weaving the threads into fabric. Other *poskim*[3] hold that combing a sheitel is not *menapetz* since the strands are not suitable for spinning.

Combing a sheitel involves other potential problems. Pulling out hairs would be *soser* (demolishing or damaging). We may only shape a sheitel by hand or brush it gently with a soft brush just as when brushing natural hair.

If the sheitel is really dishevelled to the extent that the average

---

1. See ch. 26, "*Gozez.*"
2. See Rav Dovid Ribiat, *The 39 Melochos*, p. 735.
3. See Rav Pesach Eliyahu Falk, *Zochor Veshomor*, "*Menapetz.*"

person would not wear it, even in an informal setting, it may not be made usable again as this is a form of repairing something broken, which is forbidden under the *melachah* of *makeh bepatish*.

2. *I've got a black spray to keep my shoes black. Can I use it on Shabbos morning?*

   We now move on to the next *melachah* of *tzovea* (dyeing), which is usually coloring or changing the color of fabric, etc. Here you are merely strengthening the same black color. Nevertheless this is still included in the *melachah* and is not allowed.[4]

3. *We have a simchah. It would be nice to put just a touch of eye shadow on for the kiddush. Am I allowed?*

   This is one of the chief challenges connected with this *melachah*. After all, most of us are not involved in the dyeing industry and if we were, we would know not to work on Shabbos. But we do take pride in our appearance and if our appearance lacks natural color, women have, from time immemorial, added some makeup to their faces. The question of using it on Shabbos, and even on Chol Hamoed, is discussed in the Gemara.[5]

   However, the *Shulchan Aruch*[6] concludes that it is not allowed to color one's face on Shabbos. The accepted halachah[7] is to make no exceptions, and even if the coloring has no oil base to make it stick to the face and has only a very temporary effect, it

---

4. Mishnah Berurah 327:12; Rav Dovid Ribiat, *The 39 Melachos*, p. 738.
5. *Shabbos* 95a, *Moed Katan* 8b.
6. *Orach Chaim* 303:25.
7. Heard directly from Rav Moshe Shternbuch and Rav Shraga Feivel Zimmerman.

still falls under this *melachah* of *tzovea*.⁸

Coloring with traditional lipstick or any creams involves the *melachah* of *memachek*⁹ as well as *tzovea*. Some women, on Erev Shabbos, apply cosmetics that are designed to last the whole Shabbos and this is acceptable according to all opinions.

4. *What about some colorless nail polish?*

This is also not allowed for the reasons mentioned in the previous answers.¹⁰

5. *This is very embarrassing. I've just noticed that our host's toilet has a green disinfectant that colors the water every time it is flushed. What do I do?*

This is indeed a serious question of *tzovea*. When one flushes the toilet the water will undoubtedly become green; the manufacturer intended that the disinfectant be noticeable. Unfortunately, some people who are otherwise completely Shabbos observant sometimes don't realize there could be a problem. In public places, non-Jewish staff will often attend to these matters. So what does one do if confronted by this issue? If there is no choice, one may flush the water as usual because of *kavod habriyos* (human dignity)¹¹ and other halachic considerations.¹²

---

8. Rav Shlomo Zalman Auerbach, brought in *Shemiras Shabbos KeHilchasah* 14, note 158.
9. See ch. 37.
10. *Shemiras Shabbos KeHilchasah* 14:57.
11. Rav Dovid Ribiat, *The 39 Melochos*, p. 747, note 50. Also in somebody else's bathroom you are not interested in the coloring.
12. *Grama*. In fact some people are *meikel lechatchilah* because of *grama bepsik reisha*.

6. *I was just showing off my new glasses that turn dark in the sunshine and my friend said that's a shailah on Shabbos. Is he right?*

    It is a *shailah*, but the *poskim* allow wearing such glasses outside for a variety of reasons.[13]

7. *The strawberry ice cream was delicious. Can I wipe my mouth with a napkin?*

    There is a dispute about using coloring that not only does not benefit the material, but actually causes it to deteriorate (*derech lichluch*). The *Mishnah Berurah*[14] holds that if there is no option we can be lenient. However if there is a choice, you should use a napkin that is a different color than what you are cleaning up. If it is the same color some *poskim*[15] are of the opinion that it is not called a "deterioration." In cleaning up your strawberry ice cream (I'm glad you enjoyed it), it would depend on whether there is another option. You could probably get most of, if not all, the ice cream off with water. Nowadays we tend to use paper napkins and these can be used without question.[16]

8. *My nose is bleeding. Can I stop it with a white handkerchief?*

    This is similar to the last question. As your nose is bleeding, there is no real alternative to using a handkerchief so you may do so. However, as we said in the previous answer, a red handkerchief should be avoided except in a real emergency. If you could

---

13. See Rav Dovid Ribiat, *The 39 Melochos*, p. 748; *Orchos Shabbos*, vol. 1, 15:67, note 96.
14. 320:59.
15. *Mishnah Berurah* 320:59.
16. *Shemiras Shabbos KeHilchasah* 14:19.

manage with disposable tissues, it would be even better, as explained above.

9. *Avi loves black currant juice in his yogurt. Do I have to tell him it's not allowed on Shabbos?*

According to the strict halachah, we are allowed to mix foods or drinks even though one item might cause a change in the color in the other[17] and even if we are interested in producing that color. Therefore if Avi happens to like his yogurt with black currant juice, even if he really likes the red color, there's no problem. Some *poskim* are *machmir*,[18] so although Avi can be lenient,[19] there are those who *lechatchilah* try to avoid it.

10. *We're supposed to have red wine on Seder night. Can I mix red and white wine to make a red mixture?*

Producing a certain color for an important reason such as commercial profit is not allowed on Shabbos.[20] Since in this case you want the white wine to turn red for an important reason, i.e., the

---

17. *Shulchan Aruch, Orach Chaim* 320:19.
18. *Mishnah Berurah* 320:56 in the name of the *Nishmas Adam* and *Shaar HaTziyun* 318:65.
19. Some parents feel that their children have to be strict beyond the required level of halachah, presumably in the conviction that this will educate them to be *mehadrin bemitzvos* when they grow up. This is generally not good *chinuch*. There are occasions when it might be appropriate, but in a case like this, when a *chumrah* about his yogurt would decrease Avi's enjoyment of Shabbos, it is counterproductive to be *machmir* beyond what the halachah demands.
20. *Mishnah Berurah* 320:56.

halachic preference for red wine, one should be *machmir*.[21] Yet it can be done by reversing the usual sequence. Instead of putting red wine into white, we may put white into red, since that is not the way one normally adds dye.[22] It is also correct to be *machmir* in the case of manufactured additives designed to color foods.[23]

---

21. Rav Pesach Eliyahu Falk, *Zochor Veshomor*, "*Tzovea*" 3.
22. Ibid.
23. *Mishnah Berurah* 320:56.

CHAPTER 29

THE WEAVING MELACHOS: טווה, מיסך, עושה בתי נירין, עורג, פוצע — SPINNING, WARPING, CONSTRUCTING HEDDLES, WEAVING, UNRAVELLING THREADS FROM FABRIC

1. *This is a complicated subject. Can't we just skip it?*

    First of all, since when are we absolved from learning Torah just because it is complicated? Second, as with many subjects, after a little study, one begins to understand that what appeared to be complicated, now becomes clear. Third, today, we have *sefarim* that help explain these *melachos* on a basic level, with illustrations, like *The 39 Melochos* by Rav Dovid Ribiat, and on a deeper level, *Maaseh Oreg* by Dayan Gukovitski of London. So, we've agreed. We're not skipping it. Good.

2. *My tzitzis are unravelling. Can I twist the threads back again?*

    Toveh (spinning) involves either taking single fibers of wool or another material and twisting them around each other to produce a thread, or twisting thin threads around each other to form a thicker thread. These thicker threads are usually used to produce fabric. Each thread of our tzitzis is usually formed from eight thinner threads. If our tzitzis unravel and we twist them together again we are doing the equivalent of spinning, albeit in a less secure way. Therefore we clearly are not allowed to do this on Shabbos.

3. *The fringes at the edge of my Shabbos tablecloth need straightening. Is there any problem?*

   Meisach (warping) involves stretching the threads so that they are parallel to each other, held tight either by hand or more likely on a weaving loom. This is the first stage of weaving.[1] Although straightening out the fringes of your tablecloth would appear to be a similar activity, it is not forbidden because you are not preparing them to be woven together.[2]

4. *The threads of my tzitzis are entangled. Can I disentangle them?*

   Separating the threads of your tzitzis is also not for the purpose of weaving them together and therefore it should be no problem, like the fringes of your tablecloth. However there is a different issue here. The *Shulchan Aruch*[3] says that we have to separate

---

1. *Chayei Adam* 25:4.
2. Rav Pesach Eliyahu Falk, *Zochor Veshomor*, "Meisach."
3. *Orach Chaim* 8:7.

the threads of our tzitzis from one another.⁴ The Tur⁵ says the word "tzitzis" means "a fringe of separate threads." Therefore untangling the threads could be a form of repairing the tzitzis, which would not be allowed.⁶ Some are lenient.⁷ In practice, if they are really entangled, don't separate them on Shabbos and instead wear another tallis or *tallis katan*. If they are only slightly entangled it is permitted.⁸

5. *I'm having a great vacation by the sea. Can I help this fisherman repair his net?*

I'm not sure if this is such a great vacation for you, if you are spending Shabbos with non-Jewish fishermen. But at least you've asked a *shailah* before doing anything serious so I'll answer you right away.

"*Oseh batei nirin*" literally means making or fixing small rings through which all the lengthways threads on the loom are passed. Each alternate ring is attached to one lever or pedal while the others are attached to another lever or pedal. As the other threads are passed along the breadth of the loom, one of the levers is raised, raising half the threads of the length of the loom. As the threads come back across the breadth of the loom, the other half of the threads along the length of the loom is raised. This is how garments, etc., are woven — with the threads going

---

4. The *Mishnah Berurah* 8:18 brings from the Ari. The Hebrew letters of the word "tzitzis" hint to the phrase "*Tzaddik yafrid tzitziosav tamid* — A tzaddik always separates his tzitzis."
5. *Orach Chaim, siman* 8.
6. See *Shaarei Teshuvah* 8:8 and the *Gra* 8:7 who hold that it is an obligation for the tzitzis to be separated even nowadays, unlike the *Magen Avraham* 8:10 who holds that it is only "*zecher letecheiles.*"
7. *Yabia Omer* 5:3.
8. *Piskei Teshuvos* 13:3, note 16.

under and over the threads going in the other direction. If you can't follow this brief explanation, you could see a more detailed explanation in the *sefarim* I mentioned earlier.

So, as I said, making or fixing these rings onto the loom is the classic definition of this *melachah*.[9] The Rambam[10] holds that making netting or anything similar where the threads of material are not tightly connected but have holes in between them is also included in this *melachah*.

So helping the fisherman make his nets is not allowed on Shabbos.

6. *Oy vey! My sweater just got caught on a nail that pulled some threads. Surely there can't be a problem in just smoothing it out — lekavod Shabbos, of course.*

We have already described the basic way fabric is woven. Therefore doing those actions on Shabbos — interweaving the vertical and horizontal threads in an orderly way — is part of the *melachah* of *oreg* (weaving). When a garment catches on a nail and the threads are pulled out of position, if I straighten the threads back into position, I have transgressed *oreg*. To do this on Shabbos, *lekavod Shabbos,* is no better than cooking a sumptuous meal on Shabbos, *lekavod Shabbos*. As I mentioned earlier, some *melachos* can present more challenges than others and we need to draw on our *yiras Shamayim* to get us through.

7. *Sarahleh loves playing with her "Junior Weaving Set." Is there any leniency for children?*

---

9. Aruch Hashulchan 340:14.
10. Hilchos Shabbos 9:16, also brought in *Aruch Hashulchan* ibid. and *Mishnah Berurah* 344:11, subsection 3.

I like to look for leniencies for children but weaving is weaving, and it's not allowed on Shabbos. Find Sarahleh a special Shabbos game that she can enjoy just as much.

8. *I don't like them myself, but some young married women have sheitels that you can braid. Is the halachah the same as one's own hair, better, or worse?*

Leaving aside the question of whether a braid in a sheitel is appropriate,[11] making a braid in a sheitel is definitely not allowed on Shabbos. Although making a braid in one's own hair is a rabbinic prohibition,[12] to do so in a sheitel is almost certainly forbidden according to the Torah.[13]

9. *What about undoing the braid?*

Now we come to the last of the "weaving" *melachos* — *potzei'a*. We translated the *melachah* above as "unravelling threads from a fabric."

One aspect of this is a simple reversal of the weaving process — taking the vertical threads from the horizontal threads or vice versa.[14] Therefore it will definitely not be allowed to unbraid a sheitel.

10. *There's a loose thread protruding from my new suit. Can I bite it off?*

Another way of transgressing *potzei'a* is to remove or cut off a loose

---

11. See *Oz VeHadar Levushah*, by Rav Pesach Eliyahu Falk, on the subject.
12. *Mishnah Berurah* 344:11, subsection 6.
13. Ibid.
14. *Mishnah Berurah* 344:11, subsection 7.

thread from a garment or any material.[15] Therefore you may not cut off or even bite off your thread. This is another reason why we should prepare for Shabbos in good time so we can check for these loose threads or stains that need to be removed, so we should not be faced on Shabbos with challenging situations.

15. Ibid.

CHAPTER 30

קוֹשֵׁר — TYING KNOTS

1. *Chaya loves to tie her hair with a ribbon. How does she do it on Shabbos?*

   As we see from this question and others, *kosher* is a *melachah* that affects every member of the family. If we are not professional camel drivers or sailors who sometimes have to tie permanent, skilled knots, there is usually a permitted way of arranging things. It's just a question of learning the rules. So let's go.

   Chaya likes to tie her hair with a ribbon. Fair enough. Why shouldn't she look her best for Shabbos?[1] The question is what kind of a knot is required.

   There are four types of knots: tight and permanent, tight but not permanent, and permanent but not tight, which are not allowed to be made on Shabbos. The fourth type, not tight and not permanent, is usually allowed to be made on Shabbos.[2]

   Of course we have to define the terms but these are the basic four categories.

---

1. Someone told me recently that a non-Jewish neighbor of hers told her she is jealous of her. "Every Saturday morning I see you going to the synagogue dressed up in nice clothes. I have hardly ever any excuse to put on nice clothes."
2. See the introduction of *Mishnah Berurah* 317.

Let's get back to Chaya's ribbon. Now, it is not going to be permanent since I assume she will undo it at bedtime.³ To tie it with a double knot is not allowed as this is regarded as a tight knot.⁴ But tying with a bow even with a simple knot underneath, as we normally tie our shoes, is perfectly permitted.⁵

2. *Chaim's shoelaces are undone again. Can I tie the two loops of the bow into a simple knot?*

Let's start from the beginning. To tie a simple knot, which is how we begin to tie our shoelaces, is definitely permitted⁶ since it has no permanence. To do a bow over that knot is permitted, as we mentioned above, as long as we undo it within twenty-four hours.⁷ To do a simple knot above that is no more permanent than the original simple knot. Furthermore, merely pulling one of the laces will undo the bow and the higher knot. Therefore this is also permitted as long as it will be undone within twenty-four hours.⁸

---

3. *Mishnah Berurah* 317:6. Within twenty-four hours is called "on the same day."
4. *Rama* 317:1.
5. Ibid. 5. See *Mishnah Berurah* 29 that this is permitted only if it is going to be undone within twenty-four hours. In a case of special need, if it will be undone within a week it is also allowed (*Rama* 1, *Biur Halachah*, s.v. "she'einam."
6. *Chayei Adam* 27:1.
7. See note 5.
8. *Orchos Shabbos*, vol. 1, 10:15. *Ayil Meshulash*, "Kosher," p. 84. To say that this should be forbidden as a *kesher al gabei kesher* would appear to be a *chumrah yeseirah* since that halachah is in itself a *chumrah* (*Chazon Ish* 52:17), which is not universally accepted (see *Shaarei Teshuvah* 317:1) and also *Mishnah Berurah* (317:14) says it is only because it is a tight knot and in this case the bow in between the knots prevents it from being tight. Even the *Shemiras Shabbos KeHilchasah*, who was *machmir* in his first editions, has now changed his mind and in his latest edition says that one can be lenient if there is a need (15:46).

3. *How can I tie the bag with the fresh challos so that I can open it before the seudah?*

   Just do a simple knot with the two handles of the bag as described above and you'll be able to open it before your seudah without a problem.

4. *I need to tie my curtains back for the light to come in. How do I do it on Shabbos?*

   This halachah will depend on whether you close your curtains every night or you usually keep them open.[9] If you undo the knot and close them every night you can do a simple knot and a bow since it will not last twenty-four hours. If you generally keep them open, tied back by your knot, you will only be allowed to do a simple knot on Shabbos and after Shabbos you will do a stronger knot. You may not tie a knot and a bow with the intention to undo it after Shabbos since this is not your usual practice, and the halachah is afraid that you will forget to undo it.[10]

5. *I'd like to tie a pretty ribbon around the box of chocolates for my hostess. Can I?*

   As above, just tie a bow over a simple knot. Even if, for some reason, your hostess does not untie your knot and leaves it for some time, this will not mean that retrospectively you have made a permanent knot.[11]

---

9. In Amsterdam the general community has had a custom since the end of World War II, when they no longer had to keep their curtains closed, to keep them permanently open.
10. *Mishnah Berurah* 317:34.
11. *Orchos Shabbos*, vol. 1, ch. 10, note 32.

6. *My mother bought me a tie for my birthday and she just told me she's coming for Shabbos lunch. Can I put it on in her honor?*

If the tie is already made, you can put it on even though you will be tightening it around your neck.[12] Tying the tie from scratch will depend on what type of knot it is: Is the knot going to be undone within twenty-four hours? Do you usually leave it tied even though on this occasion you plan to untie it after Shabbos?

The tie knot known as a "Windsor knot" includes making a knot in the tie that doesn't undo even if you undo the rest of the tie, and may not be made on Shabbos. A standard tie knot is permitted but some hold[13] that it must be undone within twenty-four hours. According to this opinion, you shouldn't tie it on Shabbos, if you normally don't undo it but leave it tied, even if you intend to make an exception and undo it after Shabbos. However, seeing that this condition of undoing it within twenty-four hours is not so clear in this case,[14] and your mother might be upset if you're not wearing your new tie, make a basic knot and make sure you undo it within twenty-four hours.

7. *It's Shabbos Minchah and they've just asked me to do gelilah. Can I tie the gartel (belt)?*

The problem here is that if you tie a basic knot and a bow, which is the usual thing to do, it's not going to be undone until at least Monday morning.

Many *sifrei Torah* have a band with metal clasps or Velcro

---

12. *Shemiras Shabbos KeHilchasah* 15:58.
13. Ibid.
14. See *Orchos Shabbos*, vol. 1, ch. 10, note 43, and Rav Dovid Ribiat, *The 39 Melochos*, "Kosher," note 42.

that may be closed and opened on Shabbos in order to avoid this problem of tying or untying knots.[15] Otherwise, if the *gartel* is long enough to wrap round the *sefer Torah* tightly and then tuck in the ends, do it that way. If that is not possible, you can make the usual knot as long as it is going to be undone within seven days.[16]

8. *It's Yom Tov morning and I haven't tied my lulav. What do I do?*

I'm not happy that you didn't get your lulav ready before Yom Tov. The *Shulchan Aruch*[17] says that it is a mitzvah to bind the lulav with *hadassim* and *aravos* with a full knot, i.e., two knots, one on top of the other. On Yom Tov morning we are not allowed to do this, as we said above. So you have a problem. *Bedieved* you'll have to take a long lulav leaf and bind it round and round the lulav, *hadassim*, and *aravos* and then tuck the end of the leaf through the binding.[18]

The custom is to do three of these *kesharim* around the higher part of the lulav for beauty. Halachically they are not knots and are permitted. Many people have a kind of basket that one slips onto the lulav and puts the *hadassim* through the holder on the right side and the *aravos* on the left. This constitutes a full knot for the purpose of the mitzvah but seeing that it is already made, we can slip it on the lulav on Shabbos and Yom Tov without any question of *kosher*.

---

15. The *poskim* are also lenient with Velcro from the point of view of the *melachah* of *tofer* if it is just for a few days.
16. See note 5 above.
17. *Orach Chaim* 651:1.
18. Ibid., *Rama*.

9. *The knot on my tzitzis is loose. Can I tighten it?*

   No. All the *poskim* agree that to tighten a knot is the same as tying it for the first time. Since you intend the tzitzis knot to stay tight for as long as possible, this could be prohibited *min haTorah*.

10. *There seems to be a controversy about tying a bag with a twist tie. What is the halachah?*

    You're right that there is a controversy about this and there is no final *pesak*.[19] I would avoid it, but if someone does it, he should not be criticized. If it is only bound around once, it is certainly allowed.[20]

---

19. See *Orchos Shabbos*, vol. 1, 10:30.
20. Ibid.

CHAPTER 31

מתיר — UNDOING A KNOT

1. *Surely I'm going to get full marks this time: Isn't it the case that a knot we're not allowed to tie, we're not allowed to untie?*

   There is a lot of truth in what you're saying. In fact, the Rambam says this explicitly.[1] However, you might end up being too strict because there are cases when, for various reasons, we are allowed to untie a knot that we were not allowed to tie, as you will see in the rest of this chapter.

2. *Chaya's in tears. We've just taken her new dress out of the bag and the ribbon is tied at the back. Any solutions?*

   On the surface it is a problematic situation. We are obviously talking about a knot that we may not tie on Shabbos, for instance, a simple knot and bow that was tied over twenty-four hours ago. If we can't tie it, we can't undo it. Isn't that what the Rambam said? Let's think about it more deeply. We mentioned in the previous chapter that in a case of need we can be lenient with this kind of knot if it's going be undone within seven days. So maybe

---

1. *Hilchos Shabbos* 10:7.

this knot is also less than seven days old. If Chaya has nothing else suitable for Shabbos, I would call that a case of need.

However, in this case we can be lenient even without this. From the question it would appear that the knot was tied in the store. When they tied the knot, was it for a specific length of time? No. They tied the knot for as short or long a time as necessary, until some little girl like Chaya would buy the dress, go home, and put it on. Such a knot is deemed in halachah a temporary knot and may be undone even some time later.² So, Chaya, *titchadshi*!

3. *Now it's my turn: The bag with the chocolate raisins is tied at the top. Do I have to just look at them this Shabbos?*

To put your mind at rest, you will certainly be able to eat the chocolate raisins. However, whether you can undo the knot is another question. Very often, bags of nuts, raisins, and other small items are tied at the top with a knot that is not meant to be untied. The purchaser takes the bag home and usually tears the bag open. Therefore the knot is intended as a permanent one that may not be untied on Shabbos even if you wanted to. Having said that, you can tear the bag open in a way that it will not be usable afterward in order to reach the food, as is explained in chapter 33 on *korea* (tearing). The only remaining question is — what is the

---

2. *Mishnah Berurah* 314:30 and 317:21. Even though the second *Mishnah Berurah* brings that some are *machmir*, it would appear that the main halachah is to be lenient, especially in a case of need, especially with a simple knot and bow, which some allow even on a permanent basis (see *Gra* 5). Here there is also an extra reason to be lenient: Some hold that if the person making the knot is not the owner, somebody else's intention cannot create a prohibition for the owner. See *Chayei Adam* 27:4 and Rav Dovid Ribiat, *The 39 Melochos*, p. 807 and note 14.

correct *berachah* on chocolate raisins? See my *sefer Do You Know Hilchos Brachos?*, chapter 8, for the answer.

4. *What a day. I arrived at shul and my coat was drenched. Now somebody said that I'm not allowed to undo the knot in the belt. Is he right?*

Assuming this fellow from your shul is not a complete *am haaretz*,³ you must have tied some kind of knot that he thinks may not be undone on Shabbos. My hunch is that you did a loose double knot, which is quite common. We have learned that we are not allowed to do a double knot on Shabbos. However, if the knot is loose, it is permitted.⁴ A coat often has a belt that matches the coat and is there to be decorative. If your belt is still only loosely tied, just as it was permissible to tie it, it is permissible to untie it.

But what if as a result of the rain, the knot became tighter, possibly entangled? If this is what your friend from the shul saw, I can begin to understand what he means. However, the halachah⁵ says that an accidental knot may always be undone. Therefore thank your friend for his concern, refer him to the sources, and take your coat off. Just remember to hang it up in the normal place in the cloakroom and certainly not over a radiator, for reasons that we learn in chapter 27 on *melaben*.

5. *We came back from our vacation on Thursday, and our Shabbos clothes are in the suitcase. The problem is that I tied some thick string around the case and I didn't undo it before Shabbos. What can I do?*

---

3. Ignoramus.
4. See *Mishnah Berurah* 317:14.
5. Ibid. 23.

If you would have said you tied a knot inside your case so things don't move around, I would have assumed you tied a simple knot and bow that should have been undone within twenty-four hours. Although you forgot, since it is within seven days and it is a case of need, you could have untied it as explained in answer 2 above. However, if you tied a string around the outside of the case, you must have done a tight knot, which would not come undone even after being thown around by baggage handlers.

You probably did not do a professional knot and only intended it to last for a couple of days, but it would have been a knot we do not tie on Shabbos because it might be regarded as a skilled knot. It would only be permitted to undo this knot on Shabbos to avoid real physical discomfort. If you really have no Shabbos clothes besides these, it probably is the equivalent of physical discomfort. However, the *poskim* say that the preferred solution in this case is not to undo the knot, but to cut the string with scissors.[6] As long as you are not cutting to a particular length you will not be transgressing the *melachah* of *mechatech* (cutting).

Because people think it is not allowed to cut string or rope with scissors, we shouldn't cut the string or rope in front of an unlearned Jew,[7] even people from your own household. I mention this solution of cutting the string to the readers of this *sefer* because anyone who has worked through all the previous chapters and has reached this point cannot be described as an unlearned Jew.

6. *We were given a box of chocolates last month and the ribbon is still tied around it. Is there any leniency to open it for oneg Shabbos?*

---

6.   *Shulchan Aruch, Orach Chaim* 314:7. The cut should not be through the knot but in a different place.
7.   *Chayei Adam* 27:2, 5.

A ribbon around a box of chocolates given as a present would probably only be tied in a simple knot and a bow, or maybe a basic double knot. The trouble is that the knot has been tied for more than twenty-four hours, or even more than seven days, and may not be undone.

Similarly, a tight double knot may not be undone even just after it was knotted. Although a rabbinically forbidden knot maybe undone for a mitzvah,[8] I think it's pushing things a bit far to claim that one's *oneg Shabbos* is going to be severely compromised without these particular chocolates. But here again, the ribbon may be cut with scissors as we said in the previous answer, just not in front of an unlearned Jew. So there's your solution. *Letei'avon*.

7. *This time the knot in the string around the chocolate box is very small and tight. Is this the same halachah as in the previous question?*

The end result is the same: There is no way to undo the knot and the only solution is to cut the string.[9] The small and tight knot itself, however, is a more serious knot, as it was tied as a permanent one. It is clear that the person who tied the knot knew it would never be undone. This is similar to the knot tied in the chocolate-raisins bag in question 3.

8. *It's Shabbos Rosh Chodesh and the sefer Torah hasn't been used for quite a while. Can I undo the gartel (belt) so we can lein from it?*

This is definitely a case of a mitzvah for which we may undo a knot as long as it was not supposed to be permanent. Obviously

---

8. Shulchan Aruch, Orach Chaim 317:1; Chazon Ish, Orach Chaim 52:17.
9. See note 6 above.

it is better to check before Shabbos and undo any knots. If that didn't happen it will be permitted to undo it as I said.

9. *I tied my shoelaces in a bow but it has turned into a double knot. Do I have to sleep in my shoes?*

For two reasons you can untie your shoes and sleep normally.[10] First, we said above[11] that a knot tied by accident is not considered a knot. Second, we said that in the case of physical discomfort we can untie a knot of doubtful rabbinic status.

10. *I tied my bag of pills in a really tight knot so the children couldn't get at them. But now the doctor has said I must take one today. Can I undo the knot?*

You say you tied this knot very tightly so that the children could not undo it. That could well be a skilled knot, which we may not undo on a rabbinic level. You didn't say how often you need to take a pill. Probably not every day or else you would probably have a better system than undoing a very tight knot every day. On the other hand, it is not a permanent knot because you presumably need a pill from time to time. Therefore it is a knot that may not be undone on a rabbinic level. You're obviously ill or you wouldn't be allowed to take a pill at all.[12] I presume it isn't just a plastic bag that you could tear open because the children could also tear it open. We are not talking about a life-threatening illness because if so, everything that's required may and must be done as quickly as possible. So what can you do?

---

10. See *Yoma* 78b where it says that sleeping in shoes gives "a taste of death."
11. Answer 4.
12. See *Shulchan Aruch, Orach Chaim* 328.

In such a case the correct procedure would be to ask a non-Jew who is allowed to break a rabbinic law for a sick person.[13] If there is no non-Jew available, a Jew can also break a rabbinic law for a sick person if he does it in an unusual way.[14] I doubt if it is possible to untie a knot in an unusual way, except maybe with your teeth. If there is no option and you can't wait until after Shabbos, you may untie the knot, even in the usual way, since you are a *choleh*.[15]

---

13. Ibid. 307:5 and 328:17.
14. Ibid. 328:17 and *Mishnah Berurah* 57.
15. *Chayei Adam* 69:12 and *Mishnah Berurah* 328:102. As an extra *hiddur*, have the intention not to use this string again so that there is no *tikun* in the string. See *Biur Halachah* 317:1, s.v. "*dino.*"

CHAPTER 32

תּוֹפֵר — SEWING

1. *Moshe just fell and tore his suit. Is there anything I can do to make it respectable for now?*

   You obviously know that you can't get out your needle and thread and sew up the tear. The issue here is the old question of whether we may use a safety pin on Shabbos. Most *poskim* say it is permitted since the *melachah* of *tofer* is joining two items into one. With a safety pin the two items, even two sections of one item, are clearly only joined temporarily.[1] There are *poskim* who are more *machmir*[2] but if you make sure only to leave the pin in temporarily,[3] you can be lenient. Some[4] hold that one shouldn't use safety pins in a way that they are not visible because one is quite likely to forget and leave them on a semipermanent basis.

2. *It's Chaya's birthday party this afternoon and she wants to make some more paper chains. It doesn't seem right but can you tell me why not?*

---

1. See *Iggros Moshe, Orach Chaim* 2:84; *Chazon Ish, Orach Chaim* 126.
2. See *Minchas Yitzchak* 2:19.
3. Less than seven days.
4. Rav Pesach Eliyahu Falk, *Zochor Veshomor*, "Tofer."

Your instinct is right. Indeed making paper chains, which involves sticking or stapling small pieces of paper together, is included in this *melachah*.

3. *Avi loves sticking shapes into his coloring book. Do I have to stop him on Shabbos?*

From what we have learned already we know that sticking shapes into a coloring book is *tofer*. Do you have to stop your toddler from doing it?

When a child reaches the age when he understands that some things are not allowed on Shabbos,[5] parents are responsible for stopping him from transgressing even a rabbinic law.[6] A toddler presumably has that ability. So Avi, leave your stickers and come and play with your new Shabbos toys!

4. *I was just buttoning up my sweater when a thought struck me: Is this included in tofer?*

Don't worry. Buttoning up your sweater is definitely allowed. Numerous sources show that to button two things together is not *tofer*.[7] This is partly because of the reason in answer 1 that the *melachah* of *tofer* is when two pieces of cloth or something similar become one piece as a result of the sewing. Everybody knows that buttons are designed to be done and undone and the two pieces of material have not become one. Also the *poskim*

---

5. Three years old (Rav Pesach Eliyahu Falk, *Zochor Veshomor*, "Dinei Koton"). If a child does a *melachah* because he understands that his father would be happy for him to do it, this is not permitted at any age (*Mishnah Berurah* 334:65).
6. Shulchan Aruch, Orach Chaim 343:1; Mishnah Berurah 3.
7. For instance, *Shabbos* 65b.

compare buttons with opening and closing a door, which is not forbidden under the *melachah* of *boneh* (building) because it is the normal use of a door; we are clearly not filling in a hole in the wall when we close the door.

5. *What about zippers?*

   A zipper that functions as an alternative to buttons is permitted. In other words, if it is designed to be opened and closed on a regular basis, it is not included in *tofer*. If it is being used on a long-term basis, like zippering a lining into a coat for the winter, it is better to do it during the week since some *poskim*[8] regard zippering for long-term use to be included in *tofer*. The same applies to Velcro.

6. *If I don't use a special suction cup to keep Avi's plate on his tray, the plate and the food will be on the floor, he'll be hungry, and my kitchen will be filthy. Please say it's allowed.*

   Relax. It's similar to buttons and zippers in that it's clearly just for a short time, and is allowed.[9] But don't stick hooks with suction cups onto the wall because this would be *boneh* (building).[10]

7. *I'm in a panic. Chaim's fallen, the doctor said he needs stitches, the rabbi's not in, and I don't know if it's allowed.*

   It is important to study halachos about health issues on Shabbos

---

8. *Shevet HaLevi* 3:51.
9. *Shemiras Shabbos KeHilchasah* 11:41.
10. To add anything on a permanent or semipermanent basis to a wall of a house is *boneh*. See *Chazon Ish* 52:13.

before they occur to avoid not only panic but making the wrong decision.[11]

Putting in stitches is a complex and controversial matter. You first have to establish through proper medical advice whether there is any risk to life. Serious bleeding can clearly be a situation of *pikuach nefesh*.[12]

If there is no danger but it is the normal medical practice to require it, one should ask a non-Jewish doctor to administer the stitches. If there are only Jewish doctors available, stitching should not be done but one can use a butterfly Band-Aid or Steri-Strips to close the wound.[13] If stitches are necessary to prevent scarring and if the wound is on the face, which might have long-term ramifications, expecially for girls, some *poskim* are lenient.[14] However it would seem that most *poskim*[15] make no exception for the risk of scarring.

8. *Baruch Hashem he didn't need stitches after all, only a Band-Aid. But isn't this also a shailah?*

The basic use of a Band-Aid is permitted but we still have to be mindful of certain questions that occur when using one. We are not allowed to cut a Band-Aid to a particular length.[16] *Lechatchilah* we should remove the sticky cover of the Band-Aid and then re-stick it before Shabbos. If we didn't do that, we can

---

11. *Halachos of Refuah on Shabbos*, by Rav Yisroel Pinchos Bodner and Rav Daniel B. Roth, covers many medical situations in detail.
12. A life-threatening situation in which we must do whatever is required.
13. *Tzitz Eliezer* 20:18.
14. *Teshuvos VeHanhagos* 3:103.
15. See Rav Bodner and Rav Roth, *Halachos of Refuah on Shabbos*, p. 335.
16. Because of the *melachah* of *mechatech* (cutting to a particular size).

remove it on Shabbos before use.[17] It is better not to stick one end of the Band-Aid to the other end, for instance when putting it around a finger. If one does so, one has a lenient opinion to rely on.[18]

9. *What about this one: On my fridge there are dozens of magnets advertising various businesses, which we don't usually move. But Chaim closed the fridge so wildly that they've all fallen off. Can I put them back up again or should I leave them until after Shabbos?*

I would leave them until after Shabbos for a few reasons. You say these magnets usually stay on your fridge and therefore to attach them is a question of *tofer*.[19] On a big fridge it could be *boneh*.[20] You said that they have the names of businesses and are *muktzeh*.[21] Just reading what is written on them, if they are not *divrei Torah*, will not be allowed as with all similar written material.[22] In many families they are all removed before Shabbos to help make their homes more *Shabbosdik*.

---

17. In this question there are different opinions. Some say in this case we should remove it in an unusual way, e.g., with our teeth. Others are completely lenient.
18. *Be'er Moshe* 2:29.
19. According to the opinion of the *Biur Halachah* 340:14, s.v. "*harei*." Not all *poskim* are convinced that to combine two hard things like wood or metal is *tofer*. (See *Shemiras Shabbos KeHilchasah* 9, note 77, and *Iggros Moshe, Orach Chaim* 2:84.) If the magnets are often moved around or taken off and replaced one can be lenient.
20. See *Mishnah Berurah* 314:3.
21. If they are *muktzeh* they shouldn't be on the door of the fridge, which you move on Shabbos.
22. See ch. 5, "What We May Read on Shabbos."

10. *The biggest question must be about diapers: Can you stick them down or not?*

The question of unsticking the tapes of the diaper when first unfolding it is controversial, similar to unsticking the Band-Aid as we mentioned above in answer 8. Many *poskim* do not allow it as it may have been attached for a long time since its manufacture.[23] Therefore it should be unstuck before Shabbos. If you didn't unstick it and you really need it, one who is lenient has lenient opinions to rely on.[24]

In terms of sticking the tape to the front of the diaper when it's on the baby, this was more of a problem with the older tapes, which did not come off without tearing the whole section of the diaper. Therefore it was a permanent form of *tofer*.

However, the modern type that has tapes designed to be easily removed from the diaper and stuck down again as many times as necessary, is permitted. However, sticking the tape to the diaper for the final time after it has been soiled and is ready for throwing away is again very controversial because there is a permanent connection between the tape and the diaper. Therefore we shouldn't do that on Shabbos. Just fold it up and put it in a plastic bag to be discarded.[25]

---

23. Machazeh Eliyahu 70.
24. See *Be'er Moshe* 2:29, subsection 2; *Az Nidberu* 7:34.
25. *Machazeh Eliyahu* and many other *poskim*.

CHAPTER 33

קוֹרֵעַ — TEARING

1. *Unfortunately my brother just passed away. Should I wait until after Shabbos before doing keriah or should I do it now?*

   I'm sorry to hear of the passing of your brother. *Baruch Dayan Ha'emes*. Although *keriah* is a mitzvah, it's not allowed on Shabbos. In fact, because it is a mitzvah it would be a more serious infraction of Shabbos. Tearing a garment for no good reason would be forbidden *mi'deRabbanan*. To do so for a positive reason such as the mitzvah of *keriah* would be forbidden *min haTorah*.[1]

2. *My friend has a bad habit. When he's deep in thought, he tears pieces of paper into shreds. Should I tell him that it's definitely not allowed?*

   If he will listen to you, remind him politely that you think it is not allowed on Shabbos. If you think he won't listen to you, you

---

1. Biur Halachah 340:14, s.v. "*velo*," does not require "*al menas litfor.*"

can "turn a blind eye" for a combination of reasons.[2]

3. *It became quite hot. Can I unzip the lining from my Shabbos coat that's been there the whole winter?*

As we said in the previous chapter, zipping something to be kept closed for a lengthy period is not allowed because of *tofer*. Therefore unzipping after a lengthy period is similarly not allowed because of the *melachah* of *korea*.

4. *When Moshe sneezes it's like a gale force wind coming out of his nose. Can he use a tissue even though it'll probably tear in the process?*

Don't think that Moshe's gale force sneezes are unusual. Sneezes can come out at 100 mph[3] — enough to tear any tissue. But to answer your question, Moshe may (and should[4]) use a tissue even though it might tear, seeing that it is unintentional. The *Mishnah Berurah*[5] says that if one's clothes get caught on thorns, one should try to separate them gently and if they tear, they tear.

5. *That's a shame. The price is still stuck on this box of chocolates that I'm giving our hostess. Can I tear it off?*

---

2. There is an opinion, not accepted as *halachah lemaaseh*, that the *melachah* of tearing applies only to separating two things that are stuck or woven together, and not a single item like a piece of paper. See *Biur Halachah* 340:13, s.v. "*ein*." It is presumably *mekalkel* unless he does it to feel better. Since your friend won't listen to you and there are these slight doubts, it is a case of *mutav sheyehiyu shogagin ve'al yiheyu mezidim* — it is better to transgress in ignorance than deliberately.
3. *Wikipedia, The Free Encyclopedia.*
4. For hygienic reasons.
5. 340:45.

This is a good example of *korea*. At least you can be comforted that you know the halachah. I would suspect that many people who consider themselves *shomer Shabbos* and would like to be *shomer Shabbos* are just not aware of these details. Maybe your hostess will be so pleased with the box of chocolates, she won't even notice the price!

6. *The letter with my exam results has just been delivered. I can't stand the suspense. Any advice?*

This is a question discussed at length in the classic works on halachah, though not necessarily about exam results. Their advice[6] is, in the case of special need, to tell a non-Jew that you can't read this important letter because it is in the envelope, and if he opens it for you, so be it. There are more lenient opinions, especially among the *poskim* in Eretz Yisrael, if the envelope is destroyed, on the basis that nowadays people just throw envelopes away.[7] We may still not tear through any letters printed on the envelope.

Having said that, I think that the case of exam results is problematic for other reasons. First, we have permission to read a letter that arrives on Shabbos only because it might contain vital information, like a threat of some kind.[8] If you know that this letter contains your exam results, that is not information that you need to know today rather than tomorrow, curiosity and tension notwithstanding.[9]

---

6. *Mishnah Berurah* 340:41.
7. See *Chazon Ish* 61:2, *Orchos Shabbos*, vol. 1, 11:23.
8. *Shulchan Aruch, Orach Chaim* 307:13; *Mishna Berura* 54.
9. Thank you to my friend Yaakov Ben Harush, n"y, for bringing up this point.

Secondly, we discussed earlier[10] that we should not do things that make us sad, to the extent of not playing a game if you're a bad loser.[11] If less than excellent results would upset you, you should avoid looking at your results even if there is a helpful non-Jew around. So just be optimistic, look forward to seeing your results after Shabbos, and I hope you won't be disappointed.

7. *My newspaper is still in its wrapping. Can I tear the wrapping to read the divrei Torah in it?*

Someone who lives in a thriving Jewish community will not understand this question. Since when do newspapers[12] come in a plastic cover? You just buy them from your local Jewish store! But those of us who live or have lived in places out of the *yishuv*, where the kosher newspaper mailed to us is "oxygen" to connect us to our fellow religious Jews, will understand the question very well.

Now it may be that not everyone is lenient, but I am going to stick my neck out to allow destructive tearing, to enable reading the *divrei Torah* and other Jewish news that is permitted to be read on Shabbos. Tearing open something insignificant to extract food is certainly permitted.[13] Tearing a plastic bag to extract a shofar on Rosh HaShanah or a needed item of clothing is also allowed according to most *poskim*.[14] Are *divrei Torah* that may be necessary for us to spend Shabbos constructively any less vital?

---

10. Ch. 7, "Avoiding Distress."
11. Ibid., answer 9.
12. Obviously I'm referring to kosher newspapers, not secular ones that we may not even open, never mind read.
13. *Shulchan Aruch, Orach Chaim* 314:8.
14. See *Shemiras Shabbos KeHilchasah* 15:80, note 249.

If one can learn Torah in other ways or see the newspaper at other times, don't tear it open. But if it is your lifeline to Torah and your fellow Jews, as I wrote before, I think one can be lenient.[15]

8. *The pages of this zemiros book are stuck together in the corner. Can I gently separate them?*

I understand from your question that the pages are stuck together with dried food or something similar. Then you can separate the pages as long as you won't tear any letters.[16] If pages of a new *sefer* or book were never properly separated and are joined by even the slightest amount, we are not allowed to cut or tear them apart.[17]

9. *Chaim always enjoys his fruity yogurt for shalosh seudos. I forgot to peel the top off before Shabbos. He would be really disappointed if he can't have it.*

No problem. Just tear the top off the yogurt, taking care not to damage letters or pictures. You should have no intention of reusing even part of the top.[18] Chaim can enjoy his fruit yogurt as usual.

10. *I also forgot to open the bag of Chaya's favorite cookies. She assures me that we can tear it open. Can I trust her?*

I'm sure Chaya is a model *bas Yisrael* or soon will be. But since

---

15. See note 7.
16. *Mishnah Berurah* 340:45.
17. Ibid.
18. *Shemiras Shabbos KeHilchasah* 9:11–12.

the bag contains her favorite cookies I don't think you can rely on her.

You imply that you usually open all packaging before Shabbos, which is quite correct. The halachos are complex and one can transgress an array of *melachos* if one makes a mistake. *Bedieved*, since you forgot, let's consider this particular case. We mentioned that to tear packaging around food is permitted from the point of view of *korea*, as long as we do not intend to reuse the wrapping. Here, however, if you tear open the top of the bag with the intention of leaving the rest of the contents in the bag, the leniency will not apply. To open the bag, making it into a usable container might well transgress another *issur* — *boneh* (creating a vessel or building). So the only solution here is to tear the bag in a way that it will not be usable, making sure not to tear through letters or pictures.

So Chaya was right that there is a solution, but maybe she didn't know exactly what. I just had an idea. Appoint Chaya to be responsible every Erev Shabbos to open all the bags, bottles, cartons, and cans to be used *lekavod Shabbos*. This will be good for her and good for everybody else.

CHAPTER 34

צד — TRAPPING

1. *Help! Moshe! I spotted a mouse in the bedroom. What can we do?*

   I sympathize with your problem but, as you probably know, we are not allowed to trap animals on Shabbos. This applies to animals that are usually trapped, i.e., most animals and birds, as well as rodents and insects, which are not usually trapped but are subject to *tzad* on a rabbinic level.[1]

   We are not even allowed to set another animal on them, for example, to set a cat on a mouse.[2] We are allowed to own a cat for the purpose of catching any mouse it sees. If anyone could catch the mouse in an open bucket and quickly take the bucket outside[3] (where it is permitted to carry) or sweep it out with a broomstick, that would be a solution. If Moshe could do that he

---

1. *Shulchan Aruch, Orach Chaim* 316:3.
2. *Rama* 316:2.
3. Even though a mouse is *muktzeh*, we may carry it away in a bucket to make the house free of mice. This is called "*tiltul min hatzad letzorech davar hamutar*" and is allowed (*Shulchan Aruch, Orach Chaim* 311:8). The bucket is not to be covered, allowing the mouse to escape, so this is not *tzad*. If one is revolted by a mouse there is another leniency since it would be a *graf shel re'i*, which we are allowed to remove (*Shulchan Aruch, Orach Chaim* 308:34).

would earn himself the "Husband of the Year" prize. At least it's only a mouse!

2. *The neighbors have gone out, leaving their dog in their backyard. I'm afraid it might push their gate open and come into our yard. Can I bolt the gate?*

You can bolt the gate for two reasons: On the assumption that your neighbor's dog is completely domesticated, i.e., he does what he is told by his owner, the conclusion of the *poskim*[4] is that there is no question of *tzad*. Also, bolting the gate would not trap it completely as it can still roam around your neighbor's yard. You would merely be reducing the total area of freedom from two yards to one. This is also permitted.[5] Of course, if the dog has another way out of your neighbor's yard, there is no question that you can bolt the gate.

3. *Chaim's tortoise is edging toward the baby. Can I direct it back into its own enclosure?*

Certain animals, such as cows, are so domesticated that they are considered totally "trapped" and there is not even a rabbinic prohibition of *tzad*.[6]

There is an opinion that a tortoise that is slow moving and therefore unable to evade any person who wants to catch it is also

---

4. *Mishnah Berurah* 316:57. If the dog is trying to escape or chase another dog, etc., that is described as "rebelling." It would be *tzad* to grab hold of it. See question and answer 8.
5. *Shemiras Shabbos KeHilchasah* 27, note 115, in the name of Rav Shlomo Zalman Auerbach.
6. *Rama* 316:12, *Mishnah Berurah* 316:59.

considered already "trapped."[7] However, most opinions do not agree with this leniency.[8] So I would either encourage it to go in another direction, put something between the tortoise and the baby, or move the baby. To lift up the tortoise, besides this question of *tzad*, is not allowed because all animals including pets are *muktzeh*.[9]

4. *Moshe said I can't shut the wardrobe door because he thought he saw a moth fly in. Is he right?*

I'm glad that Moshe is being very careful about possible *chillul Shabbos*, but on this occasion he's being somewhat too strict. Let's examine this very interesting case. We are dealing here with the possible unintentional trapping of a moth. A moth is a type of creature that is not usually trapped and therefore this would be *tzad* on only a rabbinic level. This is a wardrobe, not a small box,[10] so even if you opened it, you might not be able to catch the moth so easily.[11] Indeed, if you opened it, it might fly

---

7. Rav Shlomo Zalman Auerbach.
8. *Orchos Shabbos*, vol. 1, ch. 14, note 21, in the name of Rav Yosef Shalom Elyashiv.
9. *Iggros Moshe, Orach Chaim* 5:22, as quoted by Rabbi Yisroel Pinchos Bodner in *Halachos of Muktza*, p. 119 and *teshuvah* 24. Please note that in *Iggros Moshe* itself, which was printed after Reb Moshe's passing, the editor has added to the end of the *teshuvah*, "…except for pets." But this was not in Reb Moshe's *teshuvah* and is only the view of the editor. Some people quote the *teshuvah* to show that Reb Moshe was lenient, but they have not noticed that the words "except for pets" are in a different font and are not part of the *teshuvah*.
10. Which the *Rama* 316:3 is talking about.
11. *Mishnah Berurah* 316:15.

away before you could catch it.[12] And Moshe's not even sure if there was a moth.[13] So, as much as I am impressed by Moshe's *yiras Shamayim* and *dikduk behalachah*, I think he was being a bit too strict.

5. *Why does closing a blind on Shabbos need yiras Shamayim?*

As in our previous answer, if we see any insects that are about to be trapped between the blind and the window, we have to leave a small gap through which they can escape in order to avoid *tzad*. If we can't see any insects, we don't need to search for them.

6. *Uncle Zevulun told me that on his farm he has a shomer Shabbos deer enclosure. What is he talking about?*

Uncle Zevulun obviously is well aware of *hilchos Shabbos* and *tzad* in particular. He has to feed the animals on his farm (even before he himself eats).[14] If he would just open a gate to bring in food, for a short time the deer would not be trapped, since the gate is open. Uncle Zevulun would then not be allowed to shut the gate since that would trap them again. Therefore he has a *shomer Shabbos* system of a small enclosure in front of the main enclosure for the deer. He opens the gate of the outer enclosure, goes in, and shuts the gate behind him. He then opens the inner gate. Now the deer are still trapped because the outer gate is closed. Now he can shut the inner gate without a question of *tzad* because the deer are trapped anyway.

---

12. One opinion in the *Rama* 316:3.
13. The *Biur Halachah*, s.v. "velachein," concludes like the *Taz* that if there is doubt whether something is being trapped at all, it is permitted.
14. *Berachos* 40a.

This question can also apply to a pet bird in a cage. We may not open the cage door to give the bird food or water and then close it again. What one should do is hold one's hand over the open space, while the door is open, so that at no time does the bird have a way of escaping. Then the door can be closed again without a question.

7. *Are you telling me I can't shut our front door on Shabbos just because our pet cat's inside?*

   I see why you are concerned. Any pet owner will have this problem. Do you have to leave your front door open when you go out on Shabbos? It's hardly practical as the *Biur Halachah* himself says.[15] However, if the reason that you want to shut the door is to keep intruders out, you may indeed shut it for a combination of halachic reasons.[16] However, if you are closing the door to make sure your pet doesn't escape, it is not allowed.[17]

8. *My sister has a pet dog. Can she take it for a walk?*

   Taking a dog for a walk on Shabbos raises certain issues of *hilchos Shabbos*, most of which have a solution. Holding a leash attached to the dog's collar is permitted even in a *reshus harabim* since it

---

15. 316:6, s.v. "*vehalach.*"
16. To trap an animal in an area that would still require a chase to actually get hold of it is *tzad* on a rabbinic level. To trap an animal that is domesticated enough that it would return in the evening like household cats and dogs is also *tzad* on a rabbinic level. If an animal was already trapped there is also more room to be lenient. The *Biur Halachah* above is lenient for these reasons.
17. *Shulchan Shlomo*, "*Tzad.*"

is necessary for the dog's protection.[18] Do not let the end of the leash protrude from your hand. You must also hold it fairly taut, without letting any part of the leash come within three inches of the ground.[19] Keeping these conditions makes it clearer to an onlooker that it is a leash and not just a detached item in the owner's hand.

If the dog is well behaved and doesn't try to get away, there will be no issue of *tzad*. Even if the dog does try to get away, for instance, to chase another dog or a cat, you may restrain it if the leash is already attached to its collar.[20] However, if there is an eiruv and you are holding the leash in your hand and the dog suddenly wants to escape, you may not restrain it by attaching the leash to its collar.

9. *We finally got the wasp into the spare bedroom. But can we shut the door?*

Well done for getting the wasp into the spare room. You must tell me how you did it! But closing the door on it to trap it there will not be allowed unless there is an open window through which it could escape. If an animal could cause serious distress to a person, trapping it would be allowed.[21] Normally wasps are a nuisance but do not threaten. If they are buzzing around a

---

18. *Shulchan Aruch, Orach Chaim* 305:1. See *Mishnah Berurah* 1 who says that it is like a person's clothes.
19. *Shulchan Aruch, Orach Chaim* 305:16.
20. Since it is already "trapped." See Rav Dovid Ribiat, *The 39 Melochos*, "*Tzod*," note 143. The author is not absolutely sure but it seems clear that since the dog is already on a leash it is *nitzud ve'omed* like an animal that is already in a small enclosure, where there is no prohibition against "trapping" it. See *Beitzah* 23b.
21. *Shulchan Aruch, Orach Chaim* 316:7.

particularly sensitive person or a baby, we may trap them if there is no alternative.

We are allowed to spray in the air to discourage wasps from approaching but not to spray directly at them.[22] We may spray only if there is a window or door open through which they can escape the poison.[23]

10. *Avi's running away because he wants to play outside instead of coming to bed. I told Moshe to run after him and bring him back. So why has he popped into the rabbi's house on the way?*

There is an interesting halachic debate whether the prohibition of *tzad* applies to people.[24] In the case of a small child who is not seriously running away but playing around, it is certainly permitted. And if he intended to run away, there is all the more reason to stop him, to keep him from danger. But Moshe just wanted to make sure. That's why he popped into the rabbi's house!

---

22. Similar to the case of the *Shulchan Aruch, Orach Chaim* 316:4.
23. *Orchos Shabbos*, vol. 1, 14:28.
24. See *Shemiras Shabbos KeHilchasah* 27, note 112. See the *Rama* 339:4 about arresting a criminal. In nearly all cases, the conclusion is that *tzad* does not apply.

CHAPTER 35

שוחט — SLAUGHTERING

1. *I've just seen a poisonous snake leaving my yard. What do I do?*

    The halachah divides animals into three categories in connection with this *melachah*: dangerous animals, animals that are not dangerous but can cause severe pain, and animals that can cause moderate pain. Dangerous animals, like the snake you saw, may be killed even if they are going away from you.[1] If they are not dangerous, but can cause severe pain, they may be killed if they are threatening someone but not otherwise.[2] We may trap but not kill animals that can cause moderate pain and are threatening.[3] In this case, the fact that the snake was leaving your yard is not relevant because it will go into someone else's yard where it would be a danger to people. Having said that, I wouldn't approach a poisonous snake unless you have some experience in dealing with them; in terms of the halachah you would be allowed to kill it.

2. *Help! There's a spider in the sink. Can Moshe wash it down the drain?*

---

1. *Mishnah Berurah* 316:45.
2. *Shulchan Aruch, Orach Chaim* 316:10.
3. *Mishnah Berurah* 316:37.

Why would you want to drown one of Hashem's beautiful creatures, especially one that saved David HaMelech's life? And we are supposed to emulate Hashem's characteristics of being "merciful to all his creatures."[4]

If there are dangerous spiders where you live *and* you recognize them,[5] you could kill them, but no method of killing is allowed with any other species.

3. *Chaim is offering to swipe the wasp with his table-tennis paddle. Should I let him?*

Although the *melachah* is *shocheit*, which implies killing by *shechitah*, killing by any method is equally forbidden. That is why we discussed drowning the spider in the previous answer and why under normal circumstances concussing this wasp with a table-tennis paddle or anything else is out of the question. Wasps are normally not dangerous, neither do they inflict serious pain, even if they sting. The only leniency would be if the wasp is threatening a baby or someone allergic to wasp stings, in which case, the risk is such that it would be permitted to kill it.[6] Nevertheless, if spraying near it would cause it to fly away,

---

4. Rav Moshe Feinstein (*Iggros Moshe, Choshen Mishpat* 2:47) wrote that cruelty even to an insect causes a person to become a cruel person. See also *Rama, Even Ha'Ezer* 5:14.

5. Most spiders are not dangerous and the *Magen Avraham* 316:23 criticizes people who kill spiders. The *Aruch HaShulchan* 316:22 is unsure even if there is good chance that it is dangerous, seeing that there is no proof that it is dangerous. See there the difference between this case and normal *safek pikuach nefesh*, where we are permitted and obligated to do whatever is necessary.

6. According to medical advice brought in Rav Dovid Ribiat, *The 39 Melochos*, "*Shocheit*," note 30.

removing the danger, you should do that and not kill it.

4. *Chaya has lice in her hair. Can I apply lotion?*

   You have asked a good question because we would have thought that it should be forbidden. The lotion will kill the lice. And while lice are a problem they are certainly not a danger and do not even cause pain. However, the Gemara *Shabbos*,[7] for technical reasons, excludes lice from this *melachah*. The *Shulchan Aruch*[8] also permits killing lice on Shabbos. While some *poskim*[9] have a doubt whether our lice are the same lice our sources are talking about and therefore do not allow the killing of lice, in the case of a child who is in distress because of the lice, one may be lenient.[10]

5. *For some reason, the pavement outside our house has swarms of ants. Do I have to stay inside?*

---

7. 107b.
8. Orach Chaim 316:9.
9. See *Orchos Shabbos*, vol. 1, 14:30. It would appear that in the case of a young child in distress we may put lotion on, although the custom is not to wet one's hair because of the danger of *sechitah*, as long as one is careful not to squeeze the hair. Just dab a towel over the hair. Also it is allowed to comb the hair very carefully with a special comb that one usually uses to check for lice, making sure not to pull out any hairs.

    Both these questions involve a rabbinic prohibition, which is waived in the case of a young child in distress who is considered a *choleh*. See *Biur Halachah* 302:10, s.v. "*delo*." Removal of lice, dead or alive, from hair is not considered *borer* because we do not consider a person and dirt a "mixture"; he is just a dirty person. See Rav Pesach Eliyahu Falk, *Zochor Veshomor*, "Borer" M(i). Rav Dovid Ribiat, *The 39 Melochos*, p. 889, however, is more *machmir*.
10. *Orchos Shabbos*, vol. 1, 14:30, note 48.

The question here is whether it is sure that you will kill an ant. If there are no gaps and you will be putting your full weight on at least one ant, I think the ant will not survive. So is there any leniency? If there is an eiruv and you can use a soft[11] brush to sweep the ants away, clearing a path to walk through, this is certainly the best option. If this is not possible and you will be killing ants if you walk through them and you can't somehow go around the whole column of ants, you can still be lenient for a combination of reasons.[12]

6. *I've found a greenfly on this lettuce. What do I do?*

Well done for spotting it! Now cut away a small piece of lettuce around the greenfly[13] and put it on a plate or an open bowl,[14] ready to throw away after Shabbos. I'm sure that you realize by now that pouring water over this greenfly, which will kill it, is not allowed.

7. *The doctor has recommended that I have a blood test. Should I wait until after Shabbos?*

Included in the *melachah* of *shocheit* is extracting blood either deliberately or by an action that will probably cause bleeding.

---

11. A brush with hard bristles that break with use is not allowed (*Rama* 337:2).
12. Similar to the blind man whose stick with a nail at the end will inevitably make holes in the ground (a question of *choresh*) that the *Biur Halachah* 301:18, s.v. "*aval*," allows. Here also it is *melachah she'ein tzerichah legufah, psik reisha delo neicha lei, mekalkel, kele'achar yad,* and other reasons. See *Orchos Shabbos*, vol. 1, ch. 14, note 43.
13. This avoids *borer*.
14. To avoid *tzad*.

According to most opinions, this is because blood is an absolute requirement for life, so drawing it is tantamount to *netilas neshamah* (taking life).[15] A nonurgent blood test may not be done on Shabbos. If there is a risk to life, of course, it is certainly permitted. If one is ill enough to have to lie in bed, a non-Jewish doctor or nurse may draw blood for testing.[16]

8. *I'm in a lot of pain and the dentist said the tooth must come out. Can I ask Dr. Jones to do it for me on Shabbos?*

   Obviously you mention Dr. Jones because you assume that a Jewish dentist may not cause bleeding. But may a non-Jewish dentist extract your tooth on Shabbos? It depends how bad the pain is. If you are in severe pain and you feel ill because of it, you may ask a non-Jew to take the tooth out.[17]

9. *It's Shabbos Shuvah right after two days of Rosh HaShanah. Is there any leniency to brush my teeth?*

   Brushing teeth in the normal way is not allowed because of *sechitah* (squeezing liquid out of the brush's bristles) and *memare'ach* (smoothing out the toothpaste). Even with a dry toothbrush, there could be a problem if it is very likely to make one's gums bleed. If this is not the case with you, it is permitted.

10. *Why does the mohel want to know exactly what time on Friday afternoon the baby was born?*

---

15. Biur Halachah 316:8, s.v. "vehachovel."
16. See ch. 21, "*Tochen*," answer 10.
17. Rama 328:3, Mishnah Berurah 10.

According to what we have learned, that doing something that causes bleeding is not allowed, we could ask why we sometimes celebrate a bris on Shabbos; there is always some bleeding at least for a short time. The answer is that the Torah allows it.[18] The *pasuk* says, "On the eighth day you shall perform a bris." And the Gemara[19] learns from this *pasuk* that we must do the bris, assuming the baby is well, on the eighth day even if it is Shabbos. On the seventh day it is never allowed, as it is too soon. On the ninth or succeeding day, even though there is is still a mitzvah to do the bris as soon as possible, it is not allowed on Shabbos. As I'm sure you know, the Jewish day begins not at midnight but at sunset. In fact, a baby born just after sunset on Friday would not have his bris on Shabbos because there is a doubtful time called *bein hashemashos*[20] between sunset and the time that it is definitely considered night. There are different opinions when this time is. Your *rav* will tell what is the custom in your community. But at least we understand why the mohel is asking the exact time of birth. Mazal tov.

---

18. *Vayikra* 12:3.
19. *Shabbos* 131b.
20. Literally, between the suns.

CHAPTER 36

מפשיט, מעבד, משרטט —
SKINNING, TANNING, AND RULING GUIDELINES

1. *I'm on a low-cholesterol diet. Can I peel the skin off the roast chicken?*

   The *melachah* of *mafshit* is skinning an animal. Unless we work in an abattoir it will not be relevant to us. However, skinning chickens is also included in this *melachah* and can be relevant, as you point out. The *poskim*[1] say, though, that the prohibition is only with a raw chicken. The chicken we enjoy on Shabbbos is cooked, so *mafshit* does not apply. Is taking off the skin to eat the meat not allowed because of *borer*?[2] This also is not a worry because chicken skin, which people generally eat, is regarded as just another part of the chicken and may be taken off.[3]

---

1. Aruch HaShulchan 321:26.
2. See ch. 20 above.
3. Iggros Moshe, Orach Chaim 4:74. Ayal Meshulash in the name of Rav Yosef Shalom Elyashiv. This applies to both roast chicken and boiled chicken. A minority view says that one should do it just before eating, so if possible, it is better to do it then.

מפשיט, מעבד, משרטט — Skinning, Tanning, and Ruling Guidelines

2. *Moshe's new shoes are very stiff. Can he bend them a few times to soften them up?*

    Let's visit the abattoir and see what happens. The skins are bought by leather merchants and then prepared for manufacture into furniture, briefcases, handbags, shoes, and so forth,[4] by the complex process of tanning, which causes a very unpleasant smell. Incidentally we may not, except under special conditions, sell a shul to become a tannery as it is not *kavod beis hakenesses*.[5] Someone who works there might not be included in the mitzvah of *aliya leRegel* because nobody will walk with him![6] Part of the process of tanning is the softening and moulding of the leather into the required shape. Trying to loosen up our shoes in the way that you are suggesting falls under this *melachah* and is not allowed.[7]

3. *I just got caught in a torrential shower and my shoes are soaked. Can I stuff them with newspaper so they keep their shape?*

    Since your purpose is not to stretch the leather but merely to prevent the shoes from getting out of shape, it is definitely permitted.[8]

4. *Chaim likes to sprinkle his cucumber with salt. I told him that he*

---

4. Tefillin are made from the leather of a kosher animal and have to be processed under rabbinic supervision.
5. Which is still important even when a shul is disused (*Shulchan Aruch, Orach Chaim* 153:9).
6. See *Chagigah* 4a.
7. Rav Dovid Ribiat, *The 39 Melochos*; Rav Pesach Eliyahu Falk, *Zochor Veshomor*.
8. See previous note.

can't do it on Shabbos. Moshe thought there was a way to do it. Who is right?

Part of the process of tanning leather is either covering the skins with salt or soaking them in a brine solution. This dehydrates and preserves them.

Because certain foods are often also salted or soaked in the same way to preserve them, this is not allowed on Shabbos. But preserving food by salting requires the salt to remain on the food for quite some time, so salting one piece of cucumber in order to eat it immediately is allowed.[9] To sprinkle salt on two pieces even for a short time is not allowed.[10] One opinion[11] says that if there are other pieces nearby, we may not put salt on a single piece in case we make a mistake. It seems to me that in your family you were all right. Chaim can have salt on his cucumber, one piece at a time. You are correct in general that salting vegetables is not allowed except under special circumstances. And Moshe is right that there is a permissible way to do it.

5. *I'm a bit partial to avocado with a touch of salt. Is this allowed?*

The halachah of not salting only applies to those foods that are normally salted to preserve them; this is not the case with avocado. There are other exceptions based on the same principle; it is not usual to salt pieces of tomato to preserve them, only whole tomatoes (including cherry tomatoes), therefore salting pieces of tomato is also allowed on Shabbos.[12] Some hold that it is also

---

9.   *Mishnah Berurah* 321:14.
10.   Ibid.
11.   Rav Dovid Ribiat, *The 39 Melochos*, p. 907, in the name of the *Taz*.
12.   *Shemiras Shabbos KeHilchasah* 1, note 6, in the name of Rav Shlomo Zalman Auerbach.

not usual to salt cucumber if it is peeled[13] but others disagree.[14]

6. *My family likes a tomato and cucumber salad for shalosh seudos. How do I prepare it?*

This seems like a problem since there are many small pieces of cucumber and tomato and normally one would add salt to the salad. The pieces of tomato are not a problem as we saw in the previous answer. In fact if there are more pieces of tomato than cucumber one could salt it even though the cucumber will be salted at the same time.[15] Even if there is more cucumber there is a solution. We may salt a salad before a meal as long as we immediately add oil, vinegar, or salad dressing, as these weaken the salt and it will not cause *me'abed*. The custom is to put the oil, etc., on before the salt to avoid any mistakes.[16] We also have to remember not to cut up the vegetables into thin slices or very small pieces because of *tochen*.

7. *Avi always does this. He takes a big piece of pickled cucumber and then can't finish it. Can we put the rest back in the jar?*

You're right that to put a cucumber into salt or brine to pickle it is not normally allowed. In this case, however, it was already in the brine and is, presumably, fully pickled.[17] So you are not achieving anything new by putting it back and it is allowed.[18] Just be

---

13. Based on the previous note. Rav Dovid Ribiat, *The 39 Melochos*, p. 909.
14. *Piskei Teshuvos* 321:1.
15. *Orchos Shabbos*, vol. 1, 7:10.
16. Rav Pesach Eliyahu Falk, *Zochor Veshomor*, "Me'abed," 4D.
17. Some types of cucumbers — "new green cucumbers" — are not fully pickled and should not be put back in the jar.
18. Rav Dovid Ribiat, *The 39 Melochos*, p. 905.

careful that the cucumber has not touched any meat or cheese, etc. If it has, it could affect the other pieces of cucumber in the jar.

One opinion[19] says that we may not reuse a jar, etc., without *toveling*,[20] it but another view is lenient.[21] If the cucumbers were in a metal can that was opened by a Jew, everybody agrees that it can be reused. If the manufacturers are Jewish there is similarly no question.

8. *I don't believe it. I thought the Seder table was ready but I forgot to prepare the salt water. Is there anything we can do now?*

I'm sorry, you won't be able to relax just yet. At least your question about whether you can make your salt water on Yom Tov does have a fairly simple answer. There are restrictions on making salt water because, as we explained above, immersing skins in a salt mixture is part of the tanning process. But when you are preparing a small amount for dipping at the Seder, it is permitted[22] as long as the proportion is less than two-thirds salt to one-third water. When the halachah says we shouldn't make a large amount, this means more than one is going to use on that day — Shabbos or Yom Tov;[23] some say more than one is going to use during the next meal.[24] So it is permitted, however many guests you have for your Seder. To prepare for a second Seder,

---

19. *Chelkas Yaakov* 2:57.
20. Immersing it in a mikveh as per the halachah of *tevilas kelim*.
21. *Iggros Moshe, Yoreh Deah* 2:40.
22. *Shulchan Aruch, Orach Chaim* 321:2; *Mishnah Berurah* 11; *Shaar HaTziyun* 10.
23. Rav Pesach Eliyahu Falk, *Zochor Veshomor,* "Me'abed."
24. *Orchos Shabbos*, vol. 1, 7:12 in the name of the *Ran*.

if there is one, would not be permitted. Now go and have a rest!

9. *I know that mesartet is to scratch a line before writing on parchment. So can you scratch a groove in the challah before cutting it?*

There is no doubt that to make a mark in the challah before *hamotzi*[25] is allowed since the *poskim*[26] say that the *melachah* of *mesartet* does not apply to foods. But only make the smallest groove[27] to ensure that the challah remains whole.[28]

10. *What about scoring the skin of an orange before you peel it?*

It is allowed, just as in the previous question.[29]

---

25. As mentioned in *Mishnah Berurah* 274:5.
26. *Aruch HaShulchan* 321:29, *Shemiras Shabbos KeHilchasah* 11:15.
27. Making a groove saves an unnecessary delay between saying the *berachah* and eating the bread (*Machatzis HaShekel* 274:1).
28. *Rama* 274:1.
29. *Shemiras Shabbos KeHilchasah* 11:15.

CHAPTER 37

ממחק — SMOOTHING

1. *I'm a diamond polisher and my boss asked me just for once to come in on Shabbos to finish a diamond that is needed for a customer. I'll walk to the factory, won't turn on any machines, wear my Shabbos clothes, won't accept any payment, etc. What could be wrong?*

   Have you ever heard of the "slippery slope"? Even if it would be technically permitted, once you're on a slippery slope you fall further. If you go in once "just for once" don't think your boss won't ask you again until he asks you every Shabbos. You can avoid all prohibitions? *Muktzeh*? *Maaris ayin*?[1] You can still daven *Shacharis* and *Musaf* with the minyan? Go to a *shiur*? Eat the seudah? And the message you would be giving to family? Etc., etc. And just for good measure, to polish a diamond like the smoothing of other surfaces is forbidden *min haTorah*.[2]

2. *To clean our hands properly, we need to use soap. What do we do on Shabbos?*

   I agree that it is very important to clean our hands with soap,

---

1. The prohibition of doing something that appears to involve transgressing halachah, e.g., *Shulchan Aruch, Orach Chaim* 301:45.
2. Rambam, *Hilchos Shabbos* 11:5.

especially before we eat. On Shabbos we are not allowed to use a bar of soap because by rubbing our hands we are liquidizing some of it, which is not allowed because of *nolad*.[3] Also when the bar of soap has softened somewhat, and we spread the soap over our hands, this is called *memare'ach*, which is connected to the *melachah* of *memachek*.[4] However, liquid soap, according to most *poskim*, is permitted.[5] Some[6] say that because the exact consistency that would constitute *memare'ach* is not so clear, the custom is to mix it with water either before Shabbos or as we use it. Liquid soaps also vary in their consistency and this is another reason to use them with water to be sure.

3. *The kids really enjoy making shapes with their Play-doh. Is it absolutely not allowed?*

   I'm afraid this is one of the classic examples of *memare'ach* similar to the case in the *Shulchan Aruch*[7] where we are told not to take some wax or something similar to close up a hole in a barrel. As we have said before, find or get advice about games that are permitted on Shabbos. The kids won't feel they're missing out on something because of the toys that are not for Shabbos. On the contrary they will look forward to their special Shabbos toys that are only taken out once a week.

4. *It's our eldest daughter's Shabbos kallah and she needs to smile at*

---

3. *Rama* 326:10.
4. *Mishnah Berurah* 326:30.
5. *Orchos Shabbos*, vol. 1, 17:27, note 40, in the name of Rav Yosef Shalom Elyashiv.
6. *Chut Shani*, p. 117.
7. *Orach Chaim* 314:11.

all the guests. She asked if she can clean her teeth using her finger to spread the toothpaste.

I know where you're coming from but this is also *memare'ach* according to most *poskim*.[8] My only suggestion is to mix toothpaste with water until it is watery and use that to freshen up her teeth. Tell your daughter not to worry; every bride is beautiful and I'm sure she'll be no exception.

5. *What about spraying the furniture to give it a shine?*

To spray a liquid spray onto furniture and wipe it with a cloth to give it a polished look for Shabbos is probably permitted from the point of view of *memare'ach*[9] but is not allowed because of *tzovea* (coloring).[10]

6. *Baby's quite sore. Is there any way to put some cream on?*

To spread a cream over one's skin or the skin of a baby is definitely not allowed, similar to question 4 above. A baby in distress, however, is regarded as a *choleh* (a sick person) and we are allowed to be more lenient if necessary. We're allowed to dab the cream on, in an unusual way,[11] such as with the back of a spoon. Even though when one puts a diaper on the cream will get spread out, it is permitted. If the cream has to be rubbed in to be effective, we should first try to find a liquid equivalent or a spray to avoid *memare'ach*. As an alternative, the cream could be put into

---

8. *Iggros Moshe, Orach Chaim* 1:112 and others. Rav Ovadia Yosef in *Yabia Omer* 4:30 is lenient in a case of distress.
9. See *Mishnah Berurah* 323:38, *Shaar HaTziyun* 41.
10. *Mishnah Berurah* 327:12.
11. *Chazon Ish* 52:16.

some water to make it into a watery mixture, which also avoids *memare'ach* as we discussed with soap above. If neither of these two methods is possible, assuming there is no non-Jew available, we may spread the cream so that none remains on the surface but it all gets absorbed into the skin.[12] Even this should be done in an unusual way, like with the back of the hand.

7. *The doctor prescribed a lotion that needs to be rubbed into the skin. Moshe said that it's perfectly permitted. Is he right?*

   Moshe is right and he's wrong. He's right that since it is a liquid, it is not *memare'ach*. But since this is almost certainly a skin infection rather than a debilitating illness, we may not use it on Shabbos, like other medical treatments that are not allowed unless one is ill enough to need to lie in bed.

8. *Chaya has just told me off for buttering my challah because of memare'ach. Is she right?*

   She's certainly not right about "telling you off." If she has a question about what you are doing she should ask politely, "Is it allowed to spread butter on Shabbos?"[13] As it happens, she is wrong about the halachah as well. There is no *memare'ach* with foods unless they are being shaped for esthetic reasons.[14]

---

12. Relying, *bedieved*, on an opinion that when the cream is totally absorbed into the skin, it is not called *memare'ach*. See *Shemiras Shabbos KeHilchasah* 33, note 58.
13. *Shulchan Aruch, Yoreh Deah* 240:11.
14. See *Rama* 321:19, *Mishnah Berurah* 82. Even for esthetic reasons it is not forbidden but should preferably be avoided.

9. *What about flattening the tuna salad to make it look professional?*

As mentioned in the previous answer, smoothing or flattening food for esthetic purposes is not ideal even though it is not explicitly forbidden. If we are careful not to do it, we are promised that we will merit a special *berachah*.[15] To shape food into the shape of something, e.g., a flower, is also a *shailah*.[16]

10. *This may be the first time it has snowed in Ramat Bet Shemesh. Moshe wants to go outside with the boys to make snowballs. What do I do?*

Lock the door and hide the key. Although I'm sure it's great fun, picking up snow is a question of *muktzeh*,[17] and making a snowball involves *memare'ach, boneh,* and *kosev*.[18] And throwing it down someone else's neck is a question of *bein adam lachaveiro*! After Havdalah, let them out.

---

15. See previous note.
16. See the *Chayei Adam, Hilchos Yom Tov* 92:3.
17. See Rav Dovid Ribiat, *The 39 Melochos*, "Boneh," note 280a. Rav Moshe Feinstein considered snow *muktzeh*, Rav Shlomo Zalman Auerbach did not.
18. See note 16.

CHAPTER 38

מחתך — CUTTING

1. *The bar mitzvah is just after Yom Tov but Mr. Schneider doesn't know if he'll have my new coat ready in time. Why not?*

    I hope you didn't employ Mr. Schneider too late for the bar mitzvah. Surely you knew that to make a coat involves numerous *melachos* that he will not be allowed to do on Shabbos or Yom Tov.[1] One of the *melachos* is this one of *mechatech*, which is cutting material to a particular size. The *Mishnah Berurah*[2] gives this example as one of the reasons *Chazal* forbade business dealings on Shabbos — because of the possibility that it would lead to *mechatech*.

2. *Yom Tov has come in and the candles don't fit in the candlesticks. Can I cut them to size?*

    Mechatech in the Mishkan was the cutting of animal hides to a particular size. In our previous question we discussed cutting cloth to a certain size. *Mechatech* includes cutting anything to a

---

1. Besides earning money, which is not allowed on Shabbos even if no *melachos* are involved. See ch. 8, "Earning Money on Shabbos."
2. 322:18.

particular size.³ Therefore we may not trim a candle to fit into a candlestick. Even to push a candle into a candlestick, with the intention that part of the wax will come away, is questionable.⁴

I note that you are about to light your Yom Tov candles after Yom Tov has begun. There are different customs whether to do so or to light them before Yom Tov as we do with Shabbos candles. There are reasons for both customs.⁵ On the second night, we *must* light after dark, except when it falls on Shabbos.

3. *The children are arguing over who has the bigger piece of cake. Can I cut their pieces to exactly the same size?*

Yes, that is a good way to stop them from arguing. They will be so upset about having to wait while you cut it precisely into equal portions that they won't be so fussy another time. But is this allowed on Shabbos? Well, there is no prohibition of *mechatech* with food.⁶ To make a visual estimation of how to cut two equally sized pieces is also allowed.⁷ Measuring with a ruler to get an exact size is prohibited rabbinically.⁸

4. *The rabbi said I could take a pill, but I need only half a pill twice a day. Can I cut it in two?*

You say the rabbi approved in case I might say that you shouldn't

---

3. Rambam, *Hilchos Shabbos* 11:7; *Mishnah Berurah* 322:18.
4. See *Shemiras Shabbos KeHilchasah* 13:42 and note 136.
5. See *Nitei Gavriel, Hilchos Yom Tov* 2:15.
6. *Mishnah Berurah* 322:12.
7. Ibid.
8. See ch. 10, "Measuring." Even though measuring for a mitzvah is allowed and here the purpose is to avoid an argument, it is questionable whether the leniency would extend so far.

do a *refuah* on Shabbos. So obviously you fall into one of the groups who may take medicines on Shabbos.[9] But now you're asking whether cutting the pill into two sections is *mechatech*. First, a pill could be considered food, which, as we have seen, is not considered *mechatech*. Second, although you want half the pill, you would be just as happy if it broke into small pieces and you would take half the pieces. So you are not really interested in cutting the pill to a particular size, you just want half the amount of medicine. For these reasons the *poskim*[10] are lenient. I wish you a *refuah sheleimah* but seeing that it is Shabbos, I'll say, "*Shabbos hi melizok urefuah kerovah lavo.*"[11]

5. *They may be a host of golden daffodils but they're too big for the vase. Can I cut them shorter?*

You may be surprised to learn that you can cut the flowers, with one condition. As we said above, there is no *mechatech* with food, which includes food for animals.[12] Although we don't often see dogs and cats eating flowers, other animals like deer, squirrels, and even your friendly tortoise would enjoy some juicy daffodils any day. All soft-stemmed flowers are equally edible. But be careful — taking them out of the water and putting them back is permitted only if the flowers are fully open.[13] If they are not, you'll have to cut them while they are still underwater.

---

9. See ch. 21, "*Tochen,*" answer 10.
10. Rav Shlomo Zalman Auerbach, brought in *Shemiras Shabbos KeHilchasah* 33, note 30; and Rav Nissim Karelitz in *Chut Shani*, "Mechatech."
11. See the meaning of this *berachah* in ch. 7, "Avoiding Distress," answer 7.
12. *Chayei Adam, Hilchos Shabbos* 36; and see Rav Pesach Eliyahu Falk, *Zochor Veshomor*, "Mechatech."
13. Otherwise it is not allowed because it is *nireh kezorea* (*Rama* 336:11).

6. *The hotel provides packets of ketchup. Can I cut mine open along the dotted line?*

   Here also, even if we cut it on the dotted line, we are not interested in the small packet; we will throw it away immediately. For this reason Rav Shlomo Zalmon Auerbach was lenient.[14] However, some say[15] we shouldn't cut it exactly on the dotted line because this indicates that I am interested to cut it to a certain measure even for a very temporary purpose. So to fulfill both opinions, it is better to cut it in another place.

7. *I forgot to separate the yogurts. What do I do?*

   Some argue that we want the pair of yogurts separated into two neat individual tubs, so splitting it should be considered *mechatech*.[16] Also some say that it would *makeh bepatish* (the completion of a item), in this case the container of yogurt.[17] Although other *poskim* are lenient on both questions,[18] there is certainly a doubt. To be sure, don't split them. In a family setting, however, all is not lost because two children can eat their yogurts one after the other. And if they get along really well they can eat them at the same time. That would be fun.

8. *We've made a hole in the top of the wine bottle. Now can we open it without a shailah?*

   The *poskim* discuss whether opening a bottle in the normal way

---

14. Quoted in *Shemiras Shabbos KeHilchasah* 9:4, note 25.
15. Brought in *Orchos Shabbos*, vol. 1, 11:41.
16. *Orchos Shabbos*, vol. 1, 11:42 in the name of Rav Yosef Shalom Elyashiv.
17. Ibid.
18. Ibid. in the name of Rav Shlomo Zalman Auerbach.

is prohibited because of *mechatech*.¹⁹ If part of the lid is left behind to form a ring around the top of the bottle, you have, arguably, created a bottle top of a particular size that can be taken off and put back on whenever you want. That's why you are making this hole in the lid first. But now that you have punctured the lid and made it suitable only to be thrown away, you are not interested in the way it was cut and there is no question of *mechatech*.²⁰

9. *I need to tear open a bag of cookies but there's a lot of writing on it. Can I carefully cut around the words with kitchen scissors?*

As we said above, in order for a cut to be considered *mechatech*, we must be interested in the item being cut. This is clearly not the case with a bag you are about to throw away. There is no prohibition of *korea* because you are opening the bag in order to reach the cookies inside.²¹ And, even though kitchen scissors are *kli shemelachto le'issur*,²² they may be used if nothing else is available. Since the only way to avoid destroying letters or pictures is to use scissors to open the bag, the answer is yes.

10. *I'm trying to make up my one hundred berachos. Can I cut this cinnamon stick in order to smell it?*

Well done for observing this important mitzvah of saying one hundred *berachos* every day. If we say our *berachos* with care one hundred times a day we acquire *yiras Shamayim*; in the words

---

19. See *Orchos Shabbos*, vol. 1, ch. 11, note 62. With plastic tops that have just a few narrow strips connecting the top to the ring, some *poskim* are lenient to open them *lechatchilah*. See Rav Dovid Ribiat, *The 39 Melochos*, p. 841.
20. Rav Pesach Eliyahu Falk, *Zochor Veshomor*, "Koreah."
21. See ch. 33.
22. See ch. 11.

of the Rambam, "We will remember Hashem continuously."[23] When cutting a cinnamon stick, however, you have to remember not to cut it to a particular size because of *mechatech*. The *poskim*[24] say that we have to break it by hand and not with a knife, in case we might forget and shape it into a toothpick. Incidentally, the *berachah* on smelling cinnamon is *borei minei besamim*.[25]

---

23. *Hilchos Berachos* 1:4. See the introduction to my sefer *Do You Know Hilchos Brachos?*
24. *Mishnah Berurah* 322:17.
25. *Mishnah Berurah* 216:16 (קלאפין = cinnamon), *Berachos KeHilchasan* 16:14.

CHAPTER 39

כותב — WRITING

1. *The hospital has asked me to sign a consent form. Can I do it with my left hand?*

There is obviously a medical emergency here. But before doctors will perform the required treatment, they want the patient to sign a consent form, exonerating the hospital if anything goes wrong, *chas veshalom*.

In a genuinely life-threatening situation of course you may sign, even if it involves a Torah prohibition. Having said that, if we can avoid a Torah prohibition and only trangress a rabbinic prohibition, we have to do so. Even if the patient is not in a life-threatening situation but he is ill enough to be classified as a *choleh*,[1] treatment, if it is necessary, may be done by non-Jewish staff.

In either case we should sign in an unusual way. For instance, if we are right-handed we should sign with our left hand, as you suggest. If a person is ambidextrous, he would have to sign in an unusual way, for instance, holding the pen between two fingers rather than in the normal way. Just to sign an unusual signature would not be permitted. In a life-threatening situation, no delay

---

1. See ch. 21, "*Tochen*," answer 10.

is permitted and if signing in an unusual way is going to take more time, just sign normally. Sometimes seconds can make the difference between life and death.

2. *I've noticed a mistake that needs correcting in the sefer I'm reading. Can I make a tiny dot in the margin to remind me?*

No, we may not make even a small mark.[2] We are not even allowed to make a dent in the paper with our fingernail to indicate the place we want to remember.[3] Theoretically one could fold down the corner of the page, even though this causes a crease in the paper because it is not the crease that is important but the fact that the page is folded.[4] Having said that, it does not seem respectful to a *sefer* to fold its pages. An old-fashioned bookmark would do the job just as well, without maltreating the *sefer*.

3. *I've heard they've come up with a new idea — "invisible" ink. It really is invisible until you treat it after Shabbos to make it readable. Isn't this a great permitted way of "writing"?*

Haven't you heard of the *pasuk*, "There is nothing new under the sun"?[5] The *Talmud Yerushalmi*[6] already reports people doing this two thousand years ago and concludes that even the first person who writes these "invisible" letters has transgressed *kosev*. However, in a Jewish hospital, where medical notes have to be taken anyway for seriously ill patients, it is better to use this "invisible" ink that may be only rabbinically forbidden.

---

2. Mishnah Berurah 340:25.
3. Ibid.
4. Rav Dovid Ribiat, *The 39 Melochos*, p. 932; *Piskei Teshuvos* 340:19.
5. Koheles 1:9.
6. *Shabbos* 12:4. In the *Bavli*, *Gittin* 19b, "invisible" writing is also discussed.

4. *What about writing in the air if the letters are recognizable?*

   This is definitely permitted.[7] The same is true for "writing" letters with one's finger on a surface, even though someone else would know what is being "written."[8]

5. *Our non-Jewish neighbor wants to take a picture of us sitting at the Shabbos table. Is there a problem?*

   Kosev refers not only to writing letters but also to drawing a picture or creating a picture by any method. Therefore photography is clearly not allowed.[9] Asking a non-Jew to do a *melachah* is allowed only in cases of great need[10] under strict halachically acceptable conditions,[11] so you can't ask your non-Jewish neighbor to take a picture for you. Even if you don't ask but it is for your benefit, it is similarly forbidden.[12] But if the non-Jew is taking the picture purely for his or her own benefit, e.g., a tourist is taking a picture of you to "show the folks back home" or as in your case the neighbor wants a picture of your Shabbos table to put in his album, you may be photographed.

   Present-day *poskim* discuss whether we can go within range of a security camera that will produce images of us on a screen, as is very common nowadays.[13] Most allow it in cases of need.

---

7. *Rama* 340:4.
8. *Mishnah Berurah* 340:22.
9. Ibid. 340:18.
10. *Rama* 276:2. See ch. 13, "Amirah le'akum."
11. *Mishnah Berurah* 276:25. If it involves a *melachah* on a rabbinic level see *Shulchan Aruch* 307:5 and *Mishnah Berurah* 19–24.
12. *Shulchan Aruch* 276:1.
13. See *Orchos Shabbos*, vol. 1, ch. 15, note 55.

6. *Chaya knows how to make the napkins into a flower shape. Can she do this on Shabbos?*

   I'm sure Chaya can make beautiful "flowers" but to make the shape of something like a flower with paper or anything else is included in *kosev*.[14] It can be another of her Erev Shabbos jobs.

7. *My siddur is rather old. When I close it, some torn pages join back up, recreating the words. Do I have to use a different siddur on Shabbos?*

   There is definitely a value in davening from a well-used siddur. Think of all the *tefillos* that have been said from it, how many tears that have been shed over it. However, as you obviously realize, joining two parts of a page, possibly joining two parts of a letter to form the whole letter, raises a question of *kosev*. Although it would be better to stick the two parts together during the week to avoid the question or to use another siddur, Rav Moshe Feinstein[15] held that since, almost invariably, the letter is anyway recognizable from one part or the other, one can be lenient.

8. *Another of my favorite books has our name on the edge of the pages so that closing it makes the name readable. I heard that it's a shailah. What's the conclusion?*

   You're right that it is a *shailah* — one that has occupied the minds of the *poskim* for hundreds of years. This question, which is

---

14. Rav Dovid Ribiat, *The 39 Melochos*, p. 952, and other *sefarim* in the name of the *Chayei Adam, Hilchos Yom Tov* 92:3. To join together pieces of Lego, etc., to make a boat or plane is also not allowed because of *kosev*. See *Machazeh Eliyahu* 69.
15. *Iggros Moshe, Yoreh Deah* 2:75.

brought in the *Mishnah Berurah*,¹⁶ is really dependent on whether the *melachah* of *kosev* is only writing letters or if it includes bringing together letters or parts of letters that are already written, as on the edges of the pages of a book. His conclusion is that most authorities are lenient, but still, if one has a choice it is better to avoid the question by reading something else.¹⁷

9. *One thing that would keep the kids busy on Shabbos afternoon is Scrabble. I would have thought it is definitely not allowed because you're making words. Why did Moshe say that it might still be allowed?*

Your question about playing Scrabble is really an extension of our previous discussion about the definition of *kosev*. Here too, you are not creating letters but bringing letters together to form words, which, as we said, is not forbidden according to most authorities. Some¹⁸ hold that even those who are of the opinion that bringing parts of a letter together to make a letter is *not* allowed, to bring together two whole letters even to create a word *is* allowed. Therefore we have good grounds to be lenient, especially for children.

And an adult who wants to be lenient certainly has opinions to rely on. Two further points are worth mentioning. An important opinion¹⁹ states that attaching two letters to a joint background is *kosev*. According to this opinion we may not attach Scrabble letters to a board as in Travel Scrabble, although we may lay letters on a board next to each other. Similarly, putting parts of a picture

---

16. *Mishnah Berurah* 340:17.
17. Ibid. and *Shaarei Tziyun* 340:25.
18. Rav Tzvi Pesach Frank, *Har Tzvi*, "Meleches Kosev."
19. *Magen Avraham* 340:11 brought in *Iggros Moshe, Orach Chaim* 1:135.

next to each other even if it forms a complete picture is allowed, but a jigsaw in which the pieces fit together or fit within a frame is not allowed.[20]

Bear in mind too that if you normally keep score, the *poskim*[21] are concerned that on Shabbos you might forget and write down the points, so they forbid playing such games. To answer your precise question and bearing all this in mind, yes, Moshe is right. If the children enjoy Scrabble, let them play it. But not Travel Scrabble and not if they usually play for points.

10. *The chuppah has been delayed and it's almost Shabbos. If it gets any later, will we have to push off the chuppah until tomorrow night?*

The rabbis do not allow a number of activities because of the danger that we may forget and write. Doing business is forbidden for this reason. Whether this applies to a chuppah is controversial. The Rama[22] says that even in the case of a man who has not fulfilled the mitzvah of having children, we do not allow a chuppah. But in an emergency, when the wedding is arranged for Erev Shabbos but has been delayed and cancelling it would cause great embarrassment, if the *chassan* has not fulfilled the mitzvah of having children, we can go ahead even on Shabbos. But try very hard to complete the chuppah before Shabbos. Mazal tov.

---

20. *Shemiras Shabbos KeHilchasah* 16:23.
21. Quoting the *Chayei Adam* 38:11.
22. 339:4.

CHAPTER 40

מוחק — ERASING

1. *It's really not nice; Avi drew silly pictures in the steam on the window and we've got important guests coming. Can I erase them?*

   I see your problem but erasing letters or pictures, even not for the purpose of writing more letters, is *mochek*. In this case we are dealing with *mochek* on a rabbinic level, since the letters were never meant to be permanent, but nevertheless it is not allowed. If you have a non-Jew available you could point out the offensive picture on the window and say, "We don't like this picture," and hopefully the non-Jew will understand that you want him/her to wipe the picture off. Otherwise you may have to close the curtain or serve such good food that your guests won't notice Avi's "artwork"!

2. *I just remembered that I wrote a shopping list on my hand on Erev Shabbos and forgot to wash it off. Am I allowed to wash for the Shabbos seudos?*

   Here again you've got a problem of *mochek*. If I may just comment that both this question and maybe the last one (depending on when Chaim drew the pictures) would not have been a problem had you done your Erev Shabbos preparations properly. First of all we are supposed to wash our hands and face, at least, before

Shabbos.¹ Second, assuming you have learned *hilchos Shabbos*, you would have anticipated this problem and made sure the ink was off before Shabbos.

Now let's come back to the question of *netilas yadayim* with these letters written on your hand.² If the water won't erase the letters anyway, which I suspect is the case, there isn't any *shailah* except that it doesn't look good. You'll also have to dry your hands gently where there is writing, so that it shouldn't be erased. Since the ink is in your skin rather than on top of it, it is not a *chatzitzah*,³ which could have disqualified the washing.⁴

The most important thing is not to try to erase the writing with the water or when wiping your hands because that is definitely not allowed. If it is not certain whether the water will erase the letters, you can wash your hands. If the water would definitely erase even one letter, but you are not washing for the purpose of erasing but for the mitzvah of *netilas yadayim*, if you will be happy to have clean hands, it would not be allowed. If you really don't care (which would only apply to a child), it will be allowed *bedieved*.⁵

---

1. *Shulchan Aruch* 260:1.
2. The *Chayei Adam* (*Hilchos Netilas Yadayim* 40:8 and *Nishmas Adam* there) holds that any mark, not just letters, should not be rubbed off one's hands because he holds that one may not remove anything from a surface that can be written on, even if that wasn't one's intention. Some *poskim pasken lechatchilah* like the *Chayei Adam*, some don't. See *Piskei Teshuvos* 340:3; *Chut Shani*, "Mochek."
3. The prohibition of washing our hands with an intervening substance on them.
4. *Mishnah Berurah* 161:14.
5. *Dehavei trei deRabbanan; kesav she'eini miskayem umekalkel be'eini miskaven psik reisha delo ichpas lei.* See *Shaar HaTziyun* 316:18. Even though some are *machmir* (see *Chazon Ish*, *Orach Chaim* 61), for a child one can be lenient.

But don't let it happen again!

3. *There is some food stuck on part of a page of my zemiros book. Can I unstick it so I can see all the words?*

    This question is more serious than many people realize. It is obvious that we may not remove something stuck to the page if the letters underneath are going to be torn, because of *mochek*. However the halachah does not allow the removal of the food that is stuck firmly, even if no damage would be done to the letters underneath.⁶ The *melachah* of *mochek* is erasing in order to write, i.e., create letters. Removing whatever is stuck to the letters is like erasing in order to recreate the letters that had been obliterated, therefore it is not allowed. However, if the food is stuck loosely and can be easily wiped away or it is stuck onto a laminated page, the letters are regarded as just covered and are not being recreated. This is allowed.⁷

4. *It's Chaim's birthday this Shabbos. Can I write "happy birthday" and a number nine on the cake?*

    First of all, mazal tov on Chaim's ninth birthday. In only four years he'll be bar mitzvah and won't you be proud of him, *im yirtzeh Hashem*? Your question about the icing on the cake is one of the most talked about in *mochek*. Apparently, it should certainly not be allowed to cut through the letters or a number. But there is a possible leniency if the letters are made of sugar mixed

---

6. *Mishnah Berurah* 340:10. See there for what to do if we find something stuck to a letter in a *sefer Torah* while reading from it on Shabbos. See *Biur Halachah*, s.v. "she'al," that not everyone agrees with this halachah, but the Chofetz Chaim is *machmir* in practice.
7. See *Orchos Shabbos*, vol. 1, 15:51 and note 72.

with, say, fruit juice, which does not remain solid for very long, coupled with the fact that you intend to cut the cake, and not the writing.

Letters made of harder icing, chocolate sprinkles, silver balls, etc., would not have this leniency. To cut through letters that are part of the cake itself rather than written on top of the cake is allowed by the *Mishnah Berurah*[8] but not the Chazon Ish.[9] Breaking the letters as you eat seems to be accepted by most *poskim*[10] but that only works with icing on small cupcakes. A bigger cake will have to be cut, somehow; even a "birthday boy" cannot be allowed to put a whole cake into his mouth and thereby eat up the letters.

The simple solution is to cut up the cake in between letters even though it breaks up a word. This is not *mochek*.[11] Even to cut through a piece of icing that is just connecting two letters is allowed as long as both letters are legible without the connecting bit. But don't cut through a number because it is just like cutting through a letter. Alternatively, just admire the cake today and eat it after Shabbos. However, this suggestion may get voted down!

5. *The cookies at the Chanukah kiddush are in the shape of a menorah. Can I eat them?*

We just said that eating letters is permitted. Similarly, eating a form of something, e.g., a menorah, is permitted.

---

8. 340:17.
9. *Orach Chaim* 61:1.
10. *Mishnah Berurah*, ibid.
11. *Shemiras Shabbos KeHilchasah* 9, note 48, in the name of Rav Shlomo Zalman Auerbach.

6. *I'm in a shul with an unusual paroches. They have two sections that together form a picture. Can I open them if they give me pesichah?*

   It is an unusual *paroches*. In fact it is the Jewish custom to make one single *paroches* like the one in the Beis HaMikdash.[12] Rav Moshe Feinstein did not allow such a *paroches* and held[13] that it should be replaced.

   However, if you are given *pesichah* you can open and close it. The question is similar to playing Scrabble on Shabbos, which we discussed in *kosev*. We said that if the letters are just loosely next to each other, as distinct from Travel Scrabble where they are fixed into a base, it is permitted, although not ideal. Here also, since the two halves are just hanging next to each other, if you are asked to do *pesichah*, it would be wrong to refuse. Ideally, however, the two halves should not be closed completely. A small gap should be left to avoid the *shailah*.[14] This is in terms of *kosev* and *mochek*. But it is not correct to have such a *paroches* as I quoted before.

7. *I'm just shelling the eggs before shalosh seudos and Mommy told me to be careful. Be careful about what?*

   Eggs, even after they are boiled, often have the stamp that contains letters and numbers still visible on part of the shell. As you shell the eggs, therefore, you should be careful not to break through the letters or numbers. Sometimes, unexpectedly, the

---

12. Even according to the *tanna kamma* in the mishnah (*Yoma* 51b) who held there were two *parochos* and each one was separate; there wasn't one *paroches* divided in two.
13. *Iggros Moshe, Orach Chaim*, vol. 4, 40:22.
14. Ibid.

shell cracks through the letters. If that happens it's not the "end of the world," it was an accident. But try to be even more careful next time. I presume you are shelling the eggs just before *shalosh seudos* to avoid *borer*.[15]

8. *My baby's diaper has a picture of a teddy bear on it that gets erased when the diaper is wet. My neighbor said she'd never let her baby wear such a diaper on Shabbos. Is she right?*

Although the *poskim* are quoted[16] as being lenient, I wouldn't dismiss your neighbor's *chumrah*. Seeing that it is inevitable or almost inevitable that whoever puts the diaper on the baby is causing the picture to be erased and that person is happy when it is erased because it saves opening the diaper to see if the baby needs changing, the leniency is not so straightforward.[17]

If there are pictures all over the diaper there is another possible pitfall connected to *mochek*. Sticking something over a picture or letters may be a form of erasing.[18] If the diaper is designed to be stuck down and then unstuck a few times as many are nowadays, it would not be a problem. But if one is sticking it down for the last time before discarding the diaper, besides being a question of *tofer*,[19] it is also a question of *mochek*. So if your neighbor wants to avoid diapers with pictures to be sure that she

---

15. See ch. 20, "*Borer*," question 3.
16. See *Orchos Shabbos*, vol. 1, 15:52, note 73.
17. Is it permitted to put some writing under an open window just before it rains, when the rain will definitely erase the letters — especially if I have some interest in the letters being erased?
18. See Rav Dovid Ribiat, *The 39 Melochos*, "*Mochek*," note 54, in the name of the *Yesodei HaShulchan*.
19. See Rav Dovid Ribiat, *The 39 Melochos*, pp. 812–814, for the various opinions on this subject.

doesn't come to transgress Shabbos, maybe she's got a point.

9. *My neighbor borrowed a bottle of wine last week and she has come to replace it on Shabbos. Can I accept it?*

   Just as *Chazal* forbade various activities in case we come to write, so they forbade other activities in case we erase. One of these activities is repaying a loan, even if it is not *muktzeh*, such as an item of food.[20] We may be tempted to erase a written document concerning the loan. However in this case, the *Mishnah Berurah*[21] says that if the borrower says he is returning the item rather than repaying it, it is allowed.

10. *I was just about to read from my list where all the guests are supposed to be sitting when the rebbetzin stopped me. She said she'll do it. If I can't do it, why can she?*

    Here again *Chazal* were concerned that we might change the arrangement of the guests at the last minute and erase what we have written.[22] However, only someone who is authorized to make changes is forbidden to read the table plan because they might erase. Someone else cannot erase because they have no permission to make changes. Your observant *rebbetzin* realized what you were going to do and kindly stepped into the breach. For you it wasn't allowed; for her it was.[23]

---

20. *Rama* 307:11.
21. 307:46.
22. *Shulchan Aruch, Orach Chaim* 307:12.
23. *Mishnah Berurah* 307:47.

CHAPTER 41

בונה — BUILDING

1. *We bought a beautiful picture of our rebbe. Can we hang it up in the dining room?*

   It's certainly wonderful to have a picture of your rebbe on your wall to inspire you. The Navi[1] says, "And your eyes should see your teachers." I have a picture of Reb Mattisyahu Salomon, *shlita*, in whose home I was *zocheh* to live for two years in Gateshead, on our dining room wall and he had the famous picture of his rebbe, Reb Eliya Lapian, *zt"l*, giving milk to a cat, on his wall.

   But can you hang it up on Shabbos?

   If you have already fixed a nail in the wall before Shabbos you can certainly hang up the picture on Shabbos.[2] If you haven't, however, you're not allowed to make a hole, however small, in a permanent wall on Shabbos. The very first mishnah in *HaBoneh*[3] says that one who does this will be *chayav*. "Building" is not only building a new structure but altering it or adding to it, e.g., attaching a suction hook to your bathroom wall.[4]

---

1. *Yeshayah* 30:20.
2. Even if you're planning to leave it there permanently. See *Orchos Shabbos*, vol. 1, ch. 8, note 19.
3. *Shabbos* 102b.
4. *Shemiras Shabbos KeHilchasah* 23:39.

2. *Help! The door handle has fallen off and we can't open the door. What can I do?*

You certainly have a problem if you can't open the door because the door handle has come off. But to put the door handle back on the door is applicable to what we said in the previous answer. And even doing it in a nonpermanent way is still not allowed because we might make a mistake and fix it in a permanent way.[5] In fact the handle is now *muktzeh* and may not be moved.[6] Sometimes it is possible to use the handle as a method of opening the door without attaching it and this would be permitted. If this is not possible, in an emergency you can put the handle back in an upside down way that it will definitely not be left permanently.[7] If this doesn't help, try shouting louder![8]

3. *It's too hot for our new baby in the sun. Can I attach a sunshade to the hood of the stroller?*

We are not normally allowed to build even a temporary structure. Making even a temporary roof is more serious than a temporary wall that is sometimes permitted.[9] However, if a roof or cover was already in place before Shabbos, we are allowed to add a temporary extension. The original roof can be as narrow as one *tefach* (approximately four inches). Therefore if there is a hood at least a *tefach* wide that has been attached to the stroller before

---

5. *Mishnah Berurah* 313:51.
6. Ibid. 308:35.
7. *Chut Shani*, "Boneh" 36:7.
8. If a child is locked in a room even for a few minutes, it is regarded as *pikuach nefesh* and we may do anything necessary to free him.
9. Where a temporary partition is of no halachic significance. See *Shulchan Aruch, Orach Chaim* 315:1.

Shabbos, you can attach a sunshade to that if you want.

4. *The sliding glass front of our bookcase came off its rails. Can I push it back on?*

   This is a very important question that concerns a large piece of furniture or a fridge that is bigger than 3 x 1 x 1 *amos*.[10] With such an item even a small repair is like adding something to a permanent structure and is not allowed, as we said earlier.[11] If what you are doing is part of its normal use, like opening drawers or doors or opening the glass sliding door of a bookcase, it is allowed. But in this case the glass front came off its rails, similar to a drawer falling out of a kitchen unit. Therefore to put back the drawer, etc., is not allowed.

5. *The doll's head has come off. Can I do an emergency operation to screw it on again?*

   To put together parts of even a small item, like screwing a broomstick into the head of a broom or reattaching a leg that has come off a chair, or replacing the head of a doll as in your case, is also included in *boneh*.[12] So, I'm afraid the "emergency operation" will have to wait until Motzaei Shabbos.

6. *The wheel of the crib has come out again. Can I put it back?*

   This might be allowed if the wheel is usually only loosely attached

---

10. About 54 x 18 x 18 inches.
11. *Rama* 314:1; *Mishnah Berurah* 314:2–3.
12. See *Mishnah Berurah* 314:1; *Shulchan Aruch, Orach Chaim* 313:6. See also *Shulchan Aruch, Yoreh Deah* 141:4, concerning owning a *tzuras adam*, and *Darchei Teshuvah* 141:31.

to the leg of the crib and comes out easily. Therefore it can be put back. *Boneh* applies only if the connection between the two parts is strong enough that they are not easily separated. This is why if a table needs to be lengthened on Shabbos, and involves slipping protruding pieces of wood into holes in the other piece, it is permitted. Only if a certain degree of special effort is required to separate the parts is it considered *boneh*.[13]

7. *Our couch unfolds into a bed. Can we open it for the guest?*

This is certainly allowed. Something that is sometimes folded up but can be restored to its normal state just by unfolding, is allowed.[14] This is applicable to many of our everyday items, like folding chairs, tables, and beds.

8. *Our neighbor just walked in and saw Avi playing with his building blocks. I noticed his eyebrows went up. Should I feel guilty?*

If anyone should feel guilty, it is your eyebrow-raising neighbor for casting aspersions on Avi's *shemiras Shabbos*. Although Avi is "building," the structure is so loose that it will fall down within seconds; no one would call that *boneh*. What is more questionable is building games where pieces are really connected and can stay connected for some time. Some *poskim* do not allow such games. Others, however, argue that these games are by definition designed to be regularly built up and knocked down and do not constitute *boneh*. Those who allow their children to play with them have opinions to rely on but it is preferable that the children

---

13. *Orchos Shabbos*, vol. 1, 8:45.
14. *Shulchan Aruch, Orach Chaim* 315:5.

should take apart whatever they have built within a day.[15]

9. *I heard that boneh applies to our hair. Is that right?*

Yes. Braiding is not allowed and building up one's hair into a certain shape with the help of hair spray is also a form of "building." However, some *poskim* allow styling the hair and then spraying, which merely retains the shape that has already been made. After spraying, the hair may no longer be styled.[16] Spraying a sheitel is never allowed.[17]

10. *Is there anything wrong with playing table tennis on Shabbos?*

Flattening out a floor is part of *boneh* and *Chazal* forbade certain activities in case we might be tempted to do so. One such activity is playing games that involve rolling a ball along the ground.[18] It would appear that any game, like tennis, in which a ball bounces on the ground and might cause the players to flatten out the ground, is included in this rule.[19] However, table tennis, which is obviously not played on the ground is specifically excluded from the prohibition.[20] So technically you can play table tennis. Of course an adult should ideally not be spending his Shabbos playing games.[21] For childen it's permitted.

---

15. See a discussion on the subject in *Orchos Shabbos*, vol. 1, ch. 8, note 86; and Rav Dovid Ribiat, *The 39 Melochos*, p. 1050. Also *Machazeh Eliyahu* 69.
16. Rav Dovid Ribiat, *The 39 Melochos*, p. 1061 and note 265.
17. Ibid., p. 679.
18. *Shulchan Aruch* 338:5.
19. See ch. 14, "*Choresh*," answer 6.
20. Ibid.
21. Where the circumstances demand it, it is correct and praiseworthy for parents to play permitted games with their children on Shabbos. See ch. 7, "Avoiding Distress," answer 10.

CHAPTER 42

סותר — DEMOLISHING

1. *The suction hook in the bathroom is too close to the sink. Can I move it further away?*

   Do you remember from the previous chapter whether you can attach something to a wall of your house? We said[1] that it falls under *boneh*. Well, this is going to answer our question as well. Whatever is not allowed to do because of *boneh*, to do the reverse of that action is not allowed because of *soser*.[2] So you'll have to wait until after Shabbos to change the position of your bathroom hook.

2. *Moshe's Gemara doesn't fit in the bookcase. Can he take out the higher shelf so that it will fit in?*

   I'm sure you know this answer; it's the same principle as the previous one. To put a shelf (back) into a big bookcase, like adding on to other big pieces of furniture,[3] is *boneh*. So taking out a shelf is *soser*.

---

1. Answer 1.
2. *Minchas Chinuch*, "Meleches Soser."
3. See ch. 41, "*Boneh*," answer 4, for the size required for this halachah to apply.

3. *Our Shabbos guest is a sofer and he pointed out that one of the mezuzos is upside down. Can we take out the mezuzah and put it in the right way?*

This is a somewhat more interesting question because we all know the importance of a mezuzah. We do not fulfill the mitzvah if the mezuzah is upside down[4] so maybe we would be allowed to remove the mezuzah and turn it around before replacing it. Further, it is not the parchment that is attached to the wall but rather the outer mezuzah case. Does all this make a difference?

Maybe we should start with another question. Is a mezuzah *muktzeh* on Shabbos? No, although a mezuzah is a valuable item and we might have thought that it is *muktzeh* because of *chisaron kis*,[5] this is not the case because we can read the words of a mezuzah and learn from it.[6]

However, a mezuzah that fell off the doorpost is *muktzeh* because while it's in its place, it is regarded as part of the doorpost. If something that's part of a building becomes detached, it is *muktzeh*.[7] This answers our original question. A mezuzah is regarded as attached to the doorpost and therefore it would be *soser* to remove it, as in the previous answers. It would also be *boneh* to replace it. Even just to remove the parchment from a mezuzah case or to put it back in has the same halachah.[8] The fact that you will be without a mezuzah until after Shabbos can't be helped. However,

---

4. *Chovas HaDor* 9:7.
5. See ch. 12, "Muktzeh," part II, question 1.
6. See *Mishnah Berurah* 307:63, who says that a *get* is not *muktzeh* for this reason.
7. *Mishnah Berurah* 308:35; *Shemiras Shabbos KeHilchasah* 20, note 33.
8. *Shemiras Shabbos KeHilchasah* 23, note 101. Some *poskim* are more lenient if just the mezuzah fell, not the case. See *Orchos Shabbos*, vol. 1, 8:24.

we can still learn from this episode to make sure all our mezuzos are kosher and fixed correctly.[9] And if you redecorate your home, make sure the mezuzos don't get damaged.

4. *Chaim's friends are coming round this afternoon. Can I lift up our Persian carpet before it gets ruined?*

Something that is part of a building on a permanent or semi-permanent basis may not be removed, even if it is not fixed with nails, etc. Therefore to pick up a carpet that is permanently on the floor of a building is not allowed. A small rug that is regularly moved about may be removed. Your Persian carpet, which is usually larger and more permanent than a rug, but is not a fitted carpet, falls between these two categories. If Chaim's friends come every week[10] and you always take it away to keep it clean, it sounds as though it should be compared to the rug that is not "part of the house." If they come less often, though, it may be considered attached.[11] So in this case I would cover the carpet with a sheet and not remove it.

5. *I've just noticed a cobweb on the ceiling above the guest bed. Can I clean it away?*

The *Mishnah Berurah* says specifically that we need to remove

---

9. Because of frequent *shailos* regarding the correct placing of *mezuzos*, it is a good idea to invite a qualified *rav* to your house to tell you exactly where the mezuzos should go.
10. See Rav Dovid Ribiat, *The 39 Melochos*, "Boneh," note 34a, that less than eight or nine days is not considered fixed.
11. See previous note that eight or nine days is considered fixed. I said "may" because it could be that if it is removed regularly, even at longer intervals it is not considered fixed.

cobwebs before Shabbos.[12] The *Taamei HaMinhagim*[13] brings reasons *al pi kabbalah* for removing cobwebs but the *Mishnah Berurah* implies that it is simply part of cleaning the house *lekavod Shabbos*. Anyway, for whatever reason, there is a cobweb above the guest bed that your guest might not appreciate. Removing it on Shabbos, however, is problematic. If you are disgusted by it, the problem of *muktzeh* might be resolved,[14] but some hold that is forbidden to remove it because of *soser* since it involves detaching it from part of your house as above.[15] So leave it now but remember next Erev Shabbos.

6. *Our driveway is quite icy and people could slip. Can I get a shovel and make a safe path?*

I'm sure you'll agree that to dig up the driveway itself would not be allowed.

Soser applies not just to buildings but to anything attached to the ground. Here the question is whether the ice on your driveway is considered part of the driveway. The Magen Avraham[16] does think so and therefore he would not allow you to shovel up your ice. However, others disagree[17] and the conclusion is that if there is a need, as in your case where you're afraid people might slip over Shabbos, it is allowed.

---

12. 250:3.
13. 246.
14. As it would be *kegraf shel re'i* (see ch. 12, "Muktzeh," part II, question 7).
15. *Shemiras Shabbos KeHilchasah* 23:9.
16. 320:15. See the explanation of the *Machatzis HaShekel*.
17. See *Mishnah Berurah* 320:36. Rav Yaakov Montrose feels it is possible that the *Mishnah Berurah* was only lenient in the case of ice over a river, but would be strict in the case of ice on the ground. If there is a danger that people will slip, one can certainly be lenient.

7. *Chaya's got us stumped. She asked that if we can't make cheese because of boneh, surely if we eat it, it's soser.*

   Chaya's a clever girl. The *poskim* and *acharonim* wonder too. Why are we allowed to eat foods like cheese? If making cheese is *boneh*, shouldn't eating it be *soser*? Some say that only reversing the process of *boneh* is considered *soser*. Therefore since cutting up or eating cheese does not reverse the process of making cheese, it is not considered *soser*.[18] Another answer given[19] is that *soser* is the demolition of something into small parts, not its total destruction. According to this explanation, burning down a building is not *soser*. Neither is eating food.[20] So it's a good question, but now eat your cheese *betei'avon*.

8. *The children were playing during the shluf and made a kind of tent by draping a blanket over the backs of two chairs. But we need the chairs for shalosh seudos. What can we do?*

   It's amazing what kids get up to "during the *shluf*." It seems that your kids have made a little tent for themselves, a cute activity during the week but not allowed on Shabbos.[21] The halachah states[22] that just as we are not allowed to make a permanent structure, certainly a roof, we are not allowed to build a temporary structure. And just as we are not allowed to demolish a permanent structure, we are not allowed to demolish a temporary structure.

---

18. Rav Dovid Ribiat, *The 39 Melochos*, "Boneh," note 249, in the name of some *poskim*.
19. *Chut Shani*, "Boneh," note 16.
20. Rav Dovid Ribiat, *The 39 Melochos*, p. 1101, gives another possible explanation.
21. See ch. 41, "Boneh," answer 3.
22. *Mishnah Berurah* 315:1.

So even this ad hoc tent may not be demolished.[23] As for *shalosh seudos*, if you're short of chairs, put down a rug and tell the kids they've got to eat on the floor because there aren't enough chairs. They'll enjoy it and they'll remember the halachah for next week.

9. *Dirty water is dripping onto the patio from a broken drain. I was just getting a bucket for the water to drip into and Moshe said that it's a shailah of soser. What's the shailah? Is there any solution?*

The *shailah* is as follows. We are not allowed to make a vessel unusable on Shabbos. This is the equivalent of demolishing it and is therefore *soser*.[24] As we learned earlier, certain types of *muktzeh* may not be moved at all. Dirty water that has no use falls into this category. Therefore to put a bucket in a place where dirty water is going to fall into it, renders the bucket immovable and is therefore *soser*, as explained.[25] Moshe has therefore a reason to be hesitant.

However, if the water is just rainwater, even if it is not drinkable, it probably is usable for washing one's hands. If so, you can put the bucket there. The *Biur Halachah*[26] mentions that although we don't normally use *negel vasser* for anything and we certainly wouldn't drink it, technically it is permitted to use it and there is no problem in washing *negel vasser* into a bowl as we normally do.

10. *The leg of Chaim's bed has broken. If we put a pan underneath the bed on the side of the broken leg the bed will stay level. Is this allowed?*

---

23. *Orchos Shabbos*, vol. 1, 9:12.
24. *Mishnah Berurah* 310:20.
25. *Shulchan Aruch, Orach Chaim* 338:8.
26. Ibid.

In the previous answer we said that to make a vessel halachically immovable is *soser*. To make a vessel physically immovable also falls into this category.[27] Whether we may use a pan, which although *muktzeh* may be moved if necessary for a permitted purpose, depends on whether it will become virtually immovable by having a heavy weight resting on it. In the case of Chaim's bed, it probably is not that heavy and therefore *soser* would not apply. However, if something very heavy like a bookcase is falling over, it would probably not be permitted to hold it up with anything that would be rendered immovable.

---

27. Ibid. 313:7, *Mishnah Berurah* 313:50.

CHAPTER 43

מעביר — KINDLING A FIRE

1. *When I walk past the Shabbos lights, they always flicker. Should I try to avoid them?*

    You're right to ask because even just increasing an existing fire falls under the *melachah* of *maavir*.[1] But causing a flame to flicker does not increase the flame or use up more fuel and is therefore permitted.[2]

2. *I just asked Chaim to close the window because it's drafty. He said he doesn't think it's allowed because if he closes the window, the candles will last longer. Has he got a point?*

    I appreciate Chaim's creative thinking but his argument is incorrect in halachah. The Rama[3] says that we are allowed to close a door when there is a flame behind the door, even though this will inevitably cause the flame to last longer. This is not considered *maavir*.[4]

---

1. Shulchan Aruch, Orach Chaim 277:2; Mishnah Berurah 9.
2. There is an important debate about the definition of the *melachah* of *maavir*. Is it creating the fire or consuming the fuel? However, causing a flame to flicker does neither of these.
3. 277:1.
4. Mishnah Berurah 277:4.

מעביר — Kindling a Fire

3. *On the way home from shul there's a house with a light that goes on as we pass. Is it our problem?*

   If you are causing this light to go on, even though you are not interested in the light, it *is* your problem and you should go a different way home. This is an example of the concept of *psik reisha velo yamus* that we have discussed previously. The Gemara says that we may not cut off the head of a chicken to play with it even though we don't intend for the chicken to die, seeing that the chicken's death is inevitable. We are not allowed to do an action if it will cause a *melachah* to be done, even if it is unintended.

   In your case, if there is a doubt whether the light will go on — sometimes it does, sometimes it doesn't — you may go past, but not if it will definitely go on. If there is no choice — for example, there is no other way home or your next-door neighbor's light goes on when you walk into your own house, it is a serious question. If there are street lights that enable you to see anyway and this extra light is of no significance, you can be lenient.[5]

4. *This is a nightmare scenario: I forgot and pressed an electric doorbell. Moshe says if I keep my finger on the bell, I'm continuing the electric circuit. If I take my finger off, a light goes on. What do I do? Maybe it is a nightmare!*

   Did you say it is a nightmare or a nightmare scenario? The former would be preferable on account of the impossible situation you

---

5. *Orchos Shabbos*, vol. 3, 26:31, in the name of *gedolei haposkim* because there is no *meleches machsheves*. In an emergency, even when there is no other light, one can be lenient according to this leniency. The *Orchos Shabbos* warns us not to compare this case to other cases without asking a *posek*.

are in. It's no good telling you that you should've been more careful because that doesn't help you now. If removing your finger would not make the light go on, you wouldn't have a problem. Breaking a circuit by not allowing more electricity to enter is permitted.[6] Here, however, removing your finger causes a light to go on — a *melachah min haTorah*. You have a problem.[7] Some *poskim* argue that there is room to be lenient[8] with certain conditions but it's a situation that no Jew should find himself in on Shabbos. That's why I hope it's a nightmare and not for real. At least you'll wake up from the nightmare!

5. *My friends go out on Shabbos and leave the baby asleep. They have an intercom system with the neighbors so that if the baby wakes up and cries, the neighbor will come in. Is this okay?*

Strictly speaking, assuming the intercom was set before Shabbos, it is permitted. However, it is not ideal. First, there is a strong possibility that an adult will go in and talk to the child and the adult's voice will be heard through the intercom. In fact it would be abnormal if that didn't happen. This is the equivalent of an adult talking into a microphone or telephone, which is definitely not allowed. Some intercoms have lights that go on, which may certainly not be used on Shabbos.

Second, on Shabbos we may not activate machinery, such as a washing machine, which will make a noise,[9] and this might well fall into this category.

---

6. *Shemiras Shabbos KeHilchasah* 23:47.
7. According to *Shemiras Shabbos KeHilchasah* above there is no leniency and one has to stand there for the rest of Shabbos pressing the doorbell!
8. Rav Dovid Ribiat, *The 39 Melochos*, p. 1206.
9. See ch. 21, question 9.

On the other hand, sometimes there is a special need when this latter concern could be set aside. So I don't think it should be freely used; just on a case-by-case basis subject to consulting a *rav*.[10]

6. *I'm calling a Jewish doctor for an emergency. Can I wish him a good Shabbos or do I have to say just the minimum?*

   Yes, you can speak in a normal way even on Shabbos in this emergency situation. This includes saying "good Shabbos," "thank you," etc., but the conversation has to be about the emergency that has arisen.[11]

7. *I'm running really late this week. Can I fill the sink with hot water and wash my hands and face after Shabbos comes in?*

   You obviously know that washing one's whole body is not allowed even if the water is prepared before Shabbos. This is to ensure that we are not even tempted to kindle a fire or put on an electric heater on Shabbos itself. However, washing hands, face, and feet with water prepared before Shabbos is permitted.[12]

8. *Sometimes warm water comes out of the cold tap. Can I use it?*

   If water has been been heated in a forbidden way on Shabbos we're not allowed to wash even one hand in it. But where no transgression was done, if for instance the cold water happened to be near hot water and became warm on Shabbos, we are allowed to

---

10. This is also the conclusion of Rav Dovid Ribiat, *The 39 Melochos*, p. 1206.
11. *Shemiras Shabbos KeHilchasah* 32:41 in the name of Rav Shlomo Zalman Auerbach.
12. *Shulchan Aruch, Orach Chaim* 326:1.

wash our hands, face, and feet, just like in water that was heated before Shabbos.[13]

9. *We're staying just near the hot springs of Tiberias. Can we have a dip?*

In the hot springs of Tiberias, there are no restrictions.[14] However, in practice there is a custom not to bathe even in cold water because we might come to do certain *melachos* by mistake as we mentioned in chapter 25, "*Bishul*," part II.

10. *I told my neighbor that I like reading by the light of the Shabbos candles before going to bed. She said that's not allowed. Is she right?*

It depends. Your neighbor has probably heard of the prohibition of reading by the light of a lamp on Shabbos in case one alters the wick.[15]

However the *poskim* say that this applies to oil lights, where the danger applies, but not to candlelight. Therefore who was right, you or your neighbour, depends on what type of lights you use.

---

13. *Shemiras Shabbos KeHilchasah* 14:3.
14. *Shulchan Aruch, Orach Chaim* 326:1.
15. Ibid. 275:1.

CHAPTER 44

מכבה — EXTINGUISHING

1. *Our house is small, and opening the front door affects the Shabbos candles. But some unexpected guests have come. Can I let them in?*

   I understand you are worried about possibly extinguishing your Shabbos lights and thereby transgressing this *melachah* of *mechabeh*. On the other hand, how can we say to Jews on a Friday night that they can't come in? Certainly a dilemma. If your house was bigger, I would say that your lights should have been further away from the door, on your dining room table or nearby,[1] but your house is small and your table is near the door.

   You didn't mention what the weather was like. If there is a strong wind outside, it's more or less certain that the lights will go out, so opening the door would not be allowed.[2] Even if the wind is intermittent, we may still not open the door in case the wind picks up just then.[3] However in a case of special need, when the wind has dropped or is blowing very lightly, there is room to be lenient. In these circumstances, you can let your guests in under one further condition that you open the door gently so

---

1. "Which is the correct place for Shabbos lights?" *Mishnah Berurah* 273:32.
2. *Shulchan Aruch, Orach Chaim* 277:1.
3. *Mishnah Berurah* 277:3.

that the opening of the door itself doesn't blow the flames out.[4] All these halachic issues apply equally to opening a window near a flame but there is unlikely to be an emergency comparable to leaving guests stranded outside, even if Chaya is "boiling" with the window closed!

2. *The air-conditioning is much too cold. Can I turn it off?*

   Turning on any electrical item is *maavir* and therefore turning it off is *mechabeh*. If you are really so cold that you could become ill, you can ask a non-Jew to turn the air-conditioning off.[5]

3. *I put too much oil in the Shabbos lights. Can I pour some out if it doesn't affect the flame?*

   You say that it won't affect the flame. That applies now but by reducing the supply of oil you are shortening the total time the lights will burn. This is also included in *mechabeh*.[6]

4. *When Moshe prepares the lights, he puts in some water before the oil. Isn't this also a form of extinguishing?*

   First of all, I'm glad to hear that Moshe prepares your Shabbos lights. Even though it is the woman's responsibility to kindle the Shabbos lights it is correct that the man prepares them.[7] In terms of your question about extinguishing, you're right and

---

4. Ibid.
5. Shulchan Aruch, Orach Chaim 307:5. Even according to the Chazon Ish, who would say that turning off an electric machine is *soser*, it would only be *mi'deRabbanan* since it is *shelo al menas livnos*.
6. Mishnah Berurah 265:1. The oil is also *muktzeh*.
7. Shulchan Aruch, Orach Chaim 263:3 and Mishnah Berurah 12.

you're wrong. Putting water in and thus causing the light to be extinguished when the oil is finished is not allowed on Shabbos. But to do it on Erev Shabbos shouldn't be a problem. However, this is with an oil light.[8] To put water at the bottom of a candlestick so that when the candles burn down to the level of the water, the water extinguishes the flame, is not allowed even on Erev Shabbos.[9]

The difference is that putting water under a layer of oil does not actually extinguish the flame since it would go out anyway when there is no more oil. However, when a candle burns down to the level of the water, the water actually extinguishes the flame.[10] If there is a special need, for instance, a person is afraid to go to sleep if the candles are still burning, even this can be allowed but only on Erev Shabbos, and not on Shabbos.[11]

5. *The cholent was fully cooked before Shabbos and smells delicious. The problem is that it's only nine o'clock in the evening. Can I put a blech under the pan, seeing that it makes the gas flame look smaller?*

By saying that the cholent was cooked before Shabbos, you obviously want me to know that you are not transgressing the prohibition of having uncooked food on the stovetop without a *blech*.[12] Actually, if the food was edible[13] at sunset even though it was

---

8. *Biur Halachah* 265, s.v. "*gram kibbui.*"
9. Although we may usually prepare on Shabbos for a *melachah* to happen on Shabbos, here there is a special *gezeirah* in case we might mistakenly do it on Shabbos. See the reason in *Mishnah Berurah* 265:15.
10. *Mishnah Berurah* 265:18.
11. Ibid.
12. See above ch. 25, "*Bishul,*" part II.
13. Half-cooked or in an emergency, one-third cooked (measured in terms of the time it takes to cook the food completely).

not fully cooked, it is permitted according to the strict halachah. Most *poskim* agree though that it is still preferable that the food is cooked before Shabbos[14] and in any event to have something between the pan and the fire.[15]

There is a view that heating up a piece of metal is forbidden because of *bishul*.[16] According to this view you could not put a *blech* on a fire on Shabbos, but most authorities only forbid it if the metal would actually glow.[17] The only remaining concern is the effect that the *blech* will have on the flame. Does it in any way reduce the flame, which would mean it is prohibited because of *mechabeh*? The answer is that although it might seem to have an effect, and the flame might change shape, its strength will not be reduced because the gas supply has not been affected. So you can put the *blech* under your cholent without a question. I hope it will taste as good as it smells right now!

6. *I just checked the roast chicken that is keeping hot in the oven. A visiting seminary girl said I certainly can't shut the oven door. Why not?*

Seminary girls can be an important source of information since they are in the process of learning from their knowledgeable

---

14. To avoid making mistakes, like taking off the lid of the pan to see if it is cooked, and then, on finding that it is not, replacing the lid, which is not allowed because this would speed up the cooking.
15. To fulfill all opinions. See *Biur Halachah* 253, s.v. "*venahagu*"; Rav Shimon Eider, *Halachos of Shabbos*; Rav Pesach Eliyahu Falk, *Zochor Veshomor*, "Bishul." See also *Chut Shani*, "Shehiyah," about chicken bones that sometimes become edible after many hours of cooking. Also having the fire covered permits returning a pan to the fire in the case that it is permitted (see ch. 25).
16. *Chazon Ish, Orach Chaim* 37:11.
17. *Orchos Shabbos*, vol. 1, ch. 2, note 18.

teachers. However, it is not like hearing something from the teacher himself. A pupil can always misunderstand a teacher. Or sometimes they might have picked up one opinion and there are other opinions that the teacher might or might not have mentioned. There's nothing like your own *rav* to advise you on what you should or should not do.

I'm trying to understand what you were doing with your roast chicken. You say that it is keeping hot, implying that you know it is fully cooked. If you're not sure that it is cooked, you certainly cannot close the oven door, as this would speed up the cooking (your seminary girl might have thought the chicken wasn't cooked). If it was fully cooked and you set the oven at a low temperature and possibly set a timer to keep it hot until your Shabbos seudah, the question now is not *bishul*, but there are other issues involved in opening and closing an oven. Is there a fan or an electric light that goes on and off when you open or close the oven door? If so, you certainly can't open or close it.

A thermostat that increases the heat when cold air enters the oven and reduces the heat when the door is closed again is the most likely problem. You can test your own oven (during the week) to see how sensitive it is to changes in temperature. If opening the door for a few moments does not usually affect the thermostat, it is permitted.[18] If the thermostat is affected by opening and closing the door, even for a few moments, it will not be allowed.[19] If you don't know and you nevertheless opened the oven, listen to your seminary girl and just leave it open. At most the chicken won't be piping hot and you'll remember for another time.

---

18. *Iggros Moshe, Orach Chaim* 4:74, "*Bishul*" 28.
19. *Shemiras Shabbos KeHilchasah* 1:29.

7. *I want an early night and the lights are due to go off at midnight. Can I alter the Shabbos clock to go off earlier?*

   Shabbos clocks are a complicated question. Altering digital ones is out of the question. The ones with small tabs that you press according to the times you want the electricity to go on and off are possibly easier but there are different situations and different opinions. Some say we shouldn't touch the clock, not only because of a question of *muktzeh*, but because of confusion. One can easily do something prohibited according to the Torah. This, I would say, should be considered the default position — don't touch it.

   However, without saying something is permitted, I would say that delaying an action is better than advancing it; some prohibit even a delaying action.[20] In a case of real need, someone who initiates a delayed action has some opinions to rely on.[21] So the answer to your question about turning off the lights earlier to go to bed in the dark, the answer has to be definitely no. First, you are advancing the action, and second, it is a convenience rather than a real need.

8. *I'm alone in the house and a fire has broken out upstairs. Can I call the fire department?*

   You're by yourself in the house; presumably you can leave the house without danger, so there is no *pikuach nefesh* concerning

---

20. *Iggros Moshe, Orach Chaim* 4, 91:5; *Orchos Shabbos* 29, note 26, in the name of Rav Yosef Shalom Elyashiv.
21. *Minchas Shlomo* 2:23. If the light or an electric heater is now off and you don't want it to go on at all, and you just remove or move the tabs so that it won't go on, there is more reason to be lenient.

you. However, any fire within a city can easily spread to other homes whose residents might not be able to escape. Therefore this is a full-scale emergency situation and you must immediately phone the firefighters to put out the fire. If you can call in an unusual way, e.g., with your knuckle, without causing any extra delay, do so. This is not a situation for any imagined *chumros*. On the contrary, *kol hazariz harei zeh meshubach* — the quicker you do it the better, and hopefully the only damage will be to your house and not to people.

9. *A candle has just fallen onto the tablecloth. What do I do?*

I would have said "Don't panic," but if a person is panicking, it is useless to tell him not to. Everyone should be familiar with these halachos so that if it ever happens, one knows what to do and won't resort to panic. The most important thing to remember is that if there is even the slightest risk to life, there are no restrictions. No prohibition whether of the Torah or *mi'deRabbanan* stands in the way of *pikuach nefesh*.

As we said in the previous answer, except for the unusual situation of being in a house well away from other houses, without even a connecting line of trees, one has to treat any house fire as a potential *pikuach nefesh*. If the tablecloth has caught fire, there is a clear danger. If it is still a small fire one should douse it with a liquid, preferably not water. If flames have spread, leave the premises and call the firefighters. If the tablecloth has not caught fire one should take hold of the candle,[22] preferably in an

---

22. The solutions mentioned in *Shulchan Aruch, Orach Chaim* 277:3, are not usually relevant in our modern homes. If the candle is right near the edge of the table and you have a stone floor it could probably be indirectly pushed onto the floor.

unusual way, and put it in a safe place like a sink or on a stone floor, in such a way that the candle will go out eventually of its own accord.

10. *We live in the country; no one lives anywhere near us.[23] Last week an electrical fault caused a fire but Moshe said there was no heter to call the fire department. The whole house burned down. What am I supposed to think?*

The first thing for you to think of is the fact that your husband Moshe is an outstanding *yerei Shamayim* and you should be proud of him. He refuses to profane Shabbos even as he sees his house burning down. We don't ask for challenges, but if we get them, we have to overcome them with *emunah* and *bitachon*. Not everybody would be able to withstand such a test but your Moshe did it — a Jewish hero if ever there was one!

When we say the *Shema*, we say that we have to love Hashem "*bechol me'odecha.*" According to one explanation, this means that we have to be prepared to give up all our possessions rather than transgress the Torah. As we say the *Shema*, we should imagine just such a situation — a fire breaking out in a place where there is no danger except loss of money and we have to watch our home burning down and then we will be prepared if it actually occurs. The reward, needless to say, is very great, whether in this world or the next. Be thankful that you and Moshe are safe and I am confident that Hashem will

---

23. This is a theoretical question. Since when does a Jew live in the country away from all other Jews? What about having a minyan to daven with? Learning Torah *bechaburah*? Doing *chessed*, etc.? The question is for a place where there are no non-Jews either, or one could have said, "Anyone who extinguishes will not lose" (*Shulchan Aruch, Orach Chaim* 334:26).

help you as you rebuild your lives together.

CHAPTER 45

מכה בפטיש — THE FINAL HAMMER BLOW

1. *The music from our non-Jewish neighbors is very disturbing. Can I take some cotton wool and make myself ear plugs?*

   I'm sorry your neighbors are disturbing your *menuchas Shabbos*. At least they won't be able to complain when you're enthusiastically singing *"Chad Gadya"* next Seder night.[1] But to make earplugs on Shabbos falls into this *melachah* of *makeh bepatish*. Literally it means the final blow of a hammer to create something; it also means completing even a small item like a toothpick[2] or an oil lamp.[3] Incidentally there could be other *melachos* involved, such as *mechatech*, if you cut off a specific length of cotton wool from a larger piece, and *toveh*[4] if you would spin strands of cotton wool together to create your earplug, and some say *korea*.[5]

---

1. As long as it's not too late.
2. *Beitzah* 33b.
3. Ibid. 32a.
4. *Shaar HaTziyun* 514:52.
5. *Piskei Teshuvos* 340:27.

2. *We didn't put the belt into Chaya's new dress. She bought it especially for the simchah. Is there no solution?*

I understand your situation and Chaya may be crying as we speak but we have to look at what the halachah says. The *Mishnah Berurah*[6] says that we are not allowed to insert laces into shoes for the first time as this "completes" the shoe. Inserting a belt into the loops in a new dress is clearly a very similar act. But there could be a difference. Shoelaces, once they are put into a shoe, stay there. The laces become an intrinsic part of the shoe. Whether a belt becomes an intrinsic part of the dress depends on the type of belt. If it is indeed made of a similar pattern and "belongs" to the dress, it would be the same as the shoelaces and wouldn't be allowed. If Chaya would be prepared, just this time, to use a belt that doesn't belong to the dress, the situation could perhaps be salvaged. It doesn't sound as if she is the *baalas simchah* herself so maybe she could be convinced that not everybody will be looking just at her belt! In fact, if she learns this *sefer*, she'll learn the halachah and it won't happen again!

3. *The tissues are supposed to be separated but it seems that this packet wasn't done properly. I wouldn't mind but I've got a cold. Is it a halachah or a minhag not to separate them?*

I don't want to be pedantic but are you implying that if it's a *minhag* it can be ignored if it's not convenient? Sometimes a *minhag* can be stricter than a halachah.[7] You've surely heard of the con-

---

6. 317:18.
7. See *Pesachim* 50b where people whose fathers didn't travel to the market on Erev Shabbos had to continue their custom even though it was difficult for them.

cept of *al titosh Toras imecha* (following one's family and communal traditions). Anyway this is a question of what constitutes *makeh bepatish*, not a *minhag*.

In fact this small act of separating two tissues that are connected at one corner is a *chiyuv min haTorah*[8] and is not permitted even through a non-Jew.

In a situation that would cause severe embarrassment, such as a similar problem with bathroom tissue, we may tear the middle of a sheet in an unusual way, e.g, with one's elbow, but not where the two sheets are connected. Like many other questions, if we know the halachos and prepare carefully for Shabbos in advance, many of these difficult situations will not arise.

4. *Moshe's mad at Chaim because he just sat on his Shabbos hat. Can he repair it?*

Before we go any further, Moshe should count slowly to twenty. We men are very particular about our Shabbos hats but we should be even more particular about our children. To be in a temper, according to the Gemara,[9] is the equivalent of *avodah zarah* and we are likely to do and say things we will regret. Phew… Now let's turn to the *shailah*. If the hat has been completely flattened and is now unusable, fixing it is not allowed.[10] However, some hats are quite soft and even if they are flattened they can easily be straightened out. In fact I think they are made deliberately this way so that they can be squashed and straightened. These may be put right. Even a hard hat that is only slightly

---

8. *Mishnah Berurah* 340:45 and *Biur Halachah* there.
9. *Shabbos* 105b.
10. See Rav Dovid Ribiat, *The 39 Melochos*, "Makoh Bepatish," note 68.

out of shape can be put it back into shape.[11] We must be careful not to allow our desire to look *Shabbosdik* convince us to cut a halachic corner in this case.

5. *My shoes don't fit. Can I put in an insole?*

I'm glad you asked, but I think you could answer this yourself. Is the shoe complete? Clearly it is. It happens not to fit you personally. Therefore you can put in your insole.[12] Putting in new shoelaces is different because the shoe will fall off without the laces. The shoe is designed to be worn with laces. This shoe without the insole is completely ready, it just doesn't fit you. Another example of this would be adjusting a belt, which is already completely finished, to a wider or narrower size depending on the size of the person wearing it.[13] This should not be confused with an act of perfecting a fully functional item, which you have decided to beautify by doing something extra to it, e.g., painting a design on it. This is not allowed.[14]

6. *The door is squeaking. A spot of oil would cure it. But am I allowed?*

If the door is squeaking, something needs repairing. To repair something, even if the item is still in an almost perfect state, falls into this *melachah* of *makeh bepatish*. Therefore, in this case, when the repair is done by oiling the door, we may not do it.

7. *I'm so ashamed. The Goldsteins have come for the Shabbos seudah*

---

11. Ibid.
12. Rav Pesach Eliyahu Falk, *Zochor Veshomor*, "Makoh Bepatish."
13. Ibid.
14. *Shabbos* 75b. This would also involve the *melachah* of *kosev*.

and I just remembered that I didn't take challah. What can I do?

Not to have challah for Shabbos is a problem even without guests. With guests it would be a serious embarrassment as well. But you forgot to separate challah from the dough and we may not do this on Shabbos. It is a form of repair since bread is not permitted until challah has been taken. From a halachic point of view the challah is inedible. Taking challah makes it edible. Rabbinically it falls under *makeh bepatish*.[15] Is there a solution?

The answer, strangely enough, depends on whether you live in *chutz laAretz* or Eretz Yisrael. In *chutz laAretz*, under extenuating circumstances, it is permitted to eat the bread without having taken challah. That is on condition that you keep some of the bread until after Shabbos and then take challah from that piece on behalf of the whole dough even though the rest of it has already been eaten. Therefore if you're in *chutz laAretz* you won't have a problem. However this leniency doesn't apply to challah of Eretz Yisrael. There is no such solution in Eretz Yisrael. It does not matter where the flour comes from; it depends on where the kneading takes place.

This *chumrah* of Eretz Yisrael does result in one leniency: If one has not actually accepted Shabbos, one may separate challah during *bein hashemashos* since otherwise, there would be no way to eat the bread on Shabbos.[16] In *chutz laAretz*, since there is the solution we mentioned before, there is no leniency during *bein hashemashos*.

However, even in Eretz Yisrael there is another way that will surely be possible. That is, if you are living in a beautiful area of

---

15. *Mishnah Berurah* 261:4.
16. For a woman, lighting her Shabbos candles is her acceptance of Shabbos. Therefore someone else would have to do the separating in this situation.

Eretz Yisrael — like Ramat Bet Shemesh, where my wife and I are privileged to live — a quick visit to a few neighbors explaining the predicament will surely result in more challos being given than you and the Goldsteins could possibly eat over the whole Shabbos. *Mi ke'amcha Yisrael!*

8. *Help. I'm locked out of the house. Can I knock with the door knocker so that someone will hear me?*

Now you probably are not interested in the background to this question just at the moment, but for the sake of other readers I'll explain. As we have mentioned, repairing almost anything is *makeh bepatish*. The rabbis forbade playing any musical instrument on Shabbos in case it needs repair and we might inadvertently repair it.[17] They were obviously very worried about this possibilty because the *takanah* is very far-reaching as we shall see in this and the next two questions. The Rama[18] says that we may not even knock with the knocker fixed to a door, even though there is no attempt to play any kind of tune, since the knocker is designed to make a noise. So on Shabbos we just knock on a door with our knuckles and usually we are heard and can get in. What happens if there is an emergency — I need to get in and no one can hear me? The *Biur Halachah*[19] discusses this question and concludes that we may knock with the knocker in a real emergency, e.g., we are locked out late at night, with nowhere else to go. The knocker isn't designed for music and we are not trying to tap out any kind of tune. Otherwise we should not do it.

---

17. *Shulchan Aruch, Orach Chaim* 338:1.
18. Ibid.
19. Ibid.

9. *That was a wonderful speech. Can we clap?*

As we just said, the rabbis were worried that we might repair a musical instrument, and gave us various halachos to distance us from this possibility.

The Mishnah[20] says that we are not allowed to clap our hands to a tune for this reason. This is brought in the *Shulchan Aruch*.[21] Although the Rama brings a lenient opinion and some *poskim* rely on it,[22] others are strict and only allow clapping if it is done in an unusual way[23] unless it is for a mitzvah. This applies when one is clapping a tune or to a song that is being sung, which is not so far, conceptually, from the original prohibition. Clapping to applaud is permitted.[24]

10. *I heard that we're not allowed to dance on Shabbos. So why are we having a rekidah at this Shabbos sheva berachos?*

We are back to the question of what was included in the *takanah* that was designed to distance us from playing and thus possibly repairing a musical instrument. A simple reading of the halachah would not allow dancing, which was mentioned in the Mishnah and *Shulchan Aruch*.[25]

---

20. *Beitzah* 36b.
21. *Orach Chaim* 339:3.
22. *Iggros Moshe, Orach Chaim* 2:100. However Rav Moshe does say, "*baal nefesh yachmir.*"
23. *Mishnah Berurah* 339:10, unless it is in the case of a *mitzvah*.
24. *Shulchan Aruch, Orach Chaim* 338:1; *Mishnah Berurah* 338:2. If even banging with an instrument is permitted, if it is not in a musical way, certainly just clapping in a nonmusical way is permitted (Rav Pesach Eliyahu Falk, *Zochor Veshomor*).
25. As above.

But again there are lenient opinions and the custom is to be lenient especially for a mitzvah like *mesamei'ach chassan vekallah*. The *Aruch HaShulchan*[26] says that the original *takanah* was for dancing to live music, not just to singing, and also the very basic *rekidah* that we usually do is not similar to the *rekidah* the rabbis were talking about. More complicated dancing, however, should not be done.[27]

---

26. 339:9.
27. Rav Pesach Eliyahu Falk, *Zochor Veshomor*.

CHAPTER 46

הוצאה — TRANSFERRING OBJECTS FROM ONE DOMAIN TO ANOTHER

1. *Avi is on a sit-down strike — in the middle of Ocean Parkway! What would you advise?*

   If he's in the middle of Ocean Parkway, I would lift him onto the sidewalk first and ask questions later. Shabbos observance is always waived in a case of danger. In principle, of course, we are not allowed to carry any object in any "public domain." The exact definitions of the four domains of Shabbos are quite complicated but unless there is a rabbinically approved eiruv, a main road will be either a *reshus harabim*, in which carrying is forbidden on a Torah level, or a *karmelis*, where it is forbidden to carry on a rabbinic level.

   If Avi is sitting on the sidewalk, this is a more realistic question. Obviously you can't leave him, but do you have to stay with him until the end of Shabbos? You've tried all your tricks, waving bye-bye, offering him treats when you get home, etc. But we Jews are a "stiff-necked people" and he won't budge. There is one thing in your favor. That is the Talmudic principle that *"chai nosei es atzmo."* A living person who can normally walk, even when he is being carried, is also holding himself up. Even in a *reshus harabim* it is only forbidden rabbinically to carry him. Therefore in an emergency you could ask a non-Jew to take him home.

If this is not an option, but another Jew can help, you can lift him up, walk less than four *amos*,[1] hand him to your friend who now walks this short distance, and then he hands him back to you.[2] You carry on doing this, handing him back and forth to each other, until you get to your front door or the front gate if you have a front yard.[3] If there is no one else to help, you may lift Avi up and carry him less than four *amos*, stop for a few seconds,[4] carry him another short distance, stop for a few seconds and so on, until you reach your front door or front gate. At that point you should put him down rather than carrying him from a public to a private domain.[5] When he can see his home he will probably get up and walk in by himself. If not, put him on your shoulder or carry him inside in some other unusual way.[6]

All this is allowed only in an emergency because normally we are concerned that a person will forget and carry a full four *amos* and transgress the halachah.

The bottom line is that there are ways of getting a child home

---

1. About six feet.
2. *Shulchan Aruch, Orach Chaim* 349:3.
3. A front yard is considered a *reshus hayachid* if it is surrounded by a *mechitzah* ten *tefachim* high (32 inches [81.5 cm], or according to the Chazon Ish 38 inches [98.2 cm]. In this case even the Chazon Ish would accept the smaller measure because it is stricter).
4. Rav Dovid Ribiat in *The 39 Melochos* says that *lechatchilah* one should put the child down and pick him up every time you stop as per the stricter opinion in *Mishnah Berurah* 266:18, but Rav Pesach Eliyahu Falk in *Zochor Veshomor* does not mention it. This could be because of the additional factor of *chai nosei es atzmo*.
5. *Mishnah Berurah* 266:17.
6. Ibid.

if he won't cooperate but a person should not take out a child who is liable to stop in the street.

2. *I told Chaim that he must wear his coat. He says he doesn't need it and it would be hotzaah for him to wear it in the street. Has he got a point?*

He's a clever lad, your Chaim, but he hasn't got *hilchos Shabbos* quite clear yet. He knows that we can't carry a *masui* (literally, a burden) in the street on Shabbos. However, the definition of a *masui* is not necessarily what a person might *feel* is burdensome, like Chaim's coat when he'd rather not wear it. What is considered a "burden" in halachah is a complex subject and is not necessarily what we might have thought. Is a person allowed to wear two coats just for the purpose of bringing one to a friend?

We might be horrified at this suggestion, but the *Shulchan Aruch*[7] explicitly allows it. The *Mishnah Berurah*[8] explains that it is allowed because wearing a garment, even an unnecessary garment, is permitted. It seems that any garment is regarded as an accessory to the person, adding dignity to him and is therefore inconsequential in its own right.[9] We can see from this that for Chaim to wear a coat, even if he feels it is a "burden," is permitted. And that is the halachah.

3. *I'm the new rabbi of Siberia. Can I use a muff to keep my hands warm?*

I admire your *mesiras nefesh* in going to Siberia to bring the Torah

---

7. Orach Chaim 301:36.
8. 301:132
9. *Batel leguf*. Acharonim cite sources from the Gemara and *rishonim*.

to our far-flung fellow Jews. But it is cold there and a muff would help. The point here is that clothes are permitted as explained in our previous answer, but sometimes they are not permitted where there is a risk that we might take off those clothes and start carrying them in the street. Gloves, according to some, fall into this category since sometimes we might forget and remove them, for instance, when we want to shake hands with a friend in the street.

The halachah is that the custom is to be lenient but it is correct for a *baal nefesh*[10] to be strict.[11] A *baal nefesh* who wants to wear gloves should stitch one end of a piece of material to his glove and the other end to the sleeve of his coat. This way, even if he would forget and take the gloves off, they would just dangle from the coat, which wouldn't be regarded as a usual way of carrying.[12] Some[13] say that a muff is better than gloves because even if one takes out one hand the other hand will still be wearing it. Others[14] hold that it is worse than gloves because it can easily come off both hands. Although in normal circumstances we should not be lenient,[15] you can rely on the lenient opinion if it's

---

10. One on an elevated spiritual level.
11. *Mishnah Berurah* 301:141. The custom is for women and children to accept the lenient opinion (Rav Pesach Eliyahu Falk, *Zochor Veshomor*).
12. *Shulchan Aruch, Orach Chaim* 301:37.
13. *Taz* 301:26.
14. *Eliyah Rabbah*.
15. *Mishnah Berurah* 301:139.

extremely cold.¹⁶ If possible, before Shabbos, stitch your muff to a sleeve of your coat, as we said in connection with gloves.

4. *I'm going to help set up the kiddush at shul. Can I wear my apron so my dress won't get dirty as I set up?*

There are two questions to answer in respect to an apron. First, is an apron a garment? Second, if it is not a garment, are you wearing it to protect you or is it just to protect your dress? Let's answer these questions in order.¹⁷ Some aprons are garments, some are not. The eifod of the *kohen gadol* is a form of apron that is one of the holy *bigdei kehunah*. Some ladies have a tradition to wear a white apron on Shabbos to enhance their appearance *lekavod Shabbos kodesh*. These are certainly garments and one can wear these in the street.¹⁸ A full garment like a housecoat, even if it is only worn in private and even if it is only to protect other clothes, may also be worn in the street. Or even an apron that extends around most of the body would also be acceptable.¹⁹

---

16. See the *Be'er Heteiv* 301:31. According to the reason the *Mishnah Berurah* gives why people are lenient with gloves, the same reason would allow a muff according to the strict halachah. If the general custom in Siberia is to be strict concerning a muff, which I doubt, the *rav* can't be lenient. Get a coat with warm pockets! The advice about stitching it to one's sleeve would also be a solution.
17. *Pirkei Avos* 5:9.
18. Whether a *kohen gadol* can wear his *bigdei kehunah* outside the Beis HaMikdash is a question discussed in *Yoma* 69a. (See there for the story of the famous meeting between Shimon HaTzaddik wearing his *bigdei kehunah* and Alexander the Great.)
19. *Chayei Adam, Hilchos Shabbos* 56:4. Anything that surrounds most of the body offers warmth and protection. See Rav Pesach Eliyahu Falk, *Zochor Veshomor*, "*Hotza'ah*."

But an apron that only covers one's front[20] and is not worn to enhance one's appearance is not a garment. You want it to prepare for the kiddush. Will you wear it for the kiddush itself? No way. We have answered the first question: It is not a garment. We have really answered the second question as well. You say yourself that you only want to wear the apron in order to prepare for the kiddush so you don't dirty your dress. It is not to protect you. So, I'm afraid that it is not allowed. Try a housecoat as we said, or maybe there will be a spare apron there.

5. *Moshe sprained his ankle and his shoe will not fit over the thick bandage. Can he go out with one shoe on?*

Even items that are definitely garments are sometimes prohibited because of a danger that one might take them off and carry them in the street as we mentioned before in answer 3. One reason that might cause a person to take a garment off is that it looks strange and people might laugh at him. Going in the street with only one shoe on is rather strange and indeed under normal circumstances we are not allowed to go out wearing only one shoe.[21] However if someone has a broken foot or a sprained ankle or something similar that will enable people to understand why he is wearing only one shoe, no one is going to laugh. There is therefore no danger that a person will take off the remaining shoe and it is allowed.[22]

---

20. The fact that the straps go around the whole body is not relevant (Rav Pesach Eliyahu Falk, *Zochor Veshomor*, ibid.).
21. *Shulchan Aruch, Orach Chaim* 301:7.
22. See *Biur Halachah*, s.v. "*be'oso*," that in a *reshus harabbim deOraisa* it is correct to be *machmir* not to go out wearing just one shoe even if the other foot is wounded.

6. *Today is the day after Purim and Chaim wants to wear his Haman mask for shul. Is it allowed?*

From question 2 above I thought Chaim was a clever young man who wanted to avoid any question of carrying even to the extent of not wearing a coat when his mother told him to. And now he wants to wear his Haman mask to shul? Maybe he is not so mature after all. I'm afraid a mask in the street on Shabbos is specifically prohibited in the *Shulchan Aruch*.[23] Besides, it's not really the thing to wear in shul — except on Purim. He can wear it at home — as long as he doesn't frighten his little sister!

7. *I've just noticed that I left the dry-cleaning label in my suit. What do I do?*

Seeing that it is completely unimportant, it is *batel*[24] to your garment and is permitted.[25] If it is by any chance on the outside of the garment, visible to people, some *poskim* do not allow it because the wearer would be particular to remove it after Shabbos.[26]

8. *I'm already late for the kiddush and I've noticed that a button on my outfit is loose. Do I have to find something else to wear?*

Anything that is an intrinsic part of a garment is like the garment

---

23. *Orach Chaim* 301:20.
24. Annulled.
25. *Shulchan Aruch, Orach Chaim* 301:39.
26. Rav Dovid Ribiat, *The 39 Melochos*, p. 1366 and note 389; *Orchos Shabbos* 28:184. However the *Minchas Yitzchak* 3:36 seems to be lenient. He says that were we to be *machmir* like this, we could not go out with any dirt on our clothes or shoes that we intend to remove after Shabbos, which we have not heard of. See also *Teshuvos VeHanhagos* 1:240.

itself.²⁷ It can be something required for the garment to function or it can be something that adds to the garment's appearance. A button can be both of these. If it can be used but is a bit out of position, it is still helping the garment to function. If a button is too loose to use but is still in the right position it still adds to the appearance of the garment. If it can't be used and is not in position, it can still be permitted if it is an easily replaceable button. I would not care if it fell off, so it is permitted because it is *batel*, as in the previous answer.²⁸

However, it would not be allowed if it is not easily replaceable and I would not want it to be lost. I would have thought that a button on women's clothing is not so easily replaceable, so if you can't use it and it is not in the correct position you'll have to change your outfit. If you noticed it when you were already outside, and there is no practical option of changing, you may walk home.²⁹

9. *My neighbor lives just across the hall. Can I take the baby to her while I go to shul?*

As you probably know and as we mentioned in answer 1, under normal circumstances we are not allowed to carry in a *reshus harabim* or a *karmelis* on Shabbos. These include major and minor public roads, courtyards belonging to two or more people, and

---

27. Rama 301:23; Biur Halachah, s.v. "shedarcho."
28. Rav Pesach Eliyahu Falk, *Zochor Veshomor*, "Hotza'ah." If it is on the outside of the garment, even an unimportant button would be forbidden according to the opinion mentioned above (note 25).
29. Because of *kavod habriyos*. See *Shulchan Aruch, Orach Chaim* 13; *Mishnah Berurah* 9. To walk in a *reshus harabbim deOraisa lekol hadei'os*, through which 600,000 people go every day, would not be allowed.

even the communal stairway of a building containing private apartments. Therefore even taking a baby over to your neighbor's apartment while you go to shul, which you asked about, will not be allowed.[30]

However, if a halachically approved eiruv supervised by the local rabbinate is in place, the restrictions on carrying are cancelled. This is not always possible for a variety of reasons. Even where there is no communal eiruv, it is usually possible to set up an eiruv between Jews in a limited area, especially in an apartment block, to facilitate just such conveniences as you are asking about. Your *rav* will be able to advise you on how exactly it is done.

One point that people sometimes forget is that a box of matzos has to be kept in the home of one of the Jews to represent a kind of communal kitchen for all of the participants. It must be available for the participants to partake of if they want to. If the one in charge of the matzos goes away for Shabbos, he should give either his key or the matzos to someone who is staying at home. Usually the eiruv is renewed every year before Pesach. The standard *nusach* says that if new people move in during the year, they will be included in the eiruv.[31]

10. *We've taken over the hotel to be with the Rebbe for Shabbos. Do we need to make an eiruv?*

We said before that an eiruv combines all the participants into

---

30. If one Jew is living in a building and all the other residents are not Jewish, there are no restrictions (*Shulchan Aruch, Orach Chaim* 382:1).
31. *Shulchan Aruch, Orach Chaim* 366:9. See *Mishnah Berurah* 53 that when one makes an eiruv for the whole year, *min hastam* one has in mind any new people who come to live there during the year.

one large family theoretically eating from the same food. In a kosher hotel, where meals are served from the same kitchen to all those staying there, it is not just a theoretical concept. Since you are eating the same food together,[32] you don't need an eiruv.

HAVE A WONDERFUL SHABBOS!

---

32. In a hotel where people stay long-term and might be eating their own food, an eiruv will be required.

THE BEAUTY OF SHABBOS

Let us go out to meet the Shabbos because it is the source of all blessings.[1]

A mizmor for the Shabbos day. It is good to thank Hashem, to sing to Your Name, Most High One.[2]

You blessed it out of all the days, You sanctified it out of all the seasons.[3]

Your holy Shabbos, with love and favor, You gave to us as an inheritance.[4]

There will be a great reward for those who sanctify Shabbos in a fitting way and for those who guard it from desecration.[5]

Help those who who neither plow nor harvest on the seventh day, who take short strides and eat on it three meals to bless You.[6]

You gave it in love to the Jewish people, to the seed of Yaakov whom You have chosen.[7]

---

1. *Kabbalas Shabbos.*
2. Ibid., *Tehillim* 92.
3. *Maariv Shemoneh Esrei.*
4. Kiddush.
5. *Zemiros.*
6. Ibid.
7. *Shacharis Shemoneh Esrei.*

"The most beloved of days" is what my God and Rock called it.[8]

Eat rich foods, drink sweet drinks, because God will give clothes to wear, bread, meat, and fish to eat, to all those who cleave to Him.[9]

Those who take pleasure in it will inherit eternal honor, those who savor it have merited life, those who love its words have chosen greatness.[10]

Those who observe the Shabbos will rejoice in Your kingdom; the people who sanctify the seventh day will take pleasure in Your goodness.[11]

You gave a day of rest and sanctity to Your People…a rest of peace, serenity, tranquility…a perfect rest.[12]

A person's yearly income is decided on Rosh HaShanah, except for what he spends on Shabbos, Yom Tov, and his children's Jewish education. If he spends less, he is given less, and if he spends more, he is given more.[13]

HaKadosh Baruch Hu said to Moshe, "I have a special gift that I want to give to the Jewish people and its name is Shabbos."[14]

Rabbi Shimon ben Lakish said that on Erev Shabbos HaKadosh Baruch

---

8. *Zemiros.*
9. Ibid.
10. *Musaf Shemoneh Esrei.*
11. Ibid.
12. *Minchah Shemoneh Esrei.*
13. *Beitzah 16a.*
14. Ibid.

Hu gives an extra neshamah[15] *to a person and on Motzaei Shabbos He takes it away from him.*[16]

One who fulfills the mitzvah of eating three meals on Shabbos will be saved from three things — the birthpangs of Mashiach, the punishment of Gehinnom, and the war of Gog and Magog.[17]

Someone who fulfills the mitzvah of oneg Shabbos will merit an unlimited inheritance, will be saved from the servitude of the exile, and will be given the desires of his heart.[18]

Somebody who observes Shabbos according to the halachah, even if he serves idols like the generation of Enosh, will be forgiven.[19]

If the Jewish people would only keep two Shabbosos according to the halachah they would be redeemed immediately.[20]

Rabbi Chaninah put on his best clothes on the afternoon of Erev Shabbos and said, "Let us go out to meet the Shabbos Queen."[21]

Rebbe asked Rabbi Yishmael ben Rabbi Yosei, "In what merit have the wealthy people in Eretz Yisrael become wealthy?"

---

15. An extra capacity to rest and rejoice, to eat and drink (*Rashi*). On Shabbos a person increases his trust in Hashem and is more relaxed; therefore his appetite increases (Rav Elimelech Kornfeld).
16. Ibid.
17. *Shabbos* 118a.
18. *Shabbos* 118b.
19. Ibid.
20. Ibid.
21. Ibid.

He answered, "Because they tithe their produce."
"And the wealthy of Bavel?"
"Because they honor the Torah."
And the wealthy of other lands?"
"Because they honor the Shabbos."[22]

The Roman emperor once asked Rabbi Yehoshua ben Chananyah why Jewish food [on Shabbos] was so tasty. He answered, "We use a special 'spice' called Shabbos." The emperor asked whether he could be given some of this spice. Rabbi Yehoshua ben Chananyah said to him, "For someone who observes Shabbos, it is effective. For someone who does not observe Shabbos, it is ineffective."[23]

Rabbi Hamnuna said, "Someone who says Vayechulu on Shabbos evening is considered to be a partner with HaKadosh Baruch Hu in the creation of the world."[24]

Rabbi Chisda said in the name of Mar Ukva, "When someone says Vayechulu on Shabbos evening, two angels who accompany him put their hands on his head and say, 'Your transgression is removed, your sin is atoned.'"[25]

Rabbi Yosei ben Rabbi Yehudah says, "Two ministering angels, a good angel and a bad angel, accompany a man on Shabbos evening from his shul to his home. If, when they arrive at his home, the Shabbos lights are lit, the table is set, and the couch is tidy, the good angel says, 'May it be like this next Shabbos,' and the bad angel is forced to say amen. If they do not find

---

22. *Shabbos* 119a.
23. Ibid.
24. *Shabbos* 119b.
25. Ibid., quoting the *pasuk* in *Yeshayah* 6:7.

*that the home is ready for Shabbos, the bad angel says, 'May it be like this next Shabbos,' and the good angel is forced to answer amen."*²⁶

*A person should rise early on Erev Shabbos to prepare for Shabbos. Even if he has several servants, he should try to prepare at least something to honor Shabbos. Rabbi Chisda cut up the vegetables, Rabba and Rabbi Yosef cut wood, Rabbi Zeira lit the fire, Rabbi Nachman took out the weekday items from his home and brought in the Shabbos items. Everyone should learn from them and not say that it compromises their honor; on the contrary, this adds to his honor if he honors the Shabbos.*²⁷

*This was the custom of Rabbi Yehuda Bar Ila'i: On Erev Shabbos they brought him a bowl of hot water; he washed his face, hands, and feet; he wrapped himself in his finest linen talis with woolen tzitzis; and sat waiting for Shabbos looking like a Malach Hashem Tzevakos.*²⁸

---

26. *Shabbos* 119b.
27. *Shulchan Aruch, Orach Chaim* 250:1.
28. *Shabbos* 25b. See ch. 1, question 7.

INDEX

accepting Shabbos, 45
acquisition
   esrog, 69
   gift, 70
   non-Jews, from, 71–72
additives, food coloring, 187
air freshener, 128
air, letters in, 251
air conditioner
   drips from, 106
   non-Jew &, 280
   turning off, 280
alarm clock, 37–38, 141
algae, 109
aliyos
   selling, 74
   talking between, 73–74
allergies, wasps &, 227
amirah le'akum. See non-Jews
anger, 290
animals
   dangerous, 226
   dead, 37
   distress, in, 97
   enclosure, 222–23
   feeding, 97, 222, 245
   food for, cutting, 245
   killing, 226
   muktzeh, 36, 221
   pain-causing, 226
   riding, 112
   skinning, 232
   trapping, 36, 219–20, 223, 226
   using, 113
ants
   crumbs &, 179
   sweeping, 229
   walking on, 229
apartments, carrying between, 304

appearance
   apron &, 300
   button &, 303
   cosmetics. *See* cosmetics
   gozez &, 169
appetite
   seudah, for, 44, 46–47
apron, 300
arbaah minim, 69
attachment, boneh &, 264
automatic lights, 275
avocado
   mashing, 136
   salt &, 234
baal korei, earnings of, 65–66
baby
   babysitting, 66
   bathing, 165–67
   bottle. *See* baby bottle
   bris milah. *See* bris milah
   brush(ing), 167, 170
   carrying, 303
   cereals, 149, 150
   cleaning, 124
   cream, 240–41
   diapers. *See* diapers
   distress, in, 167, 240
   hair, washing, 167
   intercom, 276
   lotion, 124
   mixture, thick, 153
   stains &, 173
   sunshade, 263
   wasps &, 227
   weighing, 76
   wipes, 124
baby bottle
   meraked &, 143
   strainer, 147
   warming, 155, 164
babysitting, 66

bag
   handles, tying, 196
   knotted, 201, 205
   tea. *See under* tea
   tearing. *See under* tearing
   twist tie, 199
   untying, 196, 201
baking
   bishul after, 139
   challos, 33–34
ball games, 101, 266
banana, mashing, 136
Band-Aid. See plaster
barrel
   hole, stopping, 239
bassis, 85–87
batei nirin, 190
bathing. See washing
beach. See sand
beads. See also necklace
beard, drying, 124
becher, 123–24
bed
   propping, 273
   sickness &, 230, 241
   unfolding, 265
behavlaah, earnings, 65–66
bein gavra legavra, 73–74
bein hashemashos
   birth, 231
   challah, separating, 292
belt
   adjusting, 291
   decorative, 202
   gelilah &. *See* gelilah
   inserting, 289
   untying, 200, 202, 204
berachos
   chocolate raisins, 202
   cinnamon, smelling, 248
   hadassim, smelling, 49
   hundred, 49, 88, 247–48

mushrooms, 109
rosemary, smelling, 110
birds
   cage, feeding in, 223
   feeding, 223
   trapping, 219
birkas hamazon
   retzei, 50–51
birth
   bein hashemashos, 231
births, marriages, and
   deaths. See under reading
bishul
   baking after, 139
   checking, 155
   clothes, wet, 177
   coffee, 148
   metal &, 282
   potatoes, instant, 153
   speeding up, 160
   sun &, 154
   thawing &, 48
biting
   nails, 171
   thread, 192
blech
   chazarah &, 162
   Erev Shabbos, lifting, 161
   extinguishing &, 282
   flame, effect on. *See under*
     flame
   general, 160
   inserting, 281
   raw food &, 160
   removal from, 158
   soup &, 155
bleeding
   bris milah &, 231
   dentistry &, 230
   handkerchief &, 186
   pikuach nefesh &, 210
   shocheit &, 230
   stitches &, 210
   tissues &, 186
blind. See window blind
blocks, toy, 265
blood test, 229
blowing
   chametz, 126–27
   dust, 127

wind, peanut skins by, 126
zoreh &, 126
boneh
   attachment, nature of, 264
   cheese, making, 271
   container, making usable, 218
   door &, 209
   effort &, 265
   flattening, 266
   furniture, 267
   games, 265
   hair &, 266
   hairspray, sheitel &, 129
   magnets, 211
   mezuzah, replacing, 268
   repairing &, 264
   snowball, 242
   soser &, 267, 271
   suction pads, 209
bones
   borer &, 133
   fish, 133
borer
   bones, 133
   coats &, 134
   cutlery &, 131
   dirt &, 115
   eggshells &, 131, 260
   feathers &, 172
   freezer &, 48
   general, 130
   identical items &, 130
   implement &, 133
   manual, 133
   meal, proximity to, 137
   mouth, in, 134
   peeling &, 120
   plates &, 132
   skinning &, 232
   soup &, 132
   tidying &, 117
bottle
   baby. *See* baby bottle
   hot-water, 156
   opening, 70, 246–47
   strainer, 147
   warming, 155, 164
bottletop
   hole, making, 246–47
   ring &, 70, 247

bow
   knot &, 200, 203
   loops, tying, 195
   shoelaces, 195
   time elapsed, 200, 203
   tying, 195
box
   string round, 204
braiding
   Erev Shabbos, 35
   hair, 35, 192, 266
   sheitel, 192
breakfast cereal, 148–51, 150
breaking
   cinnamon stick, 248
   food, 139
   letters, 259
   matzah, 139
   mud, 140
   nails, 170
   news, 61
   twig, 110
bris milah
   birth Erev Shabbos, 231
   bleeding, 231
   mohel, earnings of, 67
   postponed, 231
broom
   head, reattaching, 264
   sweeping with, 102, 219
brush(ing)
   baby, 167, 170
   clothes, 174
   crumbs, 179
   furniture, 174
   hair, 169–70
   hand, by, 170, 174
   hat, 174
   sheitel, 182
   stains, 35
   teeth, 35, 230
bucket, 219, 272
building (melachah). See boneh
building (structure)
   burning, 271
   detachment from, 85, 268, 269
   games, 265

Index

hair, 266
stairway, communal, 304
business
  deal, closing, 73–74
  discussing, 73–74
  mechatech &, 243
  writing &, 254
butter, spreading, 241
butterfly plaster, 210
buttons
  buttoning, 208
  loose, 302–3
  opening, 209
  tofer &, 208
cage
  birds, feeding in, 223
cake
  cutting, 244, 257–58
  icing, characters on, 257
  Kiddush &, 44
  letters in, 258
  sugar on, 146
camera, 82–83, 251
can, reusing, 236
candle-lighting (Shabbos).
  See hadlakas neros
candles. *See* Shabbos lights
cane. *See* walking stick
cap. *See* bottle, opening
car
  closing, 89
  opening, 88–89
carpet
  matzah crumbs, 179
  non-Jew &, 179
  removal, 269
  spillage &, 123
  sweeper. *See* carpet sweeper
carpet sweeper
  crumbs, 179
  melaben &, 103
  non-Jew using, 179
carrying, 219
  apartments, between, 303
  baby, 303
  child, 296–98
  clothes, risk of, 301
  eiruv, within, 304
  gloves, 299
  reshus harabim, 296–98

walking stick, 100
wearing &, 298
yard, in, 81
cat
  feeding. *See* animals, feeding
  mouse &, 219
  trapping. *See* animals, trapping
catering, earnings for, 66–67
cereals, 148–51
chains, paper, 208
challah (separating)
  bein hashemashos, 292
  chutz laAretz, 292
  flour &, 292
  forgotten, 291–93
  kneading, location of, 292
  makeh bepatish, 292
  mitzvah of, 33, 291–93
  repairing &, 292
challos (loaves)
  baking, 33–34
  bassis &, 85
  buying, 33–34
  cutting, 237
  frozen, 48–49
  joined, 49
  marking, 237
  minimum to eat, 46
  thawing, 48
chametz
  blowing away, 126–27
  crumbs, 126–27
  Erev Pesach, 73
  selling, 73
characters, joining, 253
chatzitzah, ink &, 256
chazanus
  earnings, 65
  fasting &, 62–63
chazarah
  cholent, water adding to, 159
  conditions for, 161–62
  mistake after, 161–62
  reheating &, 163
checking
  cooking, 154
  stains, for, 193

threads for, 193
cheese
  cutting, 271
  making, 271
chess, 64
chicken
  checking, 154, 282
  feathers &, 172
  psik reisha. *See psik reisha*
  skinning, 232
chicken soup
  fish, after, 47
children. *See also* babies
  anger &, 290
  breakfast, 148–51
  candles &, 41
  carrying, 296–98
  Erev Shabbos, 32–33
  games. *See* games
  heating &, 90–91, 92
  lights &, 45
  medication &, 142
  muktzeh, danger from, 79
  running, 58
  sandbox, 102
  Scrabble &, 253–54
  spillages &, 121, 175
  toys, tidying, 117
  weaving &, 191
chisaron kis
  general, 82
  mezuzah &, 268
chocolate
  box. *See* ribbon
  delicacy, as, 47
  letters, 258
  raisins, 202
cholent
  hagasah &, 158–59
  pot, soup on, 155
  raw, 160
  Sephardim &, 159
  water, adding, 158–59
choresh
  drinking &, 106
  ground, flattening, 99
  stones, removing, 100
  urination &, 105–6
  water &, 36, 106, 127
chuppah

Shabbos, delayed until, 254
chutz laAretz, challah, 292
cinnamon, 247–48
clapping, 294
cleaning
    baby, 124
    clothes, 173
    napkins, using, 185
    shoes, 175
climbing tree, 110
clipper, nails, 170, See also nails, cutting
clock
    alarm, 37–38
    moving, 75
    Shabbos clock. *See* time switch
closing
    cage, 223
    car, 89
    curtains, 196
    deal, 74
    door, 209, 274
    dryer, 79
    hole, 239
    oven, 283
    paroches, 259
    siddur, torn, 252
    window, 274
    wound, 210
clothes
    belt. *See* belt
    borer &, 130, 134
    bringing in, 177–78
    carrying, risk of, 298–300
    cleaning, 173
    deodorant &, 128
    dryer in, 79–80
    drying, 37, 80, 177–78
    footprints, removing, 174
    hanging, 117, 173
    hotzaah &, 298
    laundry. *See* laundry
    lining. *See* zipper
    mixture, 131, 135
    multiple, 298
    river &, 178
    snowflakes on, 179–80
    stain on, 173
    thorns, caught on, 214
    torn, 207
    wet, 37, 79–80, 176–79
clothes brush, 174
clothes brushing, 174
cloths, floor, 124
coals, stoking, 160
coat. *See* clothes
cobweb, 270
coffee
    bishul &, 148
    davening, before, 63
    grinding, 136
    instant, 148
    kli rishon &, 148
    kli sheini &, 148
    kneading &, 148
coins, 86–87
collecting
    eggs, 115
    fruit, 114
    location, 116
    rainwater, 272
    toys, 117
    water, 272
coloring & colors
    additives, food, 187
    changing, 183
    cleaning &, 185
    cosmetics &, 183–84
    mixing, 186, 187
    napkins &, 175, 185
    shoes, 183
    spillage &, 121
    spraying, 183, 240
    strengthening, 183
    water, 184
combing
    gozez &, 35
    hair, 170, 182
    sheitel, 182
    spinning for, 182
    weaving, for, 182
combing, spinning for, 182
condensation
    pictures in, 255
confetti, 128
container
    reusing, 235
    usable, rendering, 218
cooking. See bishul
cosmetics, 183–84
cotton wool, cutting, 288
couch
    bassis, as, 86–87
    unfolding, 265
cream (edible)
    strainer &, 147
cream (skin)
    baby &, 240–41
    diapers &, 240
    diluting, 241
    spreading, 240–41
crockpot. See slow cooker
cruise. See jouney
crumbling sand, 146
crumbs
    ants &, 179
    brushing, 179
    carpet sweeper &, 179
    chametz, 126–27
    mice &, 179
crushing ice, 125
crying, 62
cucumber, salt on, 233
curtains
    closing, 196
    opening, 106–7
    plants &, 106–7
    tying, 196
    zorea &, 106–7
cutlery. See utensils
cutting
    animals, food for, 245
    bag, tearing, 247
    bottle top, 246–47
    business &, 243
    cake, 244, 257–58
    candles, 243
    challos, 237
    cheese, 271
    cinnamon stick, 247–48
    cotton wool, 288
    dotted line, on, 246
    earplugs, 288
    eggs, 138
    flower stalks, 245
    food, 244
    fruit, 121
    hair, 169

icing, 258
insect, around, 229
item, interest in, 247
letters, 257
measuring &, 75
Mishkan, in, 243
nails, 34, 35, 169, 170, 171
numbers, 258
onion, 137
pages, unseparated, 217
plaster, 210
potatoes, 137
ribbon, 204
sachet, 245–46
scissors, with. *See* scissors
size, to, 210, 243, 244, 246, 248
slices. *See* slicing
splitting &, 246
string, 203, 204
tablets, 244, 245
tailoring &, 243
thread, 192
vegetables, 137, 138
words, around, 247
dancing, repairing &, 294
danger
  animals, from, 226
  candle, from, 285–86
  muktzeh &, 79
dash (threshing)
  hair, wet, 124
  milking &, 119
  paper &, 122
  peeling &, 119
  separation &, 119
  shelling &, 119
  squeezing &, 119
davening
  accepting Shabbos, 45
  crying during, 62
  drinking before, 63
  illness &, 62
  siddur, torn, 252
dedication, reading, 54
demolishing. *See also* soser
  tent, 271
dentistry
  bleeding &, 230

Erev Shabbos, 39
oneg Shabbos &, 39
pain &, 230
deodorant
  clothes &, 128
  roll-on, 129
  spraying, 128
  stick, 129
detachment
  building, from, 85, 268
devar mitzvah
  journey for, 39
  medical matters, 39
  running for, 57–58
  talking about, 60
diamond, polishing, 238
diapers
  cream &, 240
  disposal of, 212, 260
  mochek &, 261
  picture on, 260–61
  sticking, 212, 260
  tofer &, 212, 260
  unfolding, 212
dirt, borer &, 115
discomfort
  illness, slight, 91
  knots &, 203
  untying &, 205
dishes. See utensils
distress
  animal in, 97
  avoiding, 54, 61–63
  baby in, 167, 240
  bathing &, 167
  leniencies &, 111
  lice &, 228
  trapping &, 224
doctor
  greeting, 277
  non-Jew, 210
documents, identity, 71
dogs
  excluding, 220
  leash, 223–24
  walking, 223–24
doll, repairing, 264
door
  boneh &, 209
  candles &, 279–80

car, 88–89
closing, 209, 274
dryer, of, 79
flame &, 274
fridge, 96
handle, replacing, 263
knocker, 293
oiling, 291
opening, 209, 263, 279
oven, closing, 283
squeaking, 291
trapping &, 221–22, 223, 224–25
doorbell, light &, 275
doorknocker, 293
dough
  challah forgotten, 292
  kneading, 148
draft, candles &, 274, 279–80
drawing lots, 76
dreidel, 76
drinking & drinks
  choresh &, 106
  ice &, 125
  kiddush, before, 44
  mites &, 145
  strainer &, 145, 147
  tea, 144
  yard, in, 106
  zorea &, 106
drips
  grapefruit, from, 121
  grass, onto, 106
dryer
  closing, 79
  clothes in, 79–80
  Erev Shabbos, 37
  noise level, 37, 141
  opening, 79
drying
  beard, 124
  clothes. *See under* clothes
  hair, 124
  hands, 178, 256
  towel, with, 178
  writing, 256
dud shemesh, 154
dust
  blowing away, 127

furniture, on, 174
hat, on, 174
earrings
   baal korei, 65–66
   babysitting, 66
   behavlaah, 65–66
   caterer, 66–67
   chazan, 65
   gift, 66, 68
   interest, 67
   mitzvah, for, 65–66
   mohel, 67
   non-Jew, 68
   non-monetary, 66, 67–68
   rent, 66
earplugs, 288
eating
   Erev Shabbos, 46
   kiddush, before, 44
   letters, 258
   shape, 258
   soser &, 271
effort, boneh &, 265
egg (measure), 46
eggs
   characters on, 259
   collecting, 115
   cutting, 138
   mayonnaise &, 152
   mayonnaise, onion &, 138
   new-laid, 115
   onion &, 137, 138, 151
   overnight, 131, 152
   salad, 151
   shelling, 131, 259
   slicer, 138
   sun, frying in, 154
eggshells
   borer &, 131, 260
   numbers on, 259
eggslicer. See slicer
eggtimer
   measuring &, 75
eiruv
   carrying within, 304
   hotel in, 304
   matzah for, 304
   new residents &, 304
enclosure, animals &,
   222–23

envelopes
   muktzeh, 82
   tearing, 215
erasing
   hands, from, 256
   letters, 255, 256
   pictures, 255
   sticking over, 260
   writing, for, 257
Erev Pesach
   chametz, 73, 126–27
   matzah, 83
Erev Shabbos
   alarm clock, setting, 37–38
   bassis &, 87
   birth, time of, 231
   blech, lifting, 161
   candles, water &, 281
   challos, baking, 33–34
   children, 32–33
   chuppah, 254
   cobwebs, 270
   cosmetics, 184
   dentistry, 39
   dryer, 37
   eating, 46
   hair, 35
   Kavod Shabbos, 31–34
   laundry. *See under* laundry
   lights, electric, 35
   melachah, preparing, 37
   melachah, starting, 140
   Minchah, 45
   mousetrap, 36
   neshamah, extra, 307
   oil lamp, water &, 281
   opening bags, bottles, etc., 218
   plants, curtains &, 106–7
   preparations, 31, 32–33
   purchases, 31
   slow cooker, 164
   sprinklers, 36, 140
   stain, 37
   tasting, 33
   towel, cloth, etc., 35
   washing, bathing,
      showering, etc., 34,
      35, 78, 255, 310
   work on, 39–40
esrog

acquisition, 69
moving, 87
muktzeh &, 87
smelling, 87
extinguishing
   air conditioner, 280
   blech &, 282
   draft &, 279–80
   emergency, 285
   oil, reducing, 280
   oil, water in, 280–81
extraction, soaking by, 175
eye shadow. *See* cosmetics
face
   cosmetics. *See* cosmetics
   stitches, 210
   washing (Shabbos). *See*
      washing
   washing, Erev Shabbos.
      See Erev Shabbos,
      washing, etc.
fan, moving, 80
fasting, 62–63
fat
   soup, in, 134
feathers
   chicken, removing from, 172
feeding. See under animals;
   birds
feet, washing
   Erev Shabbos. *See* Erev
      Shabbos, washing, etc.
   Shabbos. *See washing*
filing, 170
filter, tap, 144
financial matters
   reading, 52
finger, toothpaste on, 240
fire (cooking, etc.)
   blech &. *See under blech*
   hagasah &, 159
fire (dwelling, heating). See
   heating (dwelling)
fire (emergency)
   extinguishing, 285
   house, isolated, 286
   source, removing, 285
   spreading, danger of, 285

telephoning &, 285–86
fire (kindling), 274, 277
fish
  bones, 133
  eating, 47
  lemon, squeezing onto, 121
  meat, etc. after, 47
  raw, 48
flame
  blech &, 162
  door &, 274
  flicker, causing, 274
  oil, reducing, 280
flask, thermos
  hatmanah &, 165
flattening
  boneh &, 266
  choresh &, 99
  floor, 266
  food, 242
  ground, 99
flicker
  causing, 274
floor
  ball games, 101
  cloths, etc. &, 124
  covering, temporary, 179
  crumbs, 179
  flattening, 266
  spillage, 123–24
  sweeping, 102–3, 116–17
  washing, 102–3
  wine, spillage of, 123–24
flour
  challah &, 292
  muktzeh &, 48
  sifting, 143
  water &, 148
flowers
  ground, in, 83
  holding, 83
  muktzeh &, 83
  paper, 252
  receiving, 108
  stalks, cutting, 245
  tree, on, 83
  vase, in, 83, 108
  water, in, 83, 108
  water, returning to, 245

foil
  hatmanah &, 164
  insects, protection against, 164
  slow cooker &, 165
folding
  page, 250
  tallis, 180
food
  animals for, cutting, 245
  baked, *kli sheini* &, 139
  breaking, 139
  coloring, 187
  cutting, 244
  flattening, 242
  graf shel re'i, 84
  insects &, 229
  juice, squeezing onto, 120
  letters, obscuring, 257
  mechatech &, 244
  memare'ach &, 241
  raw, 160
  reheating. *See* heating (food)
  shaping, 242
  squeezing onto, 120
  stains, 173
  tablets as, 245
footprints, removing, 174
freezer
  borer &, 48
  challos from, 48–49
  muktzeh &, 48–49
Friday. See Erev Shabbos
fridge
  light, 96–97
  magnets, 211
  repair, 264
fringes
  straightening, 189
  tablecloth, 189
  threads, of, 189
  tzitzis. *See* tzitzis
fruit
  collecting, 114
  cutting, 121
  fallen, 88, 109, 114
  juice, letters &, 258
  rooting, possibility of, 104
  scattered, 115, 116

  smelling, 110
  squeezing, 119
  tree, detached from, 88, 114
furniture
  adding to, 267
  boneh &, 267
  brushing, 174
  dust on, 174
  repair, 264
  soser &, 267
  spraying, 240
  wiping, 240
furniture, ground, on, 103
games. See also toys
  ball, 101, 266
  building, 265
  chess, 63–64
  children, 64, 101
  desirability of, 266
  dreidel, 76
  jigsaw puzzle, 254
  losing, 216
  Play-doh, 239
  Scrabble, 253–54
  stones for, 100
  table tennis, 266
  writing &, 254
garden. See yard
gardening, 99
gartel. See gelilah
gelilah
  tying, 197
  untying, 204
  Velcro &, 197
gift
  acquisition, as, 70, 71
  earnings &, 66, 68
  muktzeh &, 70
  non-Jew, to, 72–73
  oneg Shabbos &, 70
  prize, 72
  use after Shabbos, 70
  wine, 70
glasses (spectacles)
  broken, 84–85
  tint, variable, 185
glasses (utensils). See utensils
gloves, 299
gozez

appearance &, 169
combing &, 35
feathers, 172
hair, brushing, 169–70
sheitel &, 182
skin, picking, 169, 170
graf shel re'i, 84
grapefruit, drips from, 121
grapes, squeezing, 120
grass
  removing object from, 81
  running, 110
  succah on, 103
  water &. *See under* water
gravy
  potatoes, mashing into, 137
  wiping, 156
greenfly, 229
greeting
  doctor, 277
  mechallel Shabbos, 81
grinding
  coffee, 136
  grinding after, 139
  noise of, 140
  stains, 174
groove, 100
ground
  ball games, 266
  choresh &, 99
  flattening, 101
  furniture on, 103
  holes, making. *See under* holes
  ice on, 270
  leash, height of, 224
  mushrooms &, 110
  picking from, 109
  produce detached from, 114
  soft, 100
  spillage on, 103
  stones, removing, 100
  uprooting from, 108
ground, flattening, 99
guest
  hadlakas neros &, 43
hachanah, sweeping &, 116
hadassim, 49, 198

hadlakas neros
  duration, 43
  early minyan &, 45
  eating or drinking after, 44
  guest &, 43
  melachah after, 43–44
  Minchah &, 45
  mitzvah on whom, 42–43
  number, 41
  oil lamps, 41–42
  purposes, 92
  relighting, 44
  seudah &, 43
  shalom bayis &, 41
  travel after, 43–44
hagasah (stirring), 158–59
hair
  baby, washing, 167
  boneh &, 266
  braiding, 35, 192, 266
  brush(ing), 169–70
  combing, 169, 182
  cutting, 169
  dash &, 124
  drying, 124
  Erev Shabbos, 35
  lice, 228
  rain &, 124
  ribbon, 194
  separating, 170
  spray, 266
  squeezing, 167
  tangles, 170
  towel &, 124
  tying, 194
  washing &, 124
hammer
  muktzeh, 78
  nutcracker, as, 78–79
hammock, 112
hamotzi, 237
handkerchief
  bleeding &, 186
handles
  bag, tying, 196
  door, replacing, 263
hands
  borer &, 133
  clapping, 294
  drying, 178, 256

  erasing from, 256
  gloves &, 299
  muff for, 298–300
  rainwater &, 272
  shaking, 73, 299
  soap &, 238
  washing (Shabbos). *See washing*
  washing, Erev Shabbos. *See* Erev Shabbos, washing, etc.
  writing on, 255–56
hanging
  clothes, 117, 173
  hat, 111, 173
  picture, 262
  tree, on, 111
happiness, 61
hat
  brushing, 174
  hanging, 111, 173
  repairing, 290
hatmanah
  bottle, warming, 164
  foil &, 164
  kli sheini &, 164
  reheating &, 164
  slow cooker &, 165
  thermos &, 165
havlaah, 67
head
  broom, of, 264
  doll's, 264
  scratching, 78
health. *See also* illness
  walking &, 58
heating (dwelling)
  children &, 90–91, 92
  illness &, 90–91
  non-Jew &, 90–91, 92
heating (food)
  baby bottle, 155, 164
  blech. See blech
  hatmanah &, 164
  hotplate. *See* hotplate
  neighbor, transferring to, 162–63
  pot, on, 155
  reheating, 155, 163–64
  returning, 155

stove, near, 155
sun, by, 154
thawing &, 48
thermostat &, 283
urn, on, 163
heating (metal), 282
heels, high, 102
holes
    barrel, in, 239
    bottletop, in, 246–47
    ground, in, 99, 100, 103
    sand, in, 102
    wall, in, 262
hooks
    suction pad. *See under* suction pads
hospital
    visiting, 63
    writing &, 250
hot springs, 278
hotel, eiruv for, 304
hotplate
    non-functioning, 162–63
    reheating &, 164
    soup on, 155
hot-water bottle, 156
hotzaah
    coat, 298
    postman &, 55–56
housecoat, 300
house-sitting, 67–68
hundred berachos. See under berachos
ice
    crushing, 125
    drinks, in, 125
    shoveling, 270
icing, characters on, 257
identity documents, 71
illness
    bed, taking to. *See under* bed
    davening &, 62
    heating &, 90–91
    life-threatening, 206
    non-Jews &, 91–92
    segulah, 35
    slight, 91
    Tehillim &, 62
    visiting. *See* visiting

ink
    chatzitzah &, 256
    invisible, 250
    washing &, 256
insects
    foil &, 164
    food, in, 229
    killing, 229
    trapping, 219, 222
inserting
    laces, 289, 291
insole, 291
intercom, 276
interest, 67
invisible ink, 250
invitations
    reading, 53–54
istanis, filter &, 144
jar
    reusing, 236
jar, reusing, 235
Jell–O, 153
jigsaw puzzle, 254
joining
    page, etc., 252
    safety pin, with, 207
journey
    devar mitzvah, for, 39
    oneg Shabbos, 39
    Shabbos, proximity to, 39
juice
    drips, 121
    letters, 258
    squeezing. *See under* squeezing
Kavod Shabbos
    delicacies, 47
    Erev Shabbos, 31–34
    intention, 47
    shalosh seudos &, 50–51
    stains &, 174
kesharim, 198
ketchup
    food, hot, 157
    sachets, 245–46
kezayis, 46
kiddush
    becher, filling, 123–24
    bemakom seudah, 47

    cake &, 44
    eating and drinking before, 44
    missing, 48
    mitzvah on whom, 42–43
    shul, in, 46
    yard, in, 106
killing
    animals, 226
    insects, 229
    snakes, 226
    spiders, 226–27
kinyan, 69
kli rishon
    coffee &, 148
    kli rishon, to, 158, 159
    soup from, 139
    water from, 148, 158
kli sheini
    baked food &, 139
    coffee &, 148
    hatmanah &, 164
    hot-water bottle &, 156
    ladle, as, 139
    urn from, 156
    washing &, 167
    water &, 159
kli shelishi, 139, 159
kneading
    cereals &, 148
    challah, location &, 292
    coffee &, 148
    consistency &, 149
    dough, 148
    egg, onion &, 151
    general, 153
    mixing &, 102, 153
    sand, water &, 102
    urination &, 105–6
knobs
    stove, controlling, 160
knocker, 293
knots
    accidental, 205
    bag. *See under* bag
    beads, 118
    bow &, 200, 203
    cutting because of, 203
    discomfort &, 203
    double, 195, 202, 204, 205

gartel. See gelilah
hair. *See* hair, tangles
loops, 195
lulav, etc. &, 198
non-Jew &, 206
professional, 203
rain, tightened by, 202
skillful, 194
string. *See* string
tie (garment), 196–97
tight, 204, 205
tightening, 199
types, 194
tzitzis, 199
untying, 200, 202, 205
Windsor, 197
korea (tearing). See tearing
kosev
 characters, joining, 253
 invisibility &, 250
 picture &, 251
 Scrabble &, 253
 shaping paper, 252
 snowball &, 242
 Travel Scrabble &, 253
kosher (tying). See tying
kotzer
 mushrooms &, 110
 picking, 109
 plants, moving, 107
kugel
 hatmanah &, 164
 reheating, 163–64
label
 dry-cleaning, 302
 tearing, 214
laces
 inserting, 289, 291
 knots. *See* knots
 rinsing, 176
 tying, 195
 untying, 195
ladle, *kli sheini,* 139
lamp
 light of, reading by, 278
lash (kneading). See
 kneading
laundry
 day for, 32
 dryer in, drying. *See under*

clothes
 Erev Shabbos, 32, 37
 line, on, 177–78
leash, 223–24
leather
 shaping, 233
 softening, 233
leaves, tea, 143
lechem mishneh
 challos. *See* challos
 frozen, 48
 matzah as, 49
lemon
 salad &, 120
 squeezing, 120
 tea &, 120
letters (characters)
 air, in, 251
 attaching, 253
 breaking, 259
 cake, part of, 258
 chocolate, 258
 cutting, 257, 258
 eating, 258
 eggshells, on, 259
 erasing, 255, 256
 finger, with, 251
 food, obscured by, 257
 forming, 252
 invisible, 250
 joining, 253
 napkins, on, 175
 page edges, on, 252
 Scrabble, 253–54
 skin, on, 255–56
 sticking over, 260
 tearing, 215, 217, 218,
  247, 257
 Travel Scrabble, 253
 washing off, 255–56
letters (communications)
 non-Jew &, 215–16
 opening, 56, 215–16
 reading, 55–56, 215–16
 receiving, 55–56
 signing for, 56
lice, hair
 killing, 228
lid
 removing, 161

replacing, 154
light (sun), plants &, 106–7
lights (electric)
 automatic, 275
 children &, 45
 doorbell &, 275
 Erev Shabbos, 35
 non-Jews &. *See under*
  non-Jews
 oven, 283
 reading &. *See under*
  reading
line
 dotted, cutting along, 246
liquids
 air fresheners &, 128
 extinguishing &. *See*
  extinguishing
 furniture spray, 240
 heat, returning to, 162
 ice &, 125
 rubbing, 241
 soap, 239
 solids, mixture with,
  148–51
 spillage. *See* spillage
 squeezing. *See* squeezing
 thinning with, 151
 uncooked, 159
lishah. See kneading
liver, 152
loan, repaying, 261
loaves. *See* challos
long life, segulos &, 33
loom, 189, 190–91
loops, tying, 195
lotion, baby, 124
lots, drawing, 76
lulav
 moving, 87
 muktzeh, 87
 tying, 198
maaris ayin, 71, 89
machinery, noise of, 37, 276
mafshit
 chicken, 232
magnets, 211
makeh bepatish
 challah, taking, 292

Index

doorknocker, 293
necklace, 118
oiling, 291
separating, 290
sheitel, 183
splitting, 246
tissues, separating, 290
makeup. See cosmetics
marking
  challos, 237
  paper, 250
  peel, 237
mashing, 136, 137
mask, going out in, 302
matzah
  breaking, 139
  crumbs, 179
  eiruv, for, 304
  Erev Pesach, 83
  lechem mishneh, for, 49
  meal, 150
  soup, in, 139
mayonnaise
  consistency, 152
  egg, onion &, 138
  eggs &, 152
  liver, chopped, 152
  salad &, 152
me'amer. See collecting
measuring
  cutting &, 75
  eggtimer &, 75
  melachah &, 75
  ruler, with, 244
  thermometer &, 75–76
meat
  fish after, 47
  hot, salad with, 157
  raw, 48
mechabeh. See extinguishing
mechallel Shabbos
  greeting, 81
mechatech. See cutting
medical matters
  devar mitzvah, as, 39
medication
  children &, 142
  non-Jew &, 91–92
  pain &, 141
  tochen &, 141

meisach, fringes &, 189
melaben
  carpet sweeper &, 103
  clothes, cleaning, 173
  clothes, washing. *See*
    laundry
  clothes, wet. *See under*
    clothes
  mud &, 140
  napkin, cloth, 175
  paper &, 122
  spillage &, 121, 123
  towel, etc., squeezing, 35
  wading &, 178
melachah
  Erev Shabbos. *See under*
    Erev Shabbos
  hadlakas neros, after, 43–44
  mitzvah, for, 95–97
  non-Jews &. *See* non-Jews
memachek
  cosmetics &, 183–84
  deodorant sticks, 129
  memare'ach &. *See*
    memare'ach
memare'ach
  butter &, 241
  cream &, 241
  foods &, 241
  furniture spray, 240
  liquid &, 241
  Play-doh &, 239
  snowball, 242
  soap &, 239
  toothpaste, 230, 240
menapetz, sheitel &, 182
menus, reading, 55
meraked. See sifting
mesartet
  challos, marking, 237
metal, heating, 282
mezuzah
  chisaron kis &, 268
  detached, 268
  muktzeh &, 268
  removing, 268
  replacing, 268
  reversal, 267–68
mice. See mouse
mikveh, hot, 168

milk, cereal with, 149
milking, dash &, 119
Minchah, 40, 45
minyan
  early, 45
  running to, 57–58
mites, drinking &, 145
mitzvah
  earnings for, 65–66
  melachah for, 95–97
mixing & mixtures
  cereals, 148–51
  clothes, 131, 135
  colors, 186
  consistency, 149, 150, 152, 153
  criss-cross action, 149
  cutlery, 131
  eggs, mayonnaise &, 152
  eggs, onion &, 137
  ice, 125
  kneading &, 102, 153
  liquid, solid &, 148–51
  liver, mayonnaise &, 152
  potato flakes, 153
  sand, water &, 102, 148
  sefarim &, 133
  soap, water &, 239
  soup, 132
  thick, 152
  thinning, 151
  toothpaste, water &, 240
  wine, 186
mochek
  cake &, 257–58
  diapers &, 260
  paroches &, 259
  pictures, non-permanent, 255
  tearing. *See* letters (characters), tearing
  washing &, 255
mohel, 67
molid rei'ach, 129
money, muktzeh, as, 78
moss, 109
moths, 221–22
Motzaei Shabbos
  tallis, folding, 181
mouse

cat &, 219
crumbs &, 179
Erev Shabbos, 36
sweeping away, 219
trapping, 219–20
mousetraps, 36
mouth
　borer in, 134
　wiping, 185
moving
　esrog, 87
　fan, 80
　plants, artificial, 81
mud, 139–40
muff, 298–300
muktzeh
　animals, 37, 221
　bassis, 85, 87
　chisaron kis, 82
　clothes, wet, 37, 79–80, 176–79
　cobweb &, 270
　coins, 86–87
　danger from, 79
　eggs &, 115
　envelopes, 82
　esrog &, 87
　flour &, 48
　flowers &, 83
　freezer, in, 48–49
　fruit, fallen, 88
　gift &, 70
　hammer, 78
　handle, detached, 263
　identity documents, 71
　lulav, 87
　magnets, 211
　matzah, Erev Pesach, 83
　mezuzah &, 268
　nail clippers, 79
　negel vasser &, 84, 177
　pan, 273
　pen, 78
　pictures &, 83
　pits, 84
　plants &, 108
　rationale, 77
　removing, 79
　repairing &, 85
　sand &, 102, 146

Shabbos lights, 85–87
sieve, 146
snow, 242
stones, 100
time switch, 284
toilet seat, detached, 85
touching, 284
walking stick &, 80
wallet, 78
washing line, clothes on, 177–78
water, dirty, 272
mushrooms, 110
nail (fastener), picture for, 262
nail clipper, 79
nails
　biting, 171
　breaking, 170
　cutting, 34–35, 169, 170, 171
　file, 170
　pain &, 171
　polish, 184
napkins (cloth)
　color &, 185
　mouth, wiping, 185
　spillage &, 175
napkins (paper)
　lettering on, 175
　mouth, wiping, 185
　pictures on, 175
　shaping, 252
　spillage &, 122, 174, 175
　squeezing, 175
　tablecloth &, 175
necklace
　assembling, 117
negel vasser
　muktzeh &, 84, 177
　pouring out, 83
　throwing out, 127
　using, 272
neighbor
　food, transfer for heating, 162–63
neshamah, extra, 308
netilas neshamah
　blood test &, 230
netilas yadayim

skin, letters on, 256
netting, making, 191
news, breaking, 61
newspaper
　financial matters, 52
　reading, 52, 56, 216–17
　wrapper, tearing, 216–17
noise
　alarm clock, 37–38, 141
　dryer, 37, 141
　grinding, 140
　intercom, 276
　machinery, 37, 276
nolad, soap &, 239
non-Jews
　acquisition from, 71–72
　air-conditioning &, 280
　animals, feeding, 97
　blood test &, 230
　carpet, cleaning, 179
　chametz &, 73
　child, carrying, 297
　dentistry &, 230
　doctor, 210
　earrings, 68
　fridge light &, 96–97
　gift to, 72–73
　hat, brushing, 174
　heating &, 90–91, 92
　illness &, 91–92
　knots &, 206
　letters &, 215–16
　light, extinguishing, 95
　light, increasing, 97–98
　lights, turning on, 45, 92–97
　medication &, 91–92
　melachah, requesting, 89, 90–98
　mitzvah, *melachah* for, 95–97
　photography &, 251
　picture, erasing, 255
　postman, 56
　tea, making, 97–98
　tissues, separating, 290
　treatment, medical, 249
numbers
　cutting, 258
　eggshells, on, 259

*nutcracker, hammer as,
    78–79*
nuts
    hammer &, 78
    shelling, 119, 120
    tree, from, 120
obituaries, reading, 61–62
oil. *See also* Shabbos lights;
        oiling
    candles or, 41–42
    door &, 291
    salad &, 152
    wipes, 124
oil lamps. *See* Shabbos lights
*oiling, makeh bepatish &,
    291*
olive(s)
    measure, 44, 46
    oil, candles or, 41–42
    squeezing, 121
oneg Shabbos
    candles &, 42
    dentistry &, 39
    Erev Shabbos, work on, 40
    gift &, 70
    journey &, 39
    pain &, 39
    reward, 308
onion
    cutting, 137
    eggs &, 137, 138, 151
opening
    bottle, 70, 246–47
    buttons, 209
    car, 88–89
    curtains, 106–7
    door, 209, 263, 279
    dryer, 79
    Erev Shabbos, 218
    letters. *See* letters
        (communications)
    oven, 283
    packaging, 217–18
    sefer. See lots, drawing
    window, 280
oreg
    threads, smoothing, 191
oven
    closing, 283
    door, closing, 282

light, 283
opening, 283
thermostat, 283
packaging, opening, 217–18
pages
    cutting, 217
    edges, letters on, 252
    folding, 250
    rejoining, 252
    stuck together, 217
    tearing, 217
pain
    animals, caused by, 226
    degree of, 142
    dentistry &, 230
    medication &, 141
    nails &, 171
    oneg Shabbos &, 39
    Shabbos, on, 39
pan. *See* pot
paper
    chains, 207
    dash &, 122
    flowers, 252
    marking, 250
    napkins. *See* napkins
        (paper)
    shaping, 252
    squeezing, 122
    sticking, 208
    tearing, 213
    tissues, towels, etc.. *See*
        tissues
parcel, 55
paroches
    closing, 259
    dedication, reading, 54
    mochek &, 259
    picture, forming, 259
peanuts
    scattered, gathering, 116
    shelling, 120
    skins, 126
peel
    marking, 237
    tidying, 84
peeling, 119–20
pei'os, 124
pens, muktzeh &, 77, 78
pets. *See* animals; birds

photographs, 83
*photography, non-Jews &,
    251*
picking
    ground, from, 109
    skin, 170
    tree, from, 109
pickle, returning, 235
picture, wiping, 255
pictures
    condensation, in, 255
    diaper, on, 260–61
    erasing, 255
    hanging, 262
    kosev &, 251
    muktzeh &, 83
    napkins on, 175
    non-Jew erasing, 255
    paroches, formed by, 259
    parts, forming from, 253
    sticking over, 260
    tearing, 217, 218, 247
pikuach nefesh
    bleeding, 210
    fire &, 285
    illness. *See* illness
pill. See tablets
pits
    muktzeh, 84
    spitting out, 84
plant pot, 109
plants
    artificial, moving, 81
    curtains &, 106–7
    light &, 106–7
    moving, 108
    smelling, 110
plaster
    butterfly, 210
    cover, removing, 210
    cutting, 210
    sticking, 211
plates. *See* utensils
*Play-doh,
    memare'ach* &, 239
polish & polishing
    diamond, 238
    nails, 184
pond, 109
postman

hotzaah &, 55–56
non-Jewish, 56
pot(s)
 blech &. *See* blech
 cholent. *See under* cholent
 hatmanah &. *See*
  hatmanah
 heating on, 155
 lid, replacing, 154
 muktzeh, 273
 propping with, 273
potatoes
 consistency, 153
 cutting, 137
 flakes, *bishul* &, 153
 mashed, instant, 153
 mashing, 137
pouring
 negel vasser, 83
 zorea &, 127
preparations
 cereals, 151
 clothes, Friday night, 130
 Erev Shabbos, 31
 melachah, for, 36–38, 37
 personal, 32–33
 weekdays, on, 31–34
present. See gift
prize, gift, as, 72
produce, detached, 114
propping bed, 273
psik reisha
 amirah le'akum &, 96–97
 light, automatic, 275
purchases
 Erev Shabbos, 31
 weekdays, on, 31
puzzle, jigsaw, 254
radio
 emergency, 38
 time switch, on, 38
rain
 collecting, 272
 hair &, 124
 knots &, 202
 running from, 58
 succah, 104–5
reading
 births, marriages, and
  deaths, 56

 candles &, 278
 dedication, 54
 financial matters, 52
 invitations, 53–54
 letters, 55–56, 215–16
 light &, 94, 97–98, 278
 magnets, 211
 menus, 55
 newspaper. *See* newspaper
 obituaries, 61–62
 oil lamps &, 278
 paroches, 54
 recipes, 53
 recommended, 54–55, 216
 science, 54
 silence, in, 53
 suitability, 52–56
 table plans, 261
 thermometer, 75–76
recipes, 53
refrigerator. See fridge
reheating food. See heating
 (food)
rejoining pages, 252
rekidah. See dancing
removing
 muktzeh, 79
 shelf, 267
 skin, 169
rent, 66
repairing
 boneh, 264
 challah, separating, 292
 dancing &, 294
 doll, 264
 doorknocker, using, 293
 fridge, 264
 furniture, 264
 glasses, 85
 hat, 290
 muktzeh &, 85
 oiling, 291
 tzitzis, separating, 190
repaying loan, 261
replacing
 lid, 154
 shelf, 267
 wheel, 264
reshus harabim
 child, carrying, 296–98

 leash, in, 223–24
restaurant, kinyan &, 71
returning
 heat, food to, 155
returning pickle, 235
retzei, 50–51
reusing container, 235
ribbon
 chocolate box, 196, 203
 cutting, 204
 hair, 194
 tying, 194, 196
rice, salt in, 146
riding animals, 113
ring, bottletop &, 70, 247
rinsing
 laces, 176
 shoes, 175, 176
 squeezing &, 175
river
 clothes &, 178
 depth, 179
 wading through, 178
roll-on deodorant, 129
rosemary, 110
ruler, measuring with, 244
running
 children, 58
 grass, through, 110
 minyan, to, 57–58
 mitzvah, for, 57–58
 rain, from, 58
sachets, cutting, 245–46
safety pin, 207
salad
 egg & onion. *See under*
  eggs
 lemon &, 120
 mayonnaise &, 152
 meat with, 157
 mixed, salting, 235
 oil &, 152
 tochen &, 235
salt
 avocado &, 234
 cucumber, on, 233
 rice in, 146
 salad, mixed, 235
 scattering, 115

sieve, 146
significance, 116
spillage, 115
sprinkling, 143
tanning &, 234
tomatoes &, 234
water. *See* salt water
salt water (general)
    preparing, 236
sand
    crumbling, 146
    handling, 102
    high heels, 102
    holes, making in, 102
    kneading, 102
    muktzeh &, 102, 146
    sandbox. *See* sandbox
    sieving, 146
    sifting, 146
    tochen &, 146
    walking on, 101, 102
    water &, 148
sandbox
    beach, contrasted with, 102
    water &, 148
scarring, stitches &, 210
scattering & scattered
    fruit, 115, 116
    peanuts, 116
    salt, 115
    sifting &, 146
    wind &, 126–27
science
    reading matter, 54
scissors
    cutting with, 203, 204, 247
    nails &, 170
Scrabble, 253–54
scratching head, 78
seats, selling, 74
sechitah. *See* squeezing
security camera, 251
seeds
    sprouting, possibility of, 104
    stones, removing, 100
sefarim, mixture &, 133
sefer Torah, 198

segulos
    illness, recovery from, 35
    long life, 33, 181
selling
    aliyos, 74
    chametz, 73
    seats, 74
separating
    bones, 134
    dash &, 119
    hairs, 170
    makeh bepatish, 290
    utensils, 132
Sephardim, 49, 159
seudah
    appetite for, 44, 46–47
    candle-lighting &, 43
    foods at, 47
    missing, 47–48
seudah shelishit. *See shalosh seudos (third meal)*
sewage, *zorea &*, 106
sewing, definition, 208
Shabbos
    early, bringing in, 35
Shabbos lights. *This entry relates to candles and oil lamps. For lighting, see hadlakas neros*
    candles, cutting, 243
    candles, oil lamps or, 41–42
    children &, 41
    danger from, 285–86
    door &, 279–80
    draft &, 274, 279–80
    duty on whom, 42
    flicker, causing, 274
    lighting. *See hadlakas neros*
    muktzeh, 85–87
    oil lamps, candles or, 41–42
    oil, reducing, 280
    oneg Shabbos &, 42
    purpose, 92
    reading by, 278
    relighting, 44
    responsibility for, 280
    reward, 42
    water &, 281

    water in, 280–81
shaking
    bassis, 87
    hands, 73, 299
    snowflakes off, 179–80
    tablecloth, 104
shalom bayis
    lights &, 41
shalosh seudos (third meal)
    food, hot, 163
    kavod Shabbos &, 50–51
    name, 50–51
    women &, 49–50
shalosh seudos (three meals)
    source, 50
shape, eating, 258
shaping
    food, 242
    leather, 233
    napkins, 252
    paper, 252
    sheitel, 182
    shoes, 233
    toothpick, 248
shearing, 169
sheitel
    braiding, 192
    brush for, 182
    combing, 182
    gozez &, 182
    hairspray &, 129
    makeh bepatish, 183
    shaping, 182
    soser, 182
    spraying, 266
    unbraiding, 192
shelf
    removal, 267
    replacing, 267
shelling & shells
    dash &, 119
    eggs, 131, 259
    nuts, 119, 120
    peanuts, 119
shemittah
    air conditioner, drips from, 106
shidduch
    talking about, 60
shivah house, visiting, 63

shocheit
   blood test &, 230
   methods, 227
shoe(s)
   cleaning, 175
   coloring, 183
   high-heeled, 102
   insole, inserting, 291
   laces. *See* laces
   mud on, 139–40
   rinsing, 176
   shaping, 233
   single, going out in, 301
   softening, 233
   spraying, 183
   stuffing, 233
   tying, 195
shoelaces. See laces
shower (rain). See rain
showering,. See washing
sick, visiting, 178
sickness. See illness
siddur
   bassis &, 85–87
   torn, 252
sieving. See sifting
sifting
   flour, 143
   muktzeh &, 146
   salt &, 146
   sand, 146
   scattering &, 146
   sprinkling &, 146
   tea, making, 143
signing
   hospital, in, 249
   letters & parcels, for, 56
silence, reading in, 53
size
   belt, adjusting to, 291
   cutting to, 75, 243, 244, *See under* cutting
skin (human)
   cream, spreading on, 240–41
   ink on, 256
   letters on, 256
   liquid remedy, 241
   picking, 170
   removing, 169

skinning, 232
skipping rope, 81
slicer
   eggs, 138
   tochen &, 138
   tomato, 139
slicing, 138, 235
slow cooker
   Erev Shabbos, 164
   foil &, 165
   hatmanah &, 165
smelling
   cinnamon, 248
   esrog, 87
   fruit, 110
   plants, 110
snakes, killing, 226
sneezing
   tissue, tearing &, 214
snow
   muktzeh, 242
   walking &, 125
snowball, 242
snowflakes, 179–80
soaking, extraction, by, 175
soap
   liquid, 239
   nolad &, 239
   washing with, 167, 238
   water, mixture of, 239
softening
   leather, 233
   shoes, 233
sorting
   toys, 117
   utensils, 132
soser
   boneh &, 267, 271
   cobweb &, 270
   eating &, 271
   furniture &, 267
   ice, shoveling, 270
   mezuzah &, 268
   propping &, 273
   sheitel &, 182
   shelf, removal of, 267
   vessel, making unusable, 272
soup
   blech &, 155

   borer &, 132
   cholent pot, on, 155
   fat in, 134
   foreign object in, 126
   hotplate, on, 155
   kli rishon, from, 139
   ladle, 139
   matzah in, 139
   mixture, as, 132
spectacles. See glasses
speech. See talking
spiders, killing, 226–27
spillage
   carpet &, 123
   children &, 121, 175
   coloring &, 121
   floor, on, 123
   ground, on, 103
   napkins (paper) &, 122, 174, 175
   salt, 115
   tablecloth, on, 121, 174
   tissues &, 123
   towels &, 124
   water, 121, 122
spinning
   combing for, 182
   tzitzis, 189
spitting out pits, 84
splitting
   makeh bepatish, 246
spraying
   air freshener, 128
   coloring &, 240
   deodorant, 128
   furniture, 240
   hair, 266
   sheitel, 266
   shoes, 183
   wasps, 225, 228
spreading
   butter, 241
   cream, skin on, 240–41
spring, hot, 278
sprinkling
   salt, 143
   sifting &, 146
   sugar, 146
sprouts, 109
squeaking door, 291

squeezing
    cleaning baby, 124
    dash &, 119
    extraction, soaking by, 175
    food, onto, 120
    fruit, 119
    hair, 167
    juice, 119
    lemon, 120
    napkins (paper), 175
    olives, 121
    rinsing &, 175
    tablecloth, 121
    toothbrush, 230
    towel, etc., 35
    towels, paper, 123
    water, 124
    wine, 122
    wiping &, 121
squirting, 127
stains
    brushing, 35
    checking for, 193
    clothing, on, 173
    dry, 173
    Erev Shabbos, 37
    food, 173
    grinding &, 174
    kavod Shabbos &, 174
stairway, 304
stalks, tomato, 120
steam, 255
    meaty, 158
    window, on. *See* condensation
stick (cane). See walking stick
stick (deodorant), 129
sticking
    diapers, 212, 260
    erasing &, 260
    letters, over, 260
    paper, 208
    pictures, over, 260
    plaster, 210
    suction pad, with. *See* suction pad
    tofer &, 208
stirring, 149, 158–59
stitches (medical), 209

stones, 100
stove
    heating near, 155
    knobs, *blech* &, 160
straightening fringes, 189
strainers & filters
    bottle, 147
    cream, 147
    drinking &, 145, 147
    istanis &, 144
    tea, 143
    washing &, 145
    water, 144, 145
string
    box, round, 204
    cutting, 203, 204
    knotting, 118
    suitcase, round, 202–3
    tea bag, 144
    untying, 204
stroller, 100
stuffing shoes, 233
succah
    grass, on, 103
    rain &, 104–5
    roof, 105
Succos
    arbaah minim, 69
    rain on, 104–5
suction pads
    boneh &, 209
    hooks &, 209, 262, 267
    plate, for, 209
sugar
    cake, on, 146
    sprinkling, 146
suitcase
    string round, 202–3
sun
    cooking &, 154
    dud shemesh, 154
sunshade, 263
sweeping
    ants, 229
    broom, with, 102, 219
    carpet sweeper. *See* carpet sweeper
    coals, 160
    floor, 102–3, 116–17
    hachanah &, 116

    mouse, 219
table plans
    reading, 261
table tennis, 101, 266
tablecloth
    covering, 121
    fringes, 189
    napkins &, 175
    plastic, 175
    shaking, 104
    spillage &, 121, 174
    squeezing, 121
    synthetic, 122
    wiping, 174
table plans, reading, 55
tablets
    cutting, 244
    food as, 245
tailoring, 243
talking
    general, 57–60
    mitzvah, about, 60
    shidduch, about, 60
    subject forbidden, 59–60
tallis
    folding, 180
    Motzaei Shabbos, 181
tangles, hair, 170
tannery, 233
tanning, salt &, 234
tap
    cold, warm water from, 277
    filter, 144
tasting, Erev Shabbos, 33
tea
    bags, 144
    cold water &, 159
    davening, before, 63
    Kiddush, before, 44
    leaves, 143
    lemon &, 120
    meraked &, 143
    non-Jew making, 97–98
    strainer, 143
tearing
    bag, 159, 201, 205, 216–17, 217–18, 247
    earplugs &, 288
    envelopes, 215

letters (characters).
  See under letters
  (characters)
packaging, 217–18
pages, unseparated, 217
paper, 213
pictures. *See under* pictures
price label, 214
tissues, 214, 290
wrapper, 216–17
writing. *See under* letters
  (characters)
zipper &, 214
teeth
  brushing, 35, 230
  extraction, 39
  finger, toothpaste on, 240
Tehillim, illness &, 62
telephone
  emergency use, 285–86
tent, demolishing, 271
thawing, 48
thermometer, 75, 76
thermos flask
  hatmanah, 165
thermostat, oven, 283
thinning, 151
thorns, clothes caught on, 214
threading
  beads, 118
  necklace, 117
threads
  biting, 192
  combing for, 182
  cutting, 193
  fringes, of, 189
  loom, on, 190
  loose, checking for, 193
  netting, 191
  smoothing, 191
  stretching, 189
  twisting, 189
  tzitzis. *See* tzitzis
  unravelling, 188, 192
  weaving, 191
threshing grain, 119
throwing
  negel vasser, 127
tidying

borer &, 117
graf shel re'i, 84
peels, 84
pei'os, 124
toys, 117
tie (garment), 196–97
tie (twist), 199
tightening knots, 199
time, wasting, 38, 58
timer, sprinkler with, 104
time switch
  altering, 284
  muktzeh, 284
  radio on, 38
tissues
  bleeding &, 186
  separating, 289
  sneezing &, 214
  spillage &, 123
  tearing, 214, 290
tochen
  medication &, 141
  mud &, 140
  noise &, 140
  salad &, 235
  sand, 146
  slicer &, 138
  slicing &, 138
  stains &, 174
  tochen, achar, 139
  tomato slicer, 139
  washing machine &, 140
tofer
  buttoning &, 208
  definition, 208
  diapers &, 212, 260
  magnets &, 211
  safety pin, 207
  sticking &, 208
  Velcro &, 209
  zipper &, 209
toilet
  seat, detached, 85
  water, coloring, 184
tomato slicer, 139
tomatoes
  salt &, 234
  stalks, 120
tooth extraction. *See*
  dentistry

toothbrush, 230
toothpaste, 230, 240
toothpick, shaping, 248
tortoise, trapping, 220–21
touching muktzeh, 284
toveh, tzitzis &, 189
tovel, 72
towels (cloth)
  drying with, 178
  Erev Shabbos, 35
  hair &, 124, 125
  spillage &, 124
  squeezing, 35
towels (paper)
  spillage &, 122
  squeezing, 123
toys. *See also games*
  beads, 118
  blocks, 265
  collecting, 117
  Play-doh, 239
  sorting, 117
  tidying, 117
trapping
  animals. *See under* animals
  birds, 219
  distress &, 224
  domestication &, 220–21
  door &. *See under* door
  doubtful, 221–22
  feeding &, 222–23
  insects, 221–22
  leash &, 224
  moth, 221
  person, of, 225
  pets, 223
  rabbinic, 219
  wasps, 224–25
  window &, 224
Travel Scrabble, 253
treatment, medical
  non-Jews &, 249
tree
  climbing, 110
  descending from, 110
  flowers on, 83
  fruit. *See* fruit
  hammock &, 112
  hanging on, 111
  nuts from, 120

picking from, 109
twig, breaking, 110
twisting
    tie, 199
    tzitzis, 189
tying
    bag, handles of, 196
    beads, 118
    bow, 195
    curtains, 196
    gelilah &, 197
    general, 194
    hair, 194
    knots. *See* knots
    laces, 195
    lulav, 198
    ribbon, 194, 196
    shoes, 195
    tie (garment), 196–97
tzad. See trapping
tzitzis
    knots, 199
    retwisting, 188
    separating, 189
    spinning, 189
    threads, formation, 189
    unravelling, 188
tzovea. See coloring & colors
umbrella, 80–81
unbraiding sheitel, 192
unfolding
    diaper, 212
    furniture, 265
unravelling, 188, 192
untying
    bag, 196, 201
    belt. *See under* belt
    discomfort &, 205
    gelilah &, 204
    knots, 200, 205
    laces, 195
    method, unusual, 206
    third party, by, 196
unzipping, korea &, 214
uprooting, 108
urination, 105–6
urn
    kli sheini, to, 156
    reheating on, 163
    steam &, 158–59

water from, 159
utensils
    borer &, 131
    separating, 132
    sorting, 132
    washing, 132, 176
    wiping, 132, 156
vase
    empty, 108
    flowers in, 83, 108
    water, filling with, 108
vegetables, cutting, 137
Velcro
    gelilah &, 197
    tofer &, 209
vending machine, 38
visiting
    shivah house, 63
    sick, 63, 178
wading, 178
walking
    ants, on, 229
    dogs, 223
    general, 57–58
    health &, 58
    sand, on, 101, 102
    snow &, 125
    stick, 80–81
    tanner, with, 233
    time, wasting, 58
walking stick
    carrying, 100
    muktzeh &, 80
    pointed, 100
    umbrella as, 80–81
wall
    holes, making in, 262
wallet, muktzeh &, 78
warming food. See heating (food)
washing. Unless otherwise indicated, this entry relates to washing oneself on Shabbos. For other types of washing, see under floor; laundry; utensils.
    baby, 165–67
    distress &, 167

Erev Shabbos. *See under* Erev Shabbos
    hair &, 124
    hot water, 167, 277
    ink &, 256
    kli sheini &, 167
    skin, writing on, 255
    soap, with, 167, 238
    strainer &, 145
washing machine
    Erev Shabbos, 32, 141
    noise, 37
    tochen &, 140
wasps
    allergies &, 227
    baby &, 227
    killing, 227
    spraying, 225, 228
    trapping, 224–25
water (general)
    choresh &, 36, 106, 127
    collecting, 272
    coloring, 184
    filter, 144
    flour &, 148
    flowers in, 83, 108
    flowers, returning, 245
    grass &, 103, 105, 106, 127
    hair &, 124
    istanis &, 144
    Kiddush, before, 44
    mites in, 145
    pei'os &, 124
    rain, collecting, 272
    salt. *See* salt water
    sand &. *See* sand; sandbox
    shoelaces &, 176
    spillage, 121, 122, 124
    sprinklers, 36, 104, 140
    squeezing, 124
    squirting, 127
    straining, 145
    succah roof, from, 105
    tea, adding to, 159
    throwing out, 127
    vase. *See* vase
    wind &, 127
    yard, 36
    zorea &, 36
    zoreh &, 127

water (heated)
  bottle, 156
  cholent, adding to, 158–59
  coffee &, 148
  dud shemesh, 154
  kli rishon, from, 148, 158
  kli sheini &, 159
  Sephardim &, 159
  urn, from, 159
  warm from tap, 277
  washing in, 167, 277
water pistol, 127
watering. See under water (general)
wearing, carrying &, 298
weaving
  children &, 191
  combing for, 182
  threads, smoothing, 191
  threads, stretching, 189
  unravelling, 192
website orders, 38–39
wedding, 53, 70, 254
weekdays
  preparations on, 31–34
  purchases on, 31
Weetabix, 150, 151
weighing baby, 76
wheel
  groove, making, 100
  replacing, 264
wind
  confetti &, 128
  peanut skins &, 126
  scattering, 126–27
  squirting into, 127
  water &, 127
  zoreh &, 126
windfalls, 109
window
  closing, 274
  condensation on, 255
  insects &. *See* insects, trapping
  opening, 280
  throwing from, 127
  trapping &, 224
window blind, insects &, 222

Windsor knot, 197
wine
  becher, 123–24
  gift, 70
  mixing, 186
  opening. *See under* bottle
  spillage, 122
wipes, baby, 124
wiping
  furniture, 240
  gravy, 156
  mouth, 185
  napkin. with. *See* napkins (cloth); napkins (paper)
  picture, 255
  plate, 156
  spillage. *See* spillage
  squeezing &, 121
  tablecloth, 174
  utensils, 132, 156
women
  shalosh seudos &, 49–50
words, cutting around, 247
work
  Erev Shabbos, 39–40
wound, closing, 210
wrapper, newspaper, 216–17
writing
  business &, 254
  erasing for, 257
  games &, 254
  hands, on, 255–56
  hospital &, 249
yard
  carrying in, 81
  drinking in, 106
  gardening, 99
  kiddush in, 106
  watering, 36
yogurts, separating, 246
Yom Tov
  candle-lighting, 243, 244
zipper
  buttoning function, 209
  lining, for, 209
  tearing &, 214
  tofer &, 209
zorea
  curtains, opening, 106–7
  drinking &, 106
  plants, moving, 108
  pouring &, 127
  sewage &, 106
  urination &, 105–6
  watering &, 36
zoreh
  air freshener &, 128
  blowing &, 126
  hairspray &, 129
  scattering &, 126–27
  water &, 127
  water pistol &, 127
  wind &, 126